Biographies and Space

Dana Arnold and Joanna Sofaer's collection is striking not only in its original-ity but in the extraordinary diversity of its contributions. In bringing together just the two words 'biography' and 'space', it cultivates a new field of study where tracks wind between Gustave Flaubert and Denis Diderot, where Deleuze rubs shoulders with Wordsworth or the romantic landscape frames the expressionist Berlin of Charlotte Salomon, and where the authors themselves find unexpected ways of saying 'I'.

Adrian Rifkin, Professor of Art Writing, Goldsmiths College,
University of London

The essays in this volume take on this familiar genre of biography in new ways. Using postmodern theory and historical methods the authors demon-strate that the spatialization of biography leads to new and compelling interpretations of images, representations, and performances.

Catherine M. Soussloff, University of California Presidential
Chair and Professor, History of Art and Visual Culture

Biographies and Space

Placing the subject in art and architecture

Edited by
Dana Arnold *and* **Joanna Sofaer**

Routledge
Taylor & Francis Group

LONDON AND NEW YORK

First published 2008
by Routledge
2 Park Square, Milton Park, Abingdon, Oxfordshire OX14 4RN

Simultaneously published in the USA and Canada
by Routledge
711 Third Avenue, New York, NY 10017

First issued in paperback 2014

Routledge is an imprint of the Taylor and Francis Group, an informa business

Typeset in Galliard by Wearset Ltd, Boldon, Tyne and Wear

British Library Cataloguing in Publication Data
A catalogue record for this book is available from the British Library

Library of Congress Cataloging in Publication Data
Biographies & space : placing the subject in art and architecture /
[edited by] Dana Arnold & Joanna Sofaer.
   p. cm.
   Includes bibliographical references and index.
   1. Space (Art) 2. Identity (Psychology) in art. 3. Space
(Architecture) 4. Identity (Psychology) in architecture. I. Arnold,
Dana. II. Sofaer, Joanna R. III. Title: Biographies and space.
   N7430.7.B56 2007
   701'.8–dc22
   2007014390

ISBN 978-0-415-36551-2 (hbk)
ISBN 978-0-415-51155-1 (pbk)
ISBN 978-0-203-01738-8 (ebk)

For our grandmothers and great grandmothers

Contents

Illustration credits

Contributors

Dana Arnold is Professor of Architectural History at the University of Southampton, UK. Her recent books include: *Rural Urbanism: London Landscapes in the Early Nineteenth Century* (Manchester University Press, 2006); *Art History: A Very Short Introduction* (Oxford University Press, 2004); *Reading Architectural History* (Routledge, 2002); and *Representing the Metropolis* (Ashgate, 2000). She has edited several volumes, which include *Cultural Identities and the Aesthetics of British-ness* (Manchester University Press, 2004); (with Margaret Iversen) *Art and Thought* (Blackwell, 2003). She has held fellowships at the University of Cambridge, Yale University and the Getty Research Institute, Los Angeles and has been a visiting professor at various institutions in the UK, USA and Canada. Her forthcoming book on the hospital in London will be published by Routledge.

Andrew Ballantyne is Professor of Architecture at Newcastle University. He studied and practised architecture, before embarking on a PhD and an academic career. His work analyses the interaction of buildings and ideas, including philosophical ideas, ranging from theory of the picturesque to American Pragmatism, and the ideas of Gilles Deleuze and Felix Guattari. His books include *Architecture, Landscape and Liberty: Richard Payne Knight and the Picturesque* (Cambridge University Press, 1997), *What is Architecture?* (Routledge, 2002), *Architectures: Modernism and After* (Blackwell, 2004), *Architecture Theory* (Continuum, 2005) and the first volume in a new series 'Thinkers for Architects', on Deleuze and Guattari (Routledge, 2007). He edited *Architecture as Experience* (Routledge, 2004) with Dana Arnold, and his bestseller, *Architecture: A Very Short Introduction* (Oxford University Press, 2003) now has a life of its own and has been translated into several languages, including Greek, Chinese and Japanese.

Hélène Lipstadt is a cultural historian who has taught at Columbia University, the Université of Montreal and the Massachusetts Institute of Technology. She has received awards and fellowships from the Getty Research Institute, the National Endowment for the Humanities, the Graham Foundation, the ACLS and the Institute Nationale de l'Histoire de l'Art (France). Her many articles and books are devoted to the history of the institutions, practices and roles that define and distinguish architecture as a field, such as illustrated publications and the architectural press, exhibitions, design competitions and the architect-intellectual. She also writes on the role of visual representation and cognition in the making of architecture and its public appreciation. Since her years of study in France at the University of Paris-Sorbonne and at the Ecole Pratique des Hautes Etudes en Sciences Sociales, she has pioneered the application of the sociology of Pierre Bourdieu to architectural history. Her book on the relationship of Pierre Bourdieu and Erwin Panofsky will be published by Pennsylvania State University Press. She is also a founding Regional Editor of the *Journal of Architecture* (United Kingdom) and a founding Director of DOCOMOMO US, the modern movement preservation organization, and currently serves as the Secretary of its Board.

Belgin Turan Özkaya is Associate Professor of Architectural History at Middle East Technical University in Ankara. She received her PhD in History of Architecture and Urbanism from Cornell University, was a fellow at the 1999 Getty Summer Institute in Visual Studies and Art History and a Visiting Scholar at the Canadian Centre for Architecture in 2000–1. She published articles on the Italian *Tendenza*, Ottoman–Venetian relations and historiography in journals such as the *Journal of Architectural Education* and *Harvard Design Magazine* and in collections such as After *Orientalism*. Her work is located at the interstices of architectural history and contemporary interdisciplinary theory. Currently, she is working on a short monograph on Aldo Rossi for the Swiss publisher in*folio* and preparing a special issue on architecture and visuality for *Architectural Theory Review*. Most recently she prepared a dossier, together with Elvan Altan Ergut, on 'Modern Architecture in the Middle East', for the *Docomomo Journal* in conjunction with the international Docomomo conference 'Other Modernisms' that they organized in 2006 with Docomomo international. The volume she co-edited with Dana Arnold and Elvan Altan Ergut, *Rethinking Architectural Historiography*, was published by Routledge in 2006 and shortlisted for the RIBA international book prize.

Griselda Pollock is Professor of Social and Critical Histories of Art and Director of Centre for Cultural Analysis, Theory and History (CATH) at the University of Leeds. Building on a substantial list of books and articles covering feminist interventions in and social histories of art, she has just edited and written for *Psychoanalysis and the Image* (Blackwell, 2006), *Museums after Modernism; Strategies of Engagement* (Blackwell, 2007), *Encountering Eva Hesse* (Prestel, 2006) and has recently written articles on Modigliani, Agnes Martin, Christine Taylor Patten, on shame, concentrationary imaginaries and life-mapping. A CATH series will be launched with the collection she has edited entitled *Conceptual Odysseys: Passages to Cultural Analysis*. Current research focuses on trauma and cultural memory, psychoanalysis and aesthetics and the means of keeping the feminist project alive. She has just completed *Encounters in the Virtual Feminist Museum* (Routledge, 2007) and *Theatre of Memory: Charlotte Salomon's Leben? oder Theater? 1941–2* (Yale University Press). She is working on a feminist study of Marilyn Monroe.

Eleanor Quince is a researcher at the University of Southampton. Her research interests centre on the history of furniture, how it has been constructed and how it can be re-read. In 2004 she convened a conference entitled ' "Back to the *Drawing Book*": re-examining furniture and furnishings 1760–1950' (based upon findings from her PhD) at MODA, the Museum of Domestic Design and Architecture, at the University of Middlesex. She is currently co-authoring *Design: Key Concepts* (forthcoming, Berg, 2008) with Mark Westgarth, University of Salford.

Dorothy Rowe lectures in the History of Art at the University of Bristol. She is author of a number of publications on two distinct areas: German modernism and contemporary diasporic art. Her first book *Representing Berlin: Sexuality and the City in German Modernism* was published by Ashgate in 2003 and she is editor (with Abigail Harrison Moore) of *Architecture and Design in Europe and America 1750–2000* (Blackwell, 2006). She is currently editing an internationally based collection of essays on women's art and globalization and researching towards a new book on German modernism in painting and the visual arts. She continues to be research active in both fields.

Sam Smiles is Professor of Art History at the University of Plymouth. He has published extensively on British art *c.*1750–1950, including *The Image of Antiquity: Ancient Britain and the Romantic Imagination* (Yale University Press, 1994), *Eye Witness: Artists and Visual Documentation in Britain 1770–1830* (Ashgate, 2000) and (as co-editor) *Envisioning the Past: Archaeology and the Image* (Blackwell, 2005). His publications on Turner include the short study *J.M.W. Turner* (Tate Publishing, 2000) and its longer successor *The Turner Book* (Tate Publishing, 2006) and the exhibition 'Light into Colour: Turner in the South West' (Tate St Ives, 2006). He recently completed a study of Turner's critical reception, *J.M.W. Turner: The Making of a Modern Artist* (Manchester University Press, 2007). He is currently researching the work of Turner's old age as part of an extensive study of the so-called 'late work' of artists.

Joanna Sofaer is a Senior Lecturer in Archaeology at the University of Southampton, UK. She has published widely on prehistory, material culture and social identity, is the author of *The Body as Material Culture: A Theoretical Osteoarchaeology* (Cambridge University Press, 2006) and editor of *Material Identities* (Blackwell, 2007) and *Children and Material Culture* (Routledge, 2000).

Joshua Sofaer is an artist, writer and Senior Research Fellow at ResCen, the Centre for Research into Creation in the Performing Arts at Middlesex University, London. Recent projects include *SFMOMA Scavengers*, a scavenger hunt and exhibition for the Museum of Modern Art in San Francisco. He is the author of *The Performance Pack* (LADA/Tate, 2004) and co-editor of *Navigating the Unknown: The Creative Process in the Contemporary Performing Arts* (Middlesex University Press/ResCen Publications, 2006), www.joshuasofaer.com

Nancy Stieber is Associate Professor of Art at the University of Massachusetts Boston where she teaches architectural history. Former editor of the *Journal of the Society of Architectural Historians* (2003–06), she writes about housing, urban representation and historiography. Supported by fellowships from the National Endowment for the Humanities and the Netherlands Institute for Advanced Study, she is completing a book entitled *The Metaphorical City: Visual representations of fin-de-siecle Amsterdam* to be published by the University of Chicago Press. Her book *Housing Design and Society in Amsterdam: Reconfiguring Urban Order and Identity 1900–1920* (University of Chicago Press, 1998) was co-winner of the 1999 Spiro Kostof Award.

Acknowledgements

The idea for this volume grew out of a conference on Biographies and Space, organized by Dana Arnold and Joanna Sofaer, held at the Paul Mellon Centre for Studies in British Art, London, on 28 March 2003. This conference formed part of a larger programme of activities involving several institutions which focused on the theme of Biography during the academic year 2002–03. These included the Getty Research Institute in Los Angeles, whose theme for that year was Biography, and CRASSH (Centre for Research in Arts, Social Sciences and Humanities) at the University of Cambridge, whose research theme for 2001–03 was The Organization of Knowledge. The Biographies and Space conference was the first of a set of exchanges between visiting fellows from both institutions. It was followed by Biographical Knowledge held in Cambridge from 31 March–3 April 2003, co-sponsored by CRASSH (University of Cambridge), the Getty Research Institute (Los Angeles) and the British Academy (London). This volume draws in part on papers given at these conferences and the lively debate these events prompted helped us to formulate ideas for commissioning the other essays in this volume. The editors wish to acknowledge the generous support both of these institutions and those involved with the Biography year – including Professor Ian Donaldson, the then Director of CRASSH, Prof. Tom Crow, Director of the Getty Research Institute and Dr Brian Allen, Director of the Paul Mellon Centre for Studies in British Art. We also wish to thank Charles Salas of the Getty Research Institute and Dr Frank Salmon of the Paul Mellon Centre for their essential input into the organization of our Biographies and Space conference.

Dana Arnold and Joanna Sofaer

Introduction
Biographies and space

Dana Arnold and
Joanna Sofaer

Biography and biographical methods of historical investigation have received much attention in recent years. And there is no doubt that biography is an essential part of human memory. We think about ourselves in terms of what we have done – our identity is constructed around our past. Are then history and biography linked or just two parallel strands? In architecture there are biographical traces in its spaces, taxonomies and histories: biography is then an essential narrative tool. This volume focuses on the relationship between biography and space and how specific subjects are used as a means of explaining sets of social, cultural and spatial relationships. Biographical methods can bring out the authentic voice of subjects, revealing personal meanings and strategies in space as well as providing a means to analyse relations between the personal and the social. It is the intention here to explore these divergent conventions in order to examine the cultural formations behind them. This volume comprises essays by internationally recognized scholars that consider issues of gender, childhood, sexuality and race in respect of actual (architectural) and imagined (pictorial) space. These chapters combine to highlight an increasing fluidity and interaction between theory, methods and history in the analysis and understanding of the relationship between biographies and space.

The volume opens with a suite of three papers that take contrasting explicitly theoretical approaches to the relationship between biographies and space. In the opening essay *(Auto)biographies and space*, Dana Arnold considers how discourse shapes our experience of architecture and the built environment as a visual object and as an agent in the formation of social identity. Her essay explores how the discourses of architecture work to perpetuate hegemonies, and to think about ways in which we can destabilize such norms. She refers to both the autobiographical and the biographical trace, both of which overlap and intersect throughout her chapter. The principal question Arnold addresses is, can architecture through its hegemonic discourses make her into/construct her as a woman – in other words do her (auto)biography and the spaces (both textual and physical) she inhabits intersect? As a means of answering this she presents a series of incremental position statements about our relationship to architecture and how the verbal and visual discourses around space and spatial experience work to form our identity. These statements touch on many of the themes developed in subsequent chapters of this volume.

The theoretical exploration of the relationship between biographies and space continues in Andrew Ballantyne's essay. He uses the work of Deleuze and Guattari to explore a notion of biography where a sense of self is insep-arable from the surroundings that the subject inhabits. Here the boundaries between named subject and environment are blurred. In *Living the roman-tic landscape (after Deleuze and Guattari)* he shows how reading Wordsworth's rapport with scenery with the work of Deleuze and Guattari in mind, makes possible a re-description in which the landscape becomes part of Wordsworth's construction of himself. The landscape is mobilized as an instrument of subject-formation, and is incorporated into the subject and the subject's self-image and life-writing. Ballantyne uses these insights to reconfigure the domain of biography by arguing for a 'rebalancing of organism plus habitat not only as the unit of survival but also as the entity whose life could be the subject for biography'.

Hélène Lipstadt moves the theme of biographies and space in a different direction by using the work of Pierre Bourdieu to explore biography in terms of movement through space. Taking Bourdieu's comment that lives should be studied as if they were 'a ride in the métro'[1] as both title and premise of her essay – in other words that the study of lives is the study of space – she addresses methodological concerns as to how this may be done and examines the implications of such an approach for architectural history. Using Bourdieu on space in place of standard linear notions of biography (Bourdieu was himself deeply opposed to the latter, believing it to be a 'rhetorical illusion'), is to highlight the dynamic matrix of social relations between an individual and a field that has its homologues in physical space, rather than a traditional single focus on a subject.

A more specific articulation of the relationship between biographies and space appears in both Eleanor Quince and Nancy Stieber's essays. The two authors respond to the theme by focusing on a particular historical moment or moments. In *'This scarlet intruder': biography interrupted in the Dining Room at Tatton Park Mansion*, Eleanor Quince draws on Denis Diderot's essay 'Regrets on parting with my old Dressing Gown'.[2] Diderot hypothe-sized that objects arranged within a space function as words within syntax that work together to form sentences that reflect the biography of the resi-dent. When one item is replaced by something new or different this biogra-phy is interrupted. Hence, when he purchases a new red robe with sudden and unexpected wealth, everything else looks shabby and old. Diderot is thus prompted to replace the rest of the room's contents so that the space is coherent and his biography is rewritten. Taking Diderot's view of interior space as a starting point, Quince examines a specific eighteenth-century interior; the dining room at Tatton Park Mansion. The current arrangement of the Dining Room tries to represent generations of the Egertons, with historically disparate items sitting side by side. The constant interruption from these overlapping signifiers produces an incoherent syntax, a confusing biography. Quince explores the ways in which the objects in the room create biography within a space, the various life stories that are being put forward, and in turn, what they mean to the visitor, asking: whose story is really being told?

We move then through space and time to Nancy Stieber's essay *Amsterdam eternal and fleeting: the individual and representations of urban space*. Stieber considers the late nineteenth-century city and the contrasting ways that two individuals, one an American, the other a Dutchman, expressed their attitudes towards Amsterdam through their visual accounts of the city. The photograph album of Sheldon Thompson Viele, an American tourist visiting Amsterdam in 1888, and the scrapbook of the native Amsterdammer John Anthony Jochems which he began to compile in 1907, both offer a visual portrayal of the city where the vision of the city is a product of a particular point of view that can only be understood as the expression of the individual's own biography. Each document is thus a visual autobiography that reflects the preoccupations of its constructor, where the role of history in self-conception affected the vision of the city. Stieber shows how, in serving their own needs to create identity, the identity of the city is manipulated by these two different men. Biography thus shapes the interpretation of space.

Attention turns to the biographical spaces of the artist in the essays by Sam Smiles and Griselda Pollock. Smiles considers one of the most famous artists of the early nineteenth century. In *Turner: space, persona, authority*, Smiles considers J.M.W. Turner and strategies for the disclosure of an identity. Turner famously attempted to frustrate any searching investigations into his domestic sphere and the explanatory force of biography seems much weaker in Turner's case than it does for many of his contemporaries. Smiles argues, however, that instead of resistance or opposition to biographical scrutiny, Turner might be imagined as enacting a professional biography in the public spaces of exhibition available to him, especially at the Royal Academy. His own gallery, as well as the homes of intimate friends/patrons, reveal his differential employment of spaces in which to produce the idea of the artist. Smiles considers these manoeuvres in the light of Turner's positioning of the contemporary and historical artist in the fictive spaces of his pictures. This essay suggests that Turner paradoxically articulated a strong identity through a strategy of deploying personas, dispersing notions of artistic identity in real and imaginary situations. Indeed Turner's triumph was in preserving the idea of the public responsibility of the professional artist. In doing so, Smiles suggests that, for Turner, outside those public spaces there was simply no worthwhile biography to be had.

Griselda Pollock also considers the biographical spaces of the artist but in her essay this is through the frame of Walter Benjamin's suggestion of an urban biography through maps. In *Mapping the 'bios' in two graphic systems with gender in mind: Reading Van Gogh through Charlotte Salomon and vice versa*, she offers a comparison of art as the space of biographical inscription in the way that Van Gogh and Charlotte Salomon are represented in various art histories. She looks at both the textual space of biographical representation and the representation of space as a visualization of the bio-graphos. These considerations lead her to 'open the space of art's multiple histories'.

These ideas are picked up on and developed by Dorothy Rowe as she takes the notion of the spaces of the artist and the idea of 'mapping' in a contrasting direction by exploring how biographical facts and spatial experience may be plotted within the arena of contemporary diasporic art in Britain. In *Biography and spatial experience in contemporary diasporic art in Britain*, she demonstrates that this occurs in a way that dislocates the essentializing conventions of ethnic cultural identity politics prevalent in much of the critical literature that still accrues to this topic. Rowe's discussion of the signifying practices of a diverse group of female artists – Mohini Chandra, Sonia Boyce, Zarina Bhimji and Oreet Ashery – demonstrates the centrality of the exploration of historical and spatial contingency as co-determinants in stories of biographical and autobiographical self-presencing. The weaving of biographical, autobiographical and spatial stories makes for a critical aesthetic practice in which there are rich and varied interrogations of transnational spaces opened by feminine diasporic subjects working in present-day, post-colonial Britain.

We return to architecture in Belgin Turan Özkaya's essay *The art of reconciliation: autobiography and objectivity in the work of Aldo Rossi*. Here the focus of enquiry moves further towards an investigation of the relationship between the biographical and the autobiographical in a consideration of what it might mean for architecture to be both. As Özkaya points out, one of the oldest genres of architectural writing is biography; architecture has long been explained and classified on the basis of individual artists and architects. We are used to perceiving architecture as a product of the lives and works of individuals. But, what about autobiography? How can the abstraction of architecture and the self-representation of autobiography come together and what does it mean for architecture to be autobiographical? She tackles these questions in relation to the work of the Italian architect Aldo Rossi. Rossi not only built and designed, but also painted, drew, wrote and even shot a film, but his persona remains elusive. When he died in 1997 he left behind an abundance of archival material but the excess in the archive, together with Rossi's solipsistic and aphorismic mode of writing that brings together short pieces of writing without leading to a logical, coherent whole, complicates any attempt to come up with a definitive portrayal of him. So, should we take the often stated claims about his 'autobiographical architecture' at face value, which is also associated with an attempt to develop objective architectural principles beyond an individual architect's 'whim'? Özkaya explores the tensions between the subjective and the objective, between autobiography and architecture, and finally between the creation and the reception of architecture in order to demonstrate how these tensions might have been reconciled in Rossi's work.

The final essay in the volume is *Disinter/est: digging up our childhood. Authenticity, ambiguity and failure in the auto/biography of the infant self* by Joanna Sofaer and Joshua Sofaer, sister and brother, archaeologist and artist. Their collaboration in the Disinter/est project challenges traditional notions of autobiography based on experiential narrative through a focus on infancy, a time about which we remember nothing. Sofaer and Sofaer ask us to rethink the relationship between self and autobiography and to consider infancy as a period that permits an exploration of the self as other; a biography of the self that is an intersubjective, rather than individual, construction. Returning to Cambridge, the place of their joint infancy, they use archaeological practice to investigate spaces they then inhabited. Their 'excavations' of infancy fail to reveal any specific insights into their infant experiences, but this 'inevitable failure' of archaeological method allows a productive destabilization and an expansion of potential meanings through the exposure of a series of tensions between the material and the auto/biographical, archaeology and arts practice. As the notion of auto/biography in relation to infancy is made meaningful through its inability to produce a singular coherent narrative, so too the archaeological method used to disinter the Cambridge years becomes itself a model under study – that of productive failure.

The contributions to this volume highlight an increasing fluidity and interaction between theory, methods and history. They explore how specific subjects are used, or not, as a means of explaining or articulating sets of social, cultural and spatial relationships. Biographical methods can bring out the authentic voice of subjects, revealing personal meanings and strategies in space, as well as providing a means to analyse relations between the personal and the social. By investigating divergent conventions in order to examine the cultural formations behind them, the contributors to this book raise questions that offer a significant re-evaluation of the relationship between biographies and space.

Notes

1 Pierre Bourdieu, 'L'illusion biographique', *Actes de la recherche en science sociale* 62/63 (1986): 69. Translated as Pierre Bourdieu, *The Biographical Illusion*, trans. Yves Winkin and Wendy Leeds-Hurwitz, reprint, 1986, Working Papers and Proceedings of the Center for Psychosocial Studies, no. 14 (Chicago: Center for Psychosocial Studies, 1987).

2 Denis Diderot, 'Regrets sur ma vielle Robe de Chambre', in *Oeuvres Complètes de Diderot, Miscellanea Philosophie*, vol. IV (Paris: Garnier Frères, 1875), pp. 5–12.

1

(Auto)biographies and space

Dana Arnold

I am interested in how discourse shapes our experience of architecture and the built environment as a visual object and as an agent in the formation of social identity. This essay seeks to investigate how the discourses of architecture work to perpetuate hegemonies, and to think about ways in which we can destabilise such norms.[1] Specific reference is made here to the auto-biographical and the biographical trace, both of which overlap and intersect throughout this essay. My starting point is can architecture through its hegemonic discourses make me into/construct me as a woman – in other words do my (auto)biography and the spaces (both textual and physical) I inhabit intersect? The intention is not to offer a hermetically sealed argument about the (auto)biographical trace in architecture. Instead, it is to present a series of incremental position statements about our relationship to architecture and how the verbal and visual discourses around space and spatial experience work to form our identity. In thinking about an ontology or system of the built environment in this way it is necessary to try to think about theories of both subjects and objects (and here I include biography) and their ties – particularly in this case feminine biographies and space. And it is helpful to think about criteria for distinguishing various types of subjects and objects for instance: concrete and abstract, existent and non-existent, real and ideal, independent and dependent and their ties in other words: relations, dependencies and predication. In addition, the notion of time is important as the (auto)biographical trace transforms itself and is transformed by time.

I think the following anecdotes are helpful in telling us something about subjects, objects, their ties and their relationship to both space and time. And, appropriately, they include elements of my own (auto)biography.

Strange bedfellows

I have been fortunate enough to hold visiting fellowships at Yale University, the Getty Research Institute and the University of Cambridge, where accommodation was generously provided. This continual turnaround of living space for the ongoing procession of international scholars made me think about how many members of the academic community had slept in the same bed. My apartment at Yale had been the residence of Henri Focillon, and I was reliably informed that he had died in the very bed in which I, and many other art historians, had subsequently slept. The wardrobes and cupboards contained some of his books that had never been removed, all containing his neat signature in the inside cover declaring both ownership and a (auto)biographical trace.

My puzzlement at this space–time phenomenon grew during my tenure at the Getty Research Institute. Here academics from across the world shared the same bed, so to speak (and in real time sat in the jacuzzi together – a very different kind of close encounter). Although all traces of the previous occupant were expunged from the apartment, remnants were sometimes to be found in the assigned mailbox. But most surprisingly an odd ritual had evolved of putting the unwanted contents of a soon to be vacated apartment, presumably too good to throw away – half-full bottles of olive oil, cleaning products, coffee or even hairdryers, on a table in the communal lounge for the remaining scholars to take as they wished. These relics, the material remains of occupation and existence, manifested to me not only choices made about what was worth keeping, but also about the nature of the legacy one left behind, as this pile of former belongings became a strange kind of epitaph. Although deracinated from the actual space of occupation, the biographical trace evoked by these objects was no less forceful. These two events prompted me to think about architecture, or rather the space it encloses, and the meanings and identities that can be conferred on objects within that space. The space and the objects do not change but our understanding of them does, and this can be influenced by social and cultural circumstances. Moreover, the fragments of material culture and of material identities – Focillon's books or half-used bottles of lavatory cleaner made me think of a kind of archaeology in both the literal and Foucauldian sense.

It took my fellowship at Cambridge for me to fully realise how these events from my own biography could help me to think about the *performative* qualities of the built environment.[2] The preceding visiting fellow and previous occupant of my set (apartment) in King's College had been Edward Said. Yes, same bed, and indeed same bath, but we've already been there … but in the bottom of the wardrobe was a pair of socks – not brightly plaid argylls in case you are interested, just plain grey ribbed wool. These became objects of fascination for me – were they Said's, and perhaps more importantly were they clean? The meaning and importance of this abandoned or forgotten item of clothing ranged from cultural relic to evidence of bad housekeeping. Were they Said's? Or did he look at them thinking they belonged to the occupant before him? The spatial location of everyday objects together with a narrative that could place them at a certain point in time made these socks potentially culturally significant in providing a biographical trace of Said. Indeed, during his stay at King's, Said wrote a new preface to the edition of *Orientalism* published in 2003. Had this been drafted at the desk where I worked, and was he wearing these very socks to keep his feet warm?

In this opening section of my discussion of biographies and space I want to give a final word to the socks, or at least the anxieties that still rest within me about them. Even though I trained as an art historian, I did not take a picture. And I left them untouched, in situ, undisturbed. But did whoever occupied the set in King's after me think they were my socks? And, would anyone really believe that I would wear grey ribbed woollen socks?

At one level my personal and perhaps initially frivolous-sounding anecdotes exemplify questions about being, and highlight the most basic problems in ontology: finding a subject, a relationship, and an object to talk about evoking questions such as 'what am I?' and 'what is describing this to me?' But these narratives also show how my biography intersects with those of others through specific spatial locations and ruptured temporal continuities. And here we begin to see the role time can play in this interaction. The spatial location of objects and subjects imposes a kind of performativity on them, as they enact or represent different biographical traces, and this is something to which I will return. I want now to extend this idea to see how the body responds to its spatial location. And conversely what kinds of performative identities can be imposed on bodies by the spaces that enclose them.

Everything round invites a caress

It is almost too obvious to state that the concept of space as it is used in this essay and indeed throughout this volume is not unproblematic. It is at once the virtual spaces of the text and the physical surroundings that are our environment. Theoretical models that foreground spatial concepts in metaphysics or more recently in spatio-temporal deconstruction are commonplace. Perhaps unsurprisingly, they have a distinctly masculinist bias. Female concepts of space, whether it be theorisation or experience, have a different grounding and now work towards dissolving the boundaries between the construction and deconstruction of theory.[3] Theories of space produced by men can work to establish unities and totalities and have specific gendered contours – what better example than Gaston Bachelard's assertion that 'everything round invites a caress'?[4] But is it the role of women/feminist theorists to shape masculine space into something feminine? Surely the maxim 'everything straight deserves a caress' only endorses the phallogocentrism that underscores masculinist theoretical models.

In a recent essay I asserted 'if I say gender, you think women'.[5] And in the field of the relationship between gender and space little work has been done on writing the male subject into the discourse – he is there by rights – not least as the linguistic predicate.[6] Conversely, much important work has been done to reconfigure the canon by queer theorists and feminist architectural historians, and I have discussed this in more detail elsewhere.[7] It is suffice to say here, in relation to questions about my own (auto)biography and space that the work of feminist scholars has repositioned women as users and producers of space, establishing new spatial locations for the interaction of feminine biographies and space.[8] In this regard the domestic environment has become an object of scrutiny.[9] For Laura Mulvey the middle-class bourgeois interiors of Walter Benjamin make no mention of a private sphere. Instead domestic space is an essential adjunct to the bourgeois marriage that associates women with the role of wife and mother.[10] Women have also been shown to be proactive in the production of space. Alice T. Friedman demonstrates that an unexpectedly large number of the most significant and original houses built in Europe and America in the twentieth century were commissioned by female clients.[11] Friedman shows that these houses represent not only the epitome of Modern design, but also innovative approaches to domestic space. This was the result of the joint efforts of client–architect pairs, such as Sarah Stein and Le Corbusier, and Edith Farnsworth and Mies van der Rohe. The history of the Modern Movement is, however, usually told as a masculinist narrative – not least the case in the articulation of its aesthetic. Terms frequently used to describe modernist design include 'clean, linear, rational, transparent' and these personify (we are told) masculinity, and therefore the masculine way in which architecture encloses space. But if we are to follow Friedman's argument do these modernist aesthetic qualities in fact do this, given the heretofore unacknowledged feminine predicates? The relationship between gender and the aesthetic is not confined to modernist architecture. Think, for instance, of the Palais Royal in Paris – an eighteenth-century building – but here I am thinking about its use nearer to our own time. Imagine visiting Colette in her rooms in the Palais Royal and seeing the outside as she saw it, and then imagine visiting Cocteau in his rooms. Neither the inside nor the outside would have seemed the same. My concern here is not to replace the male subject with the female one, or to write women into the narratives of architectural history from a revised socio/cultural perspective. Let me, instead, bring the discussion back to the intersection of (auto)biography and space. My question is does the writing of women into histories of space in any way alter or transform that space? What effect/affect does the fact we know room x was used by women or was designed by/was for a woman have on our understanding? In other words, can feminine biography be signified by space or can space be signified by feminine biography? Let me unpack this a little by suggesting that instead of thinking of the Farnsworth House or the Villa Stein as an icon of modern architecture, we think of them as (family) homes. Do we then think about the space differently. Perhaps it is 'the enclosed space that is a modality of femininity [where] woman lives her space as confined and closed around her, at least in part as projecting some small area in which she can exist as a free subject',[12] or perhaps that is what the space is not.

This ambiguity about what space can represent makes me think of

Jacques Lacan's famous analysis of the toilet signs 'Ladies' and 'Gentlemen', where he argues that the signs on the toilet door do not stand for the content of the signifier, which is the toilet, but for the chain of associated signifiers assigned by history, culture and social mores separately and reciprocally to the sexual differentiation implied in them. Lacan asserts that the relationship between signifier and signified is arbitrary and there is no one correspondence between them, still less between the signifier and the thing referred to 'no signification can be sustained other than by reference to another signification'.[13] In other words, the content of the signified is determined only by its relationship to other signifiers in the signifying chain. Is it, then, our culturally determined views that make space represent masculinity or femininity? In this specific instance the gender linguistics and the linguistic predicates of the Modern Movement would suggest this to be the case. But it is more than this. If we return to Lacan through his reworking of Freud in terms of the theory of language, woman is ascribed the status of not only the 'other' sex, but also the 'other' of language as he asserts 'there is always something about her and in her which escapes discourse'.[14] Lacan is here bringing 'woman' to the spaces of the text or the scene of writing. But this maps on to the problematic of how we write women into space as something other than a represented object. If 'woman', or the 'feminine' represents those spaces that have escaped structured symbolic discourse, then how are women as subjects of space transforming the discourses of it? Women both assume a space in history and refuse historical and temporal boundaries. These acts necessitate the making of new (textual) spaces that account for women's experiences, as well as interrogating the spatial boundaries that have worked towards their exclusion.[15] In this way the linear (dis)course of history is disrupted and transformed.

The intersection and interaction of textual and physical space can be explained further if we think about women's space and spatial experience – or spatial bodily existence – as both an object constituted by space as well as being a spatially constituted subject. Central to this is the feminine body which is positioned in space by a set of patriarchal co-ordinates that impose modes of performativity that constitute our notion of woman. These operate in a similar way to the phallogocentric linguistic predicates of the text. Iris Marion Young identifies space as an agent of confinement that restricts women's bodily movements and pushes them to absent themselves from space to become invisible, occupying no space whatsoever, 'a space surrounds us in our imagination that we are not free to move beyond; the space available to our movement is a constricted one'.[16] At one level the female body is an object for which the gaze imposes and confirms certain patterns of comportment. Restricted movements in a real or imagined space that are 'ladylike' assert woman as subject by avoiding the objectification of the gaze. Female bodily movements do not fill the spaces inhabited by woman and for Young this represents the tension between woman's immanence and transcendence, her role as subject and object.[17]

This makes me think more generally about our phenomenological, bodily sense of space. Imagine, for instance, the lights failing in a room and we have to negotiate the space through touch, crawling along feeling the floor, walls and doorframe in order to move our bodies in space. Cognitive scientists accept that the body shapes the embodied mind and that this is shaped by the experiences of the body. But the experiential world is more than just a physical place. As we have seen with the 'socks' we experience the world within a certain social and cultural milieu that conditions our view of it and imposes a kind of performativity on us as regards our occupation of that space.[18]

But my concern goes beyond the phenomenological and intersects to some extent with Foucault's argument that there is a pleasure in negotiating bodily boundaries that relates not only to the (re)construction of the self, but also to the way in which society operates. Foucault is interested in the ways in which the physical spaces of our bodily boundaries are policed. These modes of discipline (and punishment) are both external to and inscribed within the body, so the body becomes both a disciplining and self-disciplining entity. In other words, the nexus at which power is produced through action and resistance. But space for Foucault is also a textual entity. In, for instance, his *Archaeology of Knowledge* the concept of spacing is essential in order to distinguish between traditional history and its opposite variously termed effective history, genealogy or archaeology. For Foucault this textual space 'defines the blank space from which I speak, and which is slowly taking shape in a discourse that I still feel to be so precarious and so unsure'.[19]

An aetiology of self/other

I have argued that phenomenological and textual spaces intersect at the point where language operates as a means of articulating space. Here, I want to think about textual space in the production of (auto)biography – in other words the (self) writing of a life and how this interacts with the physical spaces of existence. Production of the written form has something to do with the production of subjectivities and in this way self-writing and autobiography can be seen as self-construction. Is then (auto)biography the construction of another (subject), and if so what are the constraints on this vis-à-vis language effect and performativity? We must remember that the act of writing to construct self or other belongs to the normative masculine canon. Indeed, with reference to (auto)biography does the concept of 'woman' simply become something that enables the historian to enact his/her own interpretation of another's life? And if this is the case does writing women into the discourses of space in this way become another example of masculinist methods and linguistic predicates. bell hooks addresses this in her comment:

> No need to hear your voice when I can talk about you better than you can speak about yourself. No need to hear your voice. Only tell me

about your pain. I want to know your story. And then I will tell it back
to you in a new way. Tell it back to you in such a way that it has
become my own. Re-writing you I rewrite myself anew. I am still
author, authority. I am still colonizer, the speaking subject, and you are
now the centre of my tale.[20]

The question of writing and linguistic constraints of the (auto)biographical
subject is something to which I will return. Here hook's comment highlights a connection between written language and what we can term an
aetiology of the self/other. (Auto)biography as a form of writing composes
a narrative or the architecture of the universal subject and here I want to
think about the aetiology of its discourses. In recent decades the (auto)bio-
graphical canon has been extended to include more writing of/about
women and non elites – the subaltern and the marginalised subject – which
postcolonial theory has helped bring to the fore. But can (auto)biography
be disentangled from a history of the western self? After all, I began this
essay with an (auto)biographical anecdote, but I am a white western
subject, albeit a female one.

The emergence of personhood and the self in western culture can be
understood in terms of (auto)biography which is at once a mode of cognition – and this interpretive self-history is the core of self-identity in modern
life.[21] Clearly, these spaces of the text or textual formulations of the self are
an established form of cultural practice and fashioning of identities by self
and by others. But who is the subject and how is this subject formed? I
want to suggest that alongside textual space, physical space is also a language (or a discourse of power) as it has a syntactical formulation that
constructs us and imposes modes of performativity through the repetition
and incantation of places, modes of movement, bodily inhibition and con-
tainment. In this way the confluence of biography and space is a potent
one. Who is writing/shaping and what is being written and shaped. Would
a (auto)biography be different in a different spatial location? My opening
anecdotes might help to elucidate what I mean here. Returning to the socks
– what would their narrative be had I found them in a different location,
and did my circumstantial knowledge (i.e. the identity of the previous occupant of my set) determine what they represented to me? Likewise, a bottle
of lavatory cleaner in the communal lounge at the Getty scholar apartments
may signify something different from one found on a supermarket shelf.

Space and time

Space and time are the dimensional frameworks in which we construct
experience. They are built into the perceiving process, and we cannot but
think in terms of space and time, and this is linked to our perceptions of self
and other and of (auto)biography. My first question here is can we really see
space and time as binary forces? Surely theory, whether masculinist or not,

has called in to question this notion. Temporal gaps and the spaces in between make cohesion impossible; instead space and time can be seen as being two oppositional elements vulnerable to deconstruction, so space cannot be a unified subject or object. I am thinking here of Jacques Derrida's essay *Ousia and Gramme*[22] where he argues that to differentiate in absolute terms between time and space would demolish them both and undermine the basic theoretical tenet that it is possible to define something by that which it is not; that is to say its opposite. Instead, we are left with the spaces in between – with differences that give the illusion of presence. Space becomes then, in Derrida's argument, no longer represented as a subject or object distinct from temporal events, it is instead 'the rhetoric of temporality' where

> an interval must separate the present time from what it is not in order for the present to be itself.... In constituting itself, in dividing itself dynamically, this interval is what might be called spacing, the becoming-space of time or the becoming-time of space (temporization).[23]

If we return to the socks, or indeed the lavatory cleaner, we can see how their temporisation means that neither is a unified subject or object. This surely helps to inform our theorisation of (auto)biography and space as its formulation is transformed over time. (Auto)biography becomes both subject and object and its status remains volatile and fluid within its space/time location. It represents.

Representation

If space represents both the (auto)biographical subject and object how do we then identify what is being projected? Here I return to Lacan who discusses architecture in relation to anamorphism – that is the role and function of projection. Lacan argues that behind anamorphism lies the whole history of architecture and painting which he sees as being intertwined 'their combination and the history of this combination'.[24] Lacan's thoughts about and attitudes towards architecture shift throughout the years in which the Seminars were written. Here, I want to hold on to his notion of architecture as representation which appears in Seminar 7 and which accords with the general reflective register within which Lacanian thought operates.

Lacanian theory has already been used in the exploration of the relationship between gender and space. For instance, Beatriz Colomina uses the idea of the gaze as a way of interrogating the modernist architectural interior and spatial/psychological modes of analysing power and regimes of control.[25] Colomina's argument focuses on certain interior spaces designed by Adolf Loos and Le Corbusier which are designated as either masculine or feminine. The gaze operates as a process by which the subject and object exchange places, albeit by different means, in each interior. Architecture is not just a platform for viewing the subject, it also produces that subject.[26] But Colomina attributes agency in the creation/representation of the female subject/object in space to the male architect. The discourse remains within a phallogocentric textual and spatial frame. I want to try to think of representation of (auto)biography as a subject/object outwith these linguistic conventions. Does Lacan offer me another way of thinking about my (auto)biography and space?

Certainly the concept of the gaze tells me something about myself:

> From the moment this gaze exists, I am already something other, in that I feel myself becoming an object for the gaze of others. But in this position, which is a reciprocal one, others also know that I am an object who knows himself [herself] to be seen.[27]

But what is our viewpoint bearing in mind Lacan's observation 'When, in love, I solicit a look, what is profoundly unsatisfying and always missing is that – You never look at me from the place from which I see you.'[28]

My enquiry also concerns space and at this point I mean the physical spaces of the built environment. For Lacan architecture is something '[which] can be defined as something that is organised around emptiness [and that] architecture enters the symbolic order by a process of sublimation'.[29] Architecture does indeed create an enclosure that can be seen as enclosing emptiness, but does it in fact enclose an originary lost object? A reversal may be operating here as architecture might not enclose emptiness, but instead operates like a picture surface to exclude emptiness.

Moving on from this I can perhaps see my position in space and architecture as an illusion. Representation signifies the presence of absence but I/you need to be aligned to see this just like in an architectural trompe l'oeil. The pleasure of a trompe l'oeil is the surprise of the illusion as what appears to be represented does not move when I do – as in the case of an anamorphis. Lacan's screen functions then for architecture as an absent three-dimensional architecture absent behind what it represents and trompe l'oeil which signifies the visual field is not transparent but conceals something real. This takes us beyond the spatial and textual linguistic limitations of constructions of self. Perspective is the illusion of space, it represents it and it is a means through which the unconscious material of architecture is revealed. This material operates in the same way as psychoanalytical models make the unconscious work to disrupt and unsettle linear, masculinist narratives. And anamorphis – the perspectival/spatial manipulation of representation – points to a way in which (auto)biography can operate as an originary object in space outwith phallogocentric linguistic constraints. The socks point to Said within a certain scopic, spatial regime, yet in another they could *mean* me.

Notes

1 This essay draws on a paper given at the III Mediterranean Congress of Aesthetics, 'Imagination, Sensuality, Art', Portorož, Slovenia, 20–23 September 2006 in a session on 'Performance' co-chaired by Professor Catherine M. Soussloff, University of California, Santa Cruz and Professor Maryvonne Saison, Paris X. I would like to thank the session chairs and the other participants including Prof. Bill Nichols and Prof. Thierry du Duve for their incisive comments and Prof. Adrian Rifkin for his helpful critique of this essay. Any errors and omissions remain my own.

2 I acknowledge the important work of Judith Butler on performance theory and notions of performativity. See for instance J. Butler, *Gender Trouble: Feminism and the Subversion of Identity*, London and New York: Routledge, 1990 and *Bodies that Matter*, London and New York: Routledge, 1993, on the discursive limits of 'sex'.

3 Elaine Showalter, 'Women's time, women's space: writing histories of feminist criticism', *Tulsa Studies in Women's Literature*, 3 (1984), p. 30 and Julia Kristeva, 'Women's time', in *Feminist Theory: A Critique of Ideology*, ed. Nannerl O. Keohane, Michelle Z. Rosaldo and Barbara C. Gelpi, Chicago: Chicago University Press, 1982, p. 33.

4 Gaston Bachelard, *The Poetics of Space*, trans. Maria Jolas, New York: Orion Press, p. 236.

5 D. Arnold, *Reading Architectural History*, London: Routledge, 2002, Ch. 6, p. 199.

6 Notable exceptions include Harry Brod (ed.) *The Making of Masculinities*, London: Routledge, 1987 and Joel Sanders, *Stud: Architectures of Masculinity*, Princeton: Princeton Architectural Press, 1996. Anthologies such as J. Rendell, B. Penner and I. Borden, *Gender Space Architecture*, London: Routledge, 2000 provide a useful cross-section of texts, but there is a gravitation towards gender as being a feminine category. Space can be gendered through habitual use or through metaphor; for instance Henri Lefebvre argues for a conjunction of physical, mental and social space making space the product of social relations and therefore constantly in a state of flux and change. The organisation of space shapes the way in which a body can move and we order space to facilitate established social relationships (see Elizabeth Grosz, 'Bodies-Cities', in *Space, Time and Perversion*, New York and London: Routledge, 1995, pp. 103–110).

7 D. Arnold, *Reading Architectural History*, London: Routledge, 2002, Ch. 6, pp. 199–204 esp. and D. Arnold, E. Ergut and B. Özkaya (eds) *Rethinking Architectural Historiography*, London: Routledge, 2006, Ch. 16, pp. 229–245.

8 See, for instance, Alice T. Friedman, 'Domestic differences: Edith Farnsworth, Mies van der Rohe, and the gendered body', in *Not At Home: The Suppression of Domesticity in Modern Architecture*, ed. Christopher Reed, London: Thames and Hudson, 1996 and *House and Household in Elizabethan England*, Chicago: University of Chicago Press, 1989; Dolores Hayden, *The Grand Domestic Revolution: A History of Feminist Designs for American Homes, Neighborhoods, and Cities*, Cambridge, MA: MIT University Press, 1981; Lynne Walker, 'Home making: an architectural perspective', *Signs*, vol. 27, no. 3 (Spring 2002), pp. 823–835 and Gwendolyn Wright, *Building the Dream: A Social History of Housing in America*, Cambridge, MA: MIT University Press, 1983; and *Moralism and*

the Model Home: Domestic Architecture and Cultural Conflict in Chicago, 1873–1913, Chicago: University of Chicago Press, 1980.

9 See, for instance, Gwendolyn Wright, *Moralism and the Model Home*.

10 Laura Mulvey, 'Melodrama inside and outside the home', in *Visual and Other Pleasures*, London: Palgrave Macmillan, 1989.

11 Alice T. Friedman, *Women and the Making of the Modern House*, New York: Harry N. Abrams, 1998.

12 Iris Marion Young, 'Throwing Like a Girl', in *Throwing Like a Girl and Other Essays in Feminist Philosophy and Social Theory*, Bloomington: University of Indiana Press, 1990, p. 172.

13 Jacques Lacan, *Ecrits, A Selection*, trans. Alan Sheridan, New York: Norton, 1977, pp. 150–152.

14 Ibid.

15 Feminist writers such as Theresa De Lauretis argue women have never occupied a place in discourse other than as the object of representation. By creating new spaces of discourse women can occupy a position in the discourse as well as maintaining their marginal status so they can be re-visioned rather then being viewed in the dominant discourse. See Theresa De Lauretis, *Technologies of Gender: Essays on Theory, Film and Fiction*, London: Macmillan, 1987, p. 25.

16 Iris Marion Young, op. cit., p. 146.

17 See Young, loc. cit.

18 This kind of phenomenological notion of space is not solely the pre-occupation of cognitive scientists. Kant had posed similar questions over two centuries earlier believing that space was a form imposed by our minds on the world.

19 Michel Foucault, *The Archaeology of Knowledge and the Discourse on Language*, trans. A.M. Sheridan Smith, New York: Pantheon, 1972, p. 17.

20 bell hooks, 1990, p. 343, 'Marginalizing a site of resistance', in R. Ferguson, M. Geves, T.T. Minha and C. West (eds) *Out There. Marginalization and Contemporary Culture*, New York and Cambridge, MA: Museum of Contemporary Art and MIT Press, 1990, pp. 341–343.

21 On this point see Anthony Giddens, *Modernity and Self Identity. Self and Society in the Late Modern Age*, Cambridge: Polity, 1991, pp. 52–54 and Charles Taylor, *Sources of the Self. The Making of Modern Identity*, Cambridge: Cambridge University Press, 1989, p. 289.

22 Jacques Derrida, *Margins of Philosophy*, trans. Alan Bass, Chicago: Chicago University Press, 1982, pp. 29–67.

23 Derrida, op. cit., p. 13.

24 Jacques Lacan, *The Ethics of Psychoanalysis 1959–60*, Book 7, *The Seminar of Jacques Lacan*, New York: Norton, 1992, p. 135.

25 Beatriz Colomina, 'Domestic voyeurism', in Beatriz Colomina (ed.) *Sexuality and Space*, Princeton: Princeton University Press, 1992, pp. 73–128.

26 Colomina, loc. cit. p. 83.

27 Jacques Lacan, *Freud's Papers on Technique 1953–54*, Book 1, *The Seminar of Jacques Lacan* ed. Jacques-Alain Miller, trans. John Forrester, New York: Norton, 1988, p. 215.

28 Jacques Lacan, *Four Fundamental Concepts of Psychoanalysis*, New York: Norton, 1981, p. 103.

29 *The Ethics of Psychoanalysis 1959–60*, Book 7, *The Seminar of Jacques Lacan*, New York: Norton, 1992, pp. 135 and 175.

2
Living the Romantic landscape (after Deleuze and Guattari)

Andrew Ballantyne

Gregory Bateson (1904–80) was an anthropologist whose most widely read book is *Naven*, a study of ritualised transgressions in New Guinea.[1] A collection of his essays, *Steps Toward an Ecology of Mind*, includes an essay on Balinese culture, which was taken up by Gilles Deleuze and Felix Guattari who developed his idea of the "plateau" of sustained intensity as a cultural practice. It is there in the title of Deleuze and Guattari's *Mille plateaux*, and is put into practice in a very general way in their work.[2] There is a passage in one of Bateson's essays in the collection which invites us to consider:

> what happens when you make the epistemological error of choosing the wrong unit: you end up with the species versus the other species around it or versus the environment in which it operates. Man against nature. You end up, in fact, with Kaneohe Bay polluted, Lake Erie a slimy green mess, and "Let's build atom bombs to kill off the next door neighbours." *There is an ecology of bad ideas, just as there is an ecology of weeds*, and it is characteristic of the system that basic error propagates itself. It branches out like a rooted parasite through the tissues of life, and everything gets into a rather peculiar mess. [...] You forget that the eco-mental system called Lake Erie is part of your wider eco-mental system – and that if Lake Erie is driven insane, its insanity is incorporated in the larger system of your thought and experience.[3]

Kaneohe Bay is in Hawaii. It is spectacularly beautiful, and there is a naval base there. Its coral reefs are vulnerable to the effects of sewage waste from the island. The green slime on Lake Erie – *Cladaphora glomerata* – continues to be a problem.[4] Guattari, who worked with the insane, cited this passage from Bateson and made use of it in his arguments.[5] Group identity has been an important part of the Deleuze-and-Guattari-world from the beginning of their collaborations.[6] Their view of the personality (the subject) was that it is always multiple; and likewise there are group phenomena where parts of the personalities in the group form significant interactions, which makes for the development of a group "personality" or subject – a characteristic group dynamic that is different from the personality of any "individual" in the group. Guattari wrote:

> Gregory Bateson has clearly shown that what he calls the "ecology of ideas" cannot be contained within the domain of the psychology of the individual, but organizes itself into systems or "minds", the boundaries of which no longer coincide with the participant individuals.[7]

What I want to take from Guattari's analysis is the idea of the emergence of group identity, and the idea that it is produced by the politics (the interpersonal relations) at work in a given group. An entity is always in part determined by the group, and by the role it has in that group – a role that might be designated and deliberate, or which one might just assume without noticing. In the world of Deleuze and Guattari, the "individual" is far from being indivisible, but is produced by these various identities and roles that one finds oneself playing, which have "political" relations with one another. We adopt some of them as character-defining signifiers, while others stay out of sight, or may be avoided and denied. This is most clearly apparent with public figures, who arrange to be seen in certain roles, doing certain things, while from time to time the public is entertained by learning about the non-standard practices conducted in secret that presumably help to keep the show on the road. The public and private roles are all aspects of one individual, but the politics involved means that in public places the public aspects are dominant, and it would help if the secret practices could be avoided even in private, but somehow they seem to have a way of asserting themselves when no one is looking, so the idea of political "forces" being in play (within the individual) seems apt. The term that Deleuze and Guattari coined for this politics-within-the-individual is "micropolitics" – and of course the term "individual" comes to seem very clearly to be the wrong term to be using, but language keeps repeating it back to us. To go back to Bateson's term we might prefer "unit of survival" (implying "organism plus environment") but were I to do so immediately then I think that my attempt to explain would become baffling. One of the things about the Deleuze-and-Guattari-world is how remote it is from anything like common sense. There is recognition of experience, and a very strong empirical and pragmatic streak runs through the work, but there is always an application of a strict logic that is never part of common sense. (Common sense relies rather on the repetition of experience and the recognition of repetition, rather than logical thought as such.) In the Deleuze-and-Guattari-world where politics is concerned, it seems to be all the same whether we are dealing with nation states, minority groups, familial groups, individuals or molecules. The logic runs right through the different scales, regardless of the fact that we have different common-sense ways of thinking about these things, and a different range of names for the relations in different scales of operation. What is an illness at one scale is a war at another – a virus in my body, seen at a molecular scale, might have many of the same affects as a battlefield. This leads on to a blurring of any definite distinction between the living and the inorganic. Living things are of course composed of inorganic elements – we need to ingest iron and chloride of sodium. Deleuze said, "It's organisms that die, not life."[8] And Guattari used as an epigraph to his book *The Three Ecologies*, a quotation from Bateson – from the passage above: "There is an ecology of bad ideas, just as there is an ecology of weeds."[9] So ideas are treated here as having life, but we would not normally think of them as in any sense "organic". In his text, after citing Bateson, Guattari continued:

> Now more than ever, nature cannot be separated from culture; in order to comprehend the interactions between eco-systems, the mecanosphere and social and individual Universes of reference, we must learn to think "transversally". Just as monstrous and mutant algae invade the lagoon of Venice, so our television screens are populated, saturated, by "degenerate" images and statements. In the field of social ecology, men like Donald Trump are permitted to proliferate freely, like another species of algae, taking over entire districts of New York and Atlantic City; he "redevelops" by raising rents, thereby driving out tens of thousands of poor families, most of whom are condemned to homelessness, becoming the equivalent of the dead fish of environmental ecology.[10]

The image of property tycoons as scum is startling. What Guattari was arguing for here is to see the unit of survival, not as an individual organic species, but the species plus its habitat. And the habitat is likely to include other species. However, there is a style of speaking at work in his texts, that fuses the inorganic parts of a habitat as part of the living "unit of survival" (species plus habitat). So buildings are certainly included in the equation, and Guattari also mentioned "incorporeal species such as music, the arts, cinema",[11] in the company of which the gestural art of architecture certainly belongs. Guattari's ecology is extraordinarily wide-ranging in its scope. In this sort of ecology a *genius loci* can clearly flourish, and as something a good deal more real than a poetic fancy. The "spirit of the place" cannot live as an independent entity, and as it has no body, if we try to separate it from its habitat, and the people who intuit its presences, then it not only dies but vanishes altogether. It is an emergent property, a product of transversality, of relationality, that does not inhere in the parts of the place, individually or collectively, but is produced when those material elements come into contact not only with each other but also with a suitably prepared observer. In one manner of speaking this "spirit of the place" is an illusion, and does not exist; but if we hold pedantically to that manner of speaking and insist that any other way of describing our feelings about the place is wrong, then we would for example have to insist that there is no movement in cinematic images, only twenty-four stillnesses a second as the separate frames go through the projector. The movement is just an illusion, that is produced when these stillnesses are observed, and that is indeed the truth of the matter; but in everyday situations we are normally comfortable with the idea that we would say that we see an image on the screen – one image – and that we see it move. In a similar manner our disparate fragmentary identities do not really cohere into a unified "self", but yet we are on the whole quite comfortable with claiming a degree of coherence for ourselves as individuals.

This multiplicity in a unit of survival is very much part of the Deleuzoguattarian orthodoxy, but it is far from being a novel idea. Back in the eighteenth century, David Hume found that if he started to think about the idea of the self, it became impossible to pin down as a distinct persona that persisted through everything he did and said. We are:

> nothing but a bundle or collection of different perceptions, which succeed each other with inconceivable rapidity, and are in perpetual flux and movement. Our eyes cannot turn in their sockets without varying our perceptions. Our thought is still more variable than our sight; and all our other senses and faculties contribute to this change; nor is there any single power of the soul, which remains unalterably the same, perhaps for one moment. The mind is a kind of theatre, where several perceptions successively make their appearance; pass, re-pass, glide away, and mingle in an infinite variety of postures and situations. There is properly no *simplicity* in it as one time, nor *identity* in different; whatever natural propension we may have to imagine that simplicity and identity. The comparison of the theatre must not mislead us. They are the successive perceptions only, that constitute the mind; nor have we the most distant notion of the place, where these scenes are represented, or of the materials, of which it is compos'd.
>
> What then gives us so great a propension to ascribe an identity to these successive perceptions, and to suppose ourselves possest of an invariable and uninterrupted existence thro' the whole course of our lives?[12]

The implications of this line of thought are far-reaching, and there is a danger that in trying to take note of them the line of thought of the present essay would be deflected. The important points to note are (1) that identity is presented as something that is constructed (from more or less disparate perceptions) and is therefore provisional, dependent not only on the actual state of things independently of us, but also on our propensity to ascribe identities as a way of dealing with our flux of perceptions; and (2) that Hume's document was originally published in 1739 – long before the

Romantic texts that will be cited below. Hume's thought had little immediate impact, but it was taken up by Kant, and by the time that Hume had
re-worked his thoughts into more polished and ingratiating essays, he came
to be seen as one of the great figures of the age. His ultra-rigorous scepti-
cism was not usually endorsed by others, but the way that he drew attention
to the limits of reason was important for the general "project" of Romanti-
cism. (If we look to Coleridge's philosophical lectures, for example, we find
that Hume is an important referent, but he is not held up as a general
guide.[13]) I put "project" in inverted commas here, because to call Romanti-
cism a "project", or even to see it as a movement, is to ascribe some sort of
identity to what is in fact a none-too-clearly-bounded set of phenomena,
which has come to have an identity in exactly the way that Hume calls into
question. In fact he calls this intuitive making of identities "a mistake":

> Our propensity to this mistake is so great ... that we fall into it before
> we are aware; and tho' we incessantly correct ourselves by reflexion, and
> return to a more accurate method of thinking, yet we cannot long
> sustain our philosophy, or take off this bliss from the imagination. Our
> last resource is to yield to it, and boldly assert that these different
> related objects are in effect the same. However interrupted and variable.
> In order to justify to ourselves this absurdity, we often feign some new
> and unintelligible principle, that connects the objects together, and pre-
> vents their interruption or variation. Thus we feign the continu'd exist-
> ence of the perceptions of the senses, to remove the interruption; and
> run into the notion of a *soul*, and *self*, and *substance*, to disguise the
> variation. But we may farther observe, that where we do not give rise to
> such a fiction, our propension to confound identity with relation is so
> great, that we are apt to imagine something unknown and mysterious,
> connecting the parts, beside their relation; and this I take to be the case
> with regard to the identity we ascribe to plants and vegetables. And
> even when this does not take place, we still feel a propensity to con-
> found these ideas, tho' we are not able fully to satisfy ourselves in that
> particular, nor find any thing invariable and uninterrupted to justify our
> notion of identity.[14]

So Hume sees the truth of the matter as being that we have to deal with
continually changing impressions, and that one of our ways we do this is to
see relations between different impressions and assert a continuing identity
across them. If we assert that there is continuity from an acorn through its
growth into an oak tree, then what do we suppose to be continuous in it?
And given the discrepancy between the objects, and the fact that we wander
away and focus our attention on other things, what sort of imaginative leap
is it that makes us infer the continuity? Of course it is something that we
have to do, as a practical necessity, as Hume admits, and if we focus on this
side of Hume's analysis (rather than the insistence on its non-logicality,

which is what Hume himself does) then we are taken down the line of thought that results in something like John Dewey's, or C.S. Peirce's, or William James's Pragmatism – again in naming their various thoughts as a movement I am making the same useful mistake. It is the same useful mistake as we make in the cinema when we see a continuous movement rather than twenty-four images each second, or infer a relation of continuity across establishing-shots, close-ups and reaction-shots. We know how to understand these discontinuities, and allow them to affect us as an immediate visceral experience. (We're missing out if we don't.) But the truth of the matter could be that the actors were not in the same room at one time. Their reactions were probably spliced together from different "takes", which might have been on different days. The soundtrack was certainly recorded as a separate exercise. A celebrated scene in the Roman blockbuster – *Gladiator* – was filmed after the principal actor in that scene had died (Oliver Reed) but it would easily pass without notice if the film were being watched by someone who had not been alerted to look out for it.[15] In watching such scenes innocently we are continually making mistakes about what we are seeing – that is the magic of cinema. With a well-made film, we have to train ourselves very deliberately if we are to have a sense of what is going on in the studio – to notice camera movements, edits, model-work and computer-generated images. The disparate images make sense dramatically only because of our propensity to infer continuity and identity, which involves not seeing the studio but seeing the characters playing out their interactions. We construct identities for these characters, based on the writers', directors' and cinematographers' clues that are put before us for that very purpose. The point that Hume makes is that we are doing this almost all the time – whenever we are not thinking in a specialised and rigorously philosophical way – and that ideas such as the soul and the self are generated by it, so it is deep rooted in our way of dealing with the world. Identities are therefore contingent, shifting and relational, and could be drawn in different ways if we find ourselves in different circumstances. (In this aspect of his thinking, one could make a case for Hume as a proto-poststructuralist thinker, and that is rather how he comes across in Deleuze's first book, which was about him.[16]) We might think it a superstition to suppose that an oak tree has a soul and that we should treat it reverently, but on Hume's reading it is no less a superstition, and a superstition of the same type, to suppose that we have souls ourselves (or, by extension, that cinematic images move). It is useful and even necessary to make this mistake in order to have effective dealings with the world. Indeed if the capacity to find coherence in disparate perceptions is diminished in everyday contexts – as opposed to specialised introspective moments – then we diagnose a mental incapacity or illness.

Deleuze and Guattari were to take up the idea of the divided or dispersed mind in their collaborative works, especially the two volumes that carry the title *Capitalism and Schizophrenia*.[17] The opening of *Mille plateaux* alludes to the idea in passing, as something accepted and established before we begin:

> The two of us wrote *Anti-Oedipus* together. Since each of us was several, there was already quite a crowd. Here we have made use of everything that came within range, what was closest as well as farthest away. We have assigned clever pseudonyms to prevent recognition. Why have we kept our own names? Out of habit, purely out of habit. To make ourselves unrecognizable in turn. To render imperceptible, not ourselves, but what makes us act, feel, and think. Also because it's nice to talk like everybody else, to say the sun rises, when everybody knows it's only a manner of speaking. To reach, not the point where one says I, but the point where it is no longer of any importance whether one says I. We are no longer ourselves. Each will know his own. We have been aided, inspired, multiplied.[18]

It is also worth making the point that Deleuze and Guattari are not being eccentric in taking this view. It is often the case that we find ourselves "in two minds" when it comes to making a definite judgement one way or another. This is only the most acute kind of example, when both minds are conscious, but if most of what goes on in the mind is unconscious, it would follow that many such conflicts are resolved without ever coming to the surface. We do what we usually do, and call it "instinct" or "habit", rather than trying to become self-consciously aware and calling for a fresh judgement at every repetition of a comparable event. In fact Deleuze and Guattari do not characterise the mind as being composed of two parts, but of crowds, swarms or tribes. It has a parallel in Marvin Minsky's work on artificial intelligence, which he sought to explain to a non-specialist audience in his book *The Society of Mind*.[19] Here – as the title says – he imagines the mind as a "society" of interconnected parts, each part of which has a very limited role that we would hesitate to call "thinking", but when the whole set of multifarious parts is connected with an enormous number of links (such as are to be found in the brain) then it is capable of doing something very like thinking – so much like it that we might think it was not different from thinking. The key here, as in Hume's thought, is the multiplicity of connections between the multifarious parts, and the micropolitics of the mind. Moreover the "thinking" need not all be done inside a single brain. We might assemble a team of people to do a complicated thing like putting up a building, that no individual member of the team could do alone. And part of the thinking could be delegated to computers, or other sorts of tools. In this way of thinking the subject can be dispersed. The key concept in *Anti-Oedipus* is of the machine. A machine is composed of a minimum of two parts, that are brought together in an assemblage (*agencement*) and it produces something. The things that are brought together might be different parts of the mind, or they might involve something external, such as someone else's mind, in which case the thinking and the production could be said to go on between the two. In the Guattari-world, there are machines everywhere, swarms of them, and they produce not only the things that we would ordinarily expect machines to produce, but also emotional states – especially desire, which is produced when machines break down. If this is one's view of "the subject", then there is no very clear threshold that marks its limits, and in Deleuze and Guattari's world there is no discomfort in allowing a computer or an information flow from a television programme to be part of the range of elements that constitutes the subject. Guattari says explicitly:

> Should we keep the semiotic productions of the mass media, informatics, telematics and robotics separate from psychological subjectivity? I don't think so. Just as social machines can be grouped under the general title of Collective Equipment, technological machines of information and communication operate at the heart of human subjectivity, not only within its memory and intelligence, but within its sensibility, affects and unconscious fantasms.[20]

The productions he mentions here are just the latest of the tools that engage with our various rational and irrational, conscious and unconscious states of mind. We are always already cyborgs. Of course buildings have a role to play here. Caves and labyrinths, spires and towers, have haunted our imaginations and connected with our desires. They have played a role in the way we think, usually without our consciously willing it. They have a role to play in the formation of the subject. Therefore they are part of the subject. "They are in us as much as we are in them," as Gaston Bachelard put it.[21] The building is part of the way we live, part of the unit of survival. It participates in life.

If we adopt Guattari's model of the dispersed personality that becomes inseparable from its environment and its ecology, then not only do we start to think of ourselves as having a strong rapport with our surroundings, but we start to think of them as part of ourselves – not in a fanciful metaphoric way, but in a pedantic, technical way. This brings us to the romantic investment in feeling caught up in the spiritual being of a place that we find in Wordsworth's poetry. Take, for example, the lines written in the Wye Valley, a few miles upstream from Tintern Abbey, where he describes how in his youth he scampered carelessly about among the trees and hills. Now, however, at a maturer age, he looks to natural scenery for other reasons, feeling there a sublime sense of something deeply interfused,

> A motion and a spirit that impels
> All thinking things, all objects of all thought,
> And rolls through all things. Therefore am I still
> A lover of the meadows and the woods
> And mountains, and of all that we behold

From this green earth, of all the mighty world
Of eye and ear (both what they half-create
And what perceive) – well-pleased to recognize
In nature and the language of the sense,
The anchor of my purest thoughts, the nurse,
The guide, the guardian of my heart, and soul
Of all my moral being.

(vv. 89–112)

This goes beyond an aesthetic appreciation of the landscape, to turn the hills and forests into instruments of subjectification. They are being mobilised in order to make Wordsworth into the sort of person he will become. The living being is the organism plus habitat, inseparably. The hills are as much part of him as the acorn is part of the oak tree. In fact in Deleuze and Guattari's hands the conclusion is utterly unlike the romantic attachment to place, because it is linked in their writings with ideas of nomadism, constant reformulation and re-subjectification.[22] Their concern is never to recapture the original primary sensibility of the noble savage, but to go forward in an experimental frame of mind, to produce new ways of living, new ways of becoming. If Wordsworth feels bonded to a particular region, and formed by it, there is perhaps a different more mobile sensibility in Byron, who describes in *Childe Harold* something more volatile. It is not that he has been permanently shaped by the landscapes of his youth, but that he changes and becomes a different sort of person in the different sur-roundings that he puts himself in, and sometimes this is liberating and thrilling, whereas at other times it is constraining and unwelcome:

I live not in myself, but I become
Portion of that around me; and to me
High mountains are a feeling, but the hum
Of human cities torture. I can see
Nothing to loathe in nature, save to be
A link reluctant in a fleshly chain,
Classed among creatures, when the soul can flee,
And with the sky, the peak, the heaving plain
Of ocean, or the stars, mingle and not in vain.

(Canto 3, st 72)

The Romantic landscape is presented in exactly this character-forming way in the opening pages of *Anti-Oedipus*. Writing in 1972, long before there were such things as personal computers, they cite a literary creation, *Lenz*, by Georg Büchner (1813–1837). This character Lenz was based on a real person – a German Romantic poet of the Sturm und Drang tendency, Jacob Lenz (1751–1792). In Büchner's incomplete novel, based on the journal of a pastor who briefly looked after the real Lenz, at a time when he (Lenz) was losing his mind and becoming schizophrenic. The remarkable thing about Büchner's text is that it is written trying to give an impression of events that is sympathetic to Lenz's troubled point of view.[23] It is an extraordinary feat of the imagination, and Deleuze and Guattari treat it as accurate evidence of the ways in which a schizophrenic's mind works – and this would not have been done lightly, given Guattari's professional involvement with real schizophrenic patients. In Büchner's incomplete novella, Lenz speaks with the pastor in an enclosed room, and then goes for a walk outside – there's more to the writing than that – it's really about his state of mind – but it is this spatial contrast that Deleuze and Guattari make use of, the move from confinement to expansiveness. When Lenz is with the pastor the conversation is controlled in such a way that he is allowed to situate himself only in relation to his father and mother – which is to say that he is kept in the Oedipalised relations of the family. The confinement of the room correlates with the oppression in his mind. And then here I quote Deleuze and Guattari (they in turn quote Büchner in their text). We've had Lenz talking with the pastor, and suffering.

> While taking a stroll outdoors, on the other hand, he is in the mountains, amid falling snowflakes, with other gods or without any gods at all, without a family, without a father or a mother, with nature. "What does my father want? Can he offer me more than that? Impossible. Leave me in peace." Everything is a machine. Celestial machines, the stars or rainbows in the sky, alpine machines – all of them connected to those of his body. The continual whirr of machines. "He thought that it must be a feeling of endless bliss to be in contact with the profound life of every form, to have a soul for rocks, metals, water, and plants, to take into himself, as in a dream, every element of nature, like flowers that breathe with the waxing and waning of the moon." To be a chlorophyll- or a photosynthesis-machine, or at least slip his body into such machines as one part among the others. Lenz has projected himself back to a time before the man-nature dichotomy, before all the co-ordinates based on this fundamental dichotomy have been laid down. He does not live nature as nature, but as a process of production. There is no such thing as either man or nature now, only a process that produces the one within the other and couples the machines together. Producing-machines, desiring-machines everywhere, schizophrenic machines, all of species life: the self and the non-self, outside and inside, no longer have any meaning whatsoever.[24]

So in this view of the world, the person is not isolated from the surroundings, and cannot be isolated from them. By making connection with them, different states of mind are produced and different kinds of action become possible. It's worth pointing out that these states of mind can be switched into play without actually being brought into close physical contact with the things involved. The mind-set can be produced by bringing an image or an idea into play. Wordsworth is stirred to great thoughts by the memory of the hills he knew as a child, even when he is not actually among them. Lenz is stifled by even the thought of his parents. And the kind of person he is in relation to them is utterly different from the kind of person he is when he can set them on one side and engage with the stars, snowflakes and mountains. When Byron is part of a crowd of people, he is dulled; but when he is alone among the mountains he can feel his spirits soar, and lose himself in the vastness of the ocean or the heavens, where a different range of thoughts is possible. Practicalities suggest that he needn't actually be alone among the mountains. He might be daydreaming – remembering a time when he was once alone among the mountains – or vividly imagining what it would be like to be alone among the mountains – they might all have the effect of shifting his mind-set to one where he could think thoughts that were grandiose – he certainly cultivated the thoughts that he set down in verse when he was somewhere that he could write, and might not have been on a snowy peak when he did so. Adopting Deleuze and Guattari's use of the machine, we could say that both Byron and Lenz feel diminished when they sense themselves to be engaged in a social machine – producing the things that the rest of society wants to see produced. And on the contrary they feel capable of producing much more and producing something much more worthwhile when they are machinically engaged with mountains, the ocean or snowflakes – though we might be hard-pressed to put a name to what it is that is being produced. What we do have here is a very strong correspondence between the idea of the self as a system of flows caught up in a variety of semi-autonomous machines, that in fact produce the self, or rather in their various engagements they produce aspects of a rather dispersed and none-too-coherent self – the "self" of Deleuze and Guattari's "schizo-analysis". There is a correspondence between this organism and its environment that is every bit as strong as the rapport between the human body and buildings as it was envisaged in the Renaissance, where the body was described as a finite set of perfectly proportioned parts. In the space of flows envisaged by Deleuze and Guattari, orderly geometry is beside the point. Their space is relational. What matters is whether we can connect this part with that part, and what is produced when we do so. And if we go back and look at what is produced when we connect our selves with different parts of the environment, then there are different things to value. When we connect with the expanses of natural landscape, whether they're represented by alps, rolling hills, stars or snowflakes, then what is produced is something like wonder. In the case of the highly charged Romantics above, the landscape is productive of the sublime.

Going back to Bateson, pointing out that the unit of survival is the organism plus habitat, and connecting it with the Romantic conviction that we are formed by our surroundings – and not in a superficial way, but in aspects of our most fundamental character, our moral dispositions – gives us a way to see the schizo-analytic subject of Deleuze and Guattari's discourse as a character with a past (albeit a past that has been recognised only in the modern age). Hume reasoned his way into an understanding of a nebulous pre-personal potentiality that resolved into aspects of a self when he came into contact with other people, or common-sense ways of thinking. This was not the beginning of the story, however, as there are certainly intuitions of this sort in various mystical traditions and in the practical ways of collective character-formation that are to be found in the monastery and in army drill – the breaking down of the self that comes into the institution, and its reformulation in the collective body. The experience that the Romantic poets allude to is such a character-formation, but in these cases it has been achieved by dissolving the sense of self as something distinct from a place – a landscape – so that rather than feeling like part of a collective body of people (polite society, monastic brethren or fellow squaddies) the Romantic sensibility constructs the individual as alone and isolated so far as other people are concerned, but having a profound rapport with nature. The tortured genius is a Romantic ideal – misunderstood, possibly insane, and having a distant acquaintance with common sense, nevertheless this persona gives access to perceptions that would otherwise have passed us by, and appeals to the adolescent part of all of us. The personality-cult biography that is produced by this view of the genius figure is well established, and works particularly effectively with self-dramatising subjects – Byron, Nietzsche, Chateaubriand, Napoleon. If we transfer our attentions to architecture, then it is difficult to find subjects who are so compelling, because architects who erect buildings (as opposed to those who dream of building) need to have enough common sense about them to be trusted with the management of the large sums of money that are involved in building. Pugin is perhaps the purest example of the Romantic type of architect, but he is upstaged by Ludwig II of Bavaria, who was not an architect himself, but commissioned architects to realise his projects. The successful architect can rarely sustain this role as a solitary misunderstood figure, and indeed the way that buildings come about is usually that a client or patron figure decides that a building is necessary and then employs an architect to design it. While a great architect can produce a marvellous building in response to such a commission, the architect is nevertheless put in the position of a trusted servant rather than a free spirit, and it takes unusual charisma to be able to carry off the commission with aplomb, making it appear to be the work of the solitary architect's independent will.

If we shift our attention from the idea of the architect as an isolated organism, and start to consider the habitat, then there are various transitional phases in the shift. First there is the architect's cultural context – the milieu in which the architect lived and in which his or her ideas were formed. That is to say: the ideas came from this habitat, either ready made or newly coined in response to the problems that were engendered in it. An idea that is new in architecture is usually an idea that has come into architecture from outside – an idea about what the architect might be trying to articulate in the work. Even the purest sort of formal inventiveness, if it is to be seen as meaningful rather than arbitrary, will connect with some sort of receptive culture if the work has ever been seen as worthy of attention. We easily move to the position of seeing the biography as an account of the individual as a participant in various milieux – social, intellectual, economic – even when the individual's self-mythologising might propose isolation as the distinguishing character-trait. Byron, for example, is often presented as a social outcast and a lonely wanderer, and yet he would have remained in total obscurity had not he been born to a position in society that gave him access to education and the means to support him in his taking of liberties. He did things that others only dreamed of doing, some of them high-minded, some of them less so, and did not make an income by doing so. He already had money, as a consequence of his family; as a lord he had access to some of the finest houses in Europe, and their beds, and if he squandered a fortune, he put some of his money to noble causes. His repu-tation as "mad, bad, and dangerous to know" was made through his contact with society, not by being separate from it, even if he was tortured by the hum of human cities. He does not seem to have been troubled by any lack of a sense of self, rather – at least in the passage from *Childe Harold* cited above – his sense of himself seems to have spilled out into his surroundings: "I live not in myself, but I become portion of that around me." This could be contrasted with Lenz's under-determined sense of self, but at a practical level the results are identical, as the sense that is cultivated in each is of being inseparable from the habitat, commingled with the sky, the peak, the heaving plain of ocean, or the stars. The biography of such a unit of survival clearly has a different sense of where to draw the outline of its subject than a biography that focuses exclusively on the named organism as its subject. Indeed the sense of an outline could become altogether blurred, and the methodical avoidance of putting one in place could become a point of principle. For Guattari there can be no incongruity in seeing the history of ideas as a version of biography, as these incorporeal species have their lives and participate in lives. If there can be an ecology of ideas, then there are potential biographies of ideas. Then the subject of the biography is an idea, and its habitat is variously a cultural climate and the individuals that the idea inhabits, virus-like, enabling them to have certain thoughts and do certain things. So there is a story to be told, and we could call it a biography or a line of flight, that connects the Stoics' advocacy of self-denial with the mystical abnegations and dissolutions of the self to be found in later religious traditions, and then, having been analysed by Hume, made available for the Romantic sense of being self-consciously part of nature, bringing us to the ecological awareness of Bateson and Guattari, and taking us goodness-knows-where. In fact the name that has been coined for such a story is "genealogy"; it was coined by Nietzsche in his *Genealogy of Morals*, and was importantly taken up by Michel Foucault.[25] Methodologically the important thing about the genealogy is that it estab-lishes precursors, without the need to ground the whole edifice on an origin (which much eighteenth- and nineteenth-century argument did try to do – for example in speculations about the origins of language, or indeed architecture). The genealogy is a form of biography that spans multiple generations, so the individual's life is seen as part of a broader network – a network that had much greater significance for the individual in societies where the nobility would establish their authority by this means, and titles (often also names) would be transferred from one generation to the next as if by this means the same organism were continuing to inhabit the continuing environment. The content of this form of biography is limited to the transmission of genetic inheritance, and in its purest form – a family tree, or a Biblical "begat" list – has no further narrative content.

Ideas inhabit us, just as we inhabit buildings. If ideas could have a point of view, then they would see us as their hosts, or as their habitats. Deleuze and Guattari invite us to understand ourselves as landscapes, inhabited in passing by tribes and swarms of concepts.[26] Here the balance between the organism and habitat has tipped in the direction opposite to its usual common-sense position. The usual biographical subject becomes the habitat for the non-corporeal organisms whose nomadic lives we would be aiming to trace. If we can allow ourselves to reassert our common sense and reclaim the "individual" as the proper subject of biography, then if we follow the logic, we must also allow ourselves to see the equal legitimacy of seeing the places that we inhabit as having biographies. Moreover, these places – whether they be landscapes or buildings – can be shaped by human agency, but the point of them is not so much their taking shape as the life that goes on in them and on account of them. The role of the architect in this process would be that of midwife, or more precisely of the midwife's mind – the actual activity being carried out by the midwife's hands/teams of builders. Just as the midwife's ideas and intentions might not be the most significant thing about the life of the individual being born, so the architect's ideas and intentions might not be the most significant thing about a building, and indeed most of the time we know little about what those intentions might have been. The architects who have had the social prestige to make their views known have had a disproportionate amount of attention from historians, and it might be on account of the same social prestige that they have been able to secure the commissions for the best buildings. However, what gives buildings longevity is not what they meant for their designers, but what they come to mean for others. One building will be allowed to collapse, or will be demolished to be replaced by another more profitable one, whereas another building will be lovingly maintained and restored. The meaning of the building that is maintained will shift over time, with the passing of the society that saw its creation, as it is taken up by new owners with new ideas and understandings. Whether the architect's intentions form any part of that new understanding is open to doubt, particularly as it may not even have informed the understanding of the original occupants. It would be quite possible to write a biography of a long-lived building by giving an account of the growth and development of the building, explaining what had happened there and how it had shaped the lives that had passed through it, without ever giving an account of the view of the building's designer. In the same way it would seem perverse in the biography of a person who has achieved great things, to dwell at any length, or even to notice, the views of that person's midwife.

By taking seriously Hume's inclination to dissolve the self, and the Romantics' inclination to dissolve themselves into places rather than crowds of other people, I arrive at a point where I see three clear scales at which biography operates. It should be possible to extend the series indefinitely, to the sub-molecular in one direction and to the universal in the other, but three will do for the time being. The first is the biography of the organism – the body that is born and that dies. The body inhabits places, and is inhabited by ideas. One of the ideas that it seems to need is a sense of the self, and the sense of who or what one is can vary depending on aspects of circumstances that we would not always anticipate. For example Wordsworth came to see that the Cumberland and Westmorland hills were the soul of all his moral being, which made them a part of him, even when he was far away – for example in the Wye valley – remembering them. As part of this biography of the organism, we would expect there to be something by way of genealogy, to give an idea of the subject's early years and the conditions of life into which it was born; and there would be mention of children, if the subject parented any. In the case of a historical subject (as opposed to a contemporary celebrity, say) we would expect there to be some mention of important ideas that had influenced the subject's thinking; and there would be an epilogue taking the story on after the body's death, to show the lasting influence of the things that this person had thought and done. Already here the form is becoming hybrid, and engaging with the second sort of biography: the biography of ideas. We might not be able to tell where an idea originated, but we can trace its antecedents, and its descendants, and explain how it was deployed by various people across a range of time that could be longer than any human genealogy we can trace with accuracy. The incorporeal lives of ideas are imperishable so long as there are people who find an urge to think them, which is to say for as long as they have a use. (One of the most persistent is the idea of a self.) Academic readers are comfortable with these ideas when they are seen to belong to the realm of intellectual activity, but they are sometimes given other labels which make them seem to belong to a world of spirits, that makes me (for one) feel anxious and which I would prefer to avoid. However, the construction of identities and souls and *genii loci* seem to be all of a piece and such ideas certainly have potential histories, which we can call biographies. Moving in the opposite direction, from the ethereal to the solid: the third type of biography would be a biography of place, which would be the life story of a place as it came into being and as it was inhabited by waves of settlers with their regimes of ideas and patterns of behaviour. Again there is a foreshadowing of it in the biography of the first kind, if the subject's formation is seen in relation to the places of childhood, or in the kind of place that was made or adopted by the subject as an appropriate place to dwell. However, in the third type of biography the place would be the subject, the point of narrative continuity running through, while people and the ideas that occupy them come and go. Just as some ideas help us to flourish, while others lead us into self-destructive patterns of behaviour, so places will flourish or be exhausted by different ecologies of occupants (in turn informed by their different ecologies of ideas). It would be possible in principle to have biographies of places where humans had never intervened, but the likelihood is that there would be little documentation to support such projects. That might not make them impossible. We now have not only cultural histories of the weather, but also the idea that global warming about ten thousand years ago, in the historically distant but geologically recent past, might have made possible the development of early civilisation, and therefore in a manner of speaking it seems to have been one of the necessary preconditions for history.[27] Some historical events can be inferred, even when there were no witnesses who noticed what was happening at the time. My most general conclusion is that it is possible to understand places including buildings in a satisfying way if we look at them across their whole lives. Most architectural history, taking its cue from art history, has been inclined to see the important moment in the life of a building as the act of the creative imagination that gives the building form and brings it into being. Some places, however, have been found to play important roles later in life, quite independently of their designers' intentions. Indeed in a case like the Westmorland hills (and hills are proverbially old) we would find it odd if a geologist were to suggest that they had a designer, or that the designer had any intentions whatsoever. We would see their formation as the working out of a process that had its own internal way of doing what it did. Wordsworth was not responding to any moral intent that was "designed into" the hills, when he found a way of using them imaginatively as a grounding for his moral sense, but it is wonderful and inspiring that he found a way to do that and to give it forceful expression. The rebalancing of organism plus habitat not only as the unit of survival but also as the entity whose life could be the subject for biography, will produce compelling accounts of people and places that have hitherto escaped notice.

Notes

1 Gregory Bateson, *Naven: A Survey of the Problems Suggested by a Composite Picture of the Culture of a New Guinea Tribe Drawn from Three Points of View* (1958, Leland Stanford Junior University; 2nd edition London: Wildwood House, 1980).

2 The links are set out at greater length in Andrew Ballantyne, *Architecture Theory: A Reader in Philosophy and Culture* (London: Continuum, 2005), pp. 71–3. Bateson's essay, "Bali: The Value-System of a Steady State", is reprinted in that volume, pp. 74–87.

3 Gregory Bateson, "Pathologies of Epistemology", in *Steps to an Ecology of Mind* (New York: Chandler, 1972), p. 484.

4 Scott N. Higgins, E. Todd Howell, Robert E. Hecky, Stephanie J. Guildford and Ralph E. Smith, "The wall of green: The Status of *Cladaphora glomerata* on the northern shores of Lake Erie's eastern basin, 1995–2002", *Journal of Great Lakes Research*, vol. 31, no. 4 (2005), pp. 547–63.

5 This passage is cited in Felix Guattari, *Les trois ecologies* (Paris: Galilee, 1989), translated by Ian Pindar and Paul Sutton, *The Three Ecologies* (London: Athlone, 2000), p. 71.

6 I am here taking up the idea of different "worlds" from Nelson Goodman, *Ways of Worldmaking* (Indianapolis: Hackett, 1978); see also Paul Ricoeur, "Review of Nelson Goodman. Ways of worldmaking", in Andrew Ballantyne, *Architecture Theory*, pp. 170–81.

7 Guattari, *Three Ecologies*, p. 54; and see note 56, p. 93, referencing Bateson, *Steps to an Ecology of Mind*, p. 339. (Guattari's "citation" is in fact a paraphrase.)

8 Gilles Deleuze, *Pourparlers* (Paris: Editions de Minuit, 1990), translated by Martin Jouchin, *Negotiations* (New York: Columbia University Press, 1995), p. 143.

9 Guattari, *Three Ecologies*, p. 27.

10 Guattari, *Three Ecologies*, p. 43.

11 Felix Guattari, *Chaosmose* (Paris: Galilee, 1992), translated by Paul Bains and Julian Pefanis, *Chaosmosis: an Ethico-Aesthetic Paradigm* (Sydney: Power, 1995), p. 120.

12 David Hume, *A Treatise of Human Nature* (London: John Noon, 1739), edited by L.A. Selby-Bigge, revised P.H. Nidditch (Oxford: Clarendon Press, 1978), pp. 252–3.

13 Samuel Taylor Coleridge, *Philosophical Lectures*, edited by Kathleen Coburn (London: Pilot Press, 1949).

14 Hume, *Treatise*, pp. 254–5.

15 *Gladiator*, directed by Ridley Scott (2000). The actor in question was Oliver Reed.

16 Gilles Deleuze, *Empirisme et subjectivite* (Paris: Presses Universitaires de France, 1953), translated by Constantine Boundas, *Empiricism and Subjectivity: an Essay on Hume's Theory of Human Nature* (New York: Columbia University Press, 1991).

17 Gilles Deleuze and Felix Guattari, *L'anti-Oedipe* (Paris: Editions de Minuit, 1972), translated by Robert Hurley, Mark Seem and Helen R. Lane, *Anti-Oedipus: Capitalism and Schizophrenia* (New York: Viking, 1977); Gilles Deleuze and Felix Guattari, *Mille plateaux* (Paris: Editions de Minuit, 1980), translated by Brian Massumi, *A Thousand Plateaus* (Minneapolis: University of Minnesota Press, 1988).

18 Deleuze and Guattari, *A Thousand Plateaus*, p. 3.

19 Marvin Minsky, *The Society of Mind* (London: Heinemann, 1987).

20 Guattari, *Chaosmosis*, p. 4.

21 Gaston Bachelard, *La poetique de l'espace* (Paris: Presses Universitaires de France, 1958), translated by Maria Jolas, *The Poetics of Space* (Boston: Beacon Press, 1964).

22 The romantic attachment to place was of course explored very significantly by Heidegger, but along very different lines from those followed here.

23 Georg Büchner, *Lenz* (Deutscher Klassiker Verlag Frankfurt am Main, 1999), translated by Richard Sieburth, *Lenz* (New York: Archipelago Books, 2004).

24 Deleuze and Guattari, *Anti-Oedipus*, p. 2.

25 Friedrich Nietzsche, *Zur Genealogie der Morale, Eine Streitschrift* (Leipzig, 1887), translated by Walter Kaufmann and R.J. Hollingdale, *The Genealogy of Morals: a Polemic* (New York: Random House, 1967); Michel Foucault, "Nietzsche, genealogie, histoire", in *Hommage a Jean Hyppolite* (Paris: Presses Universitaires de France, 1971), translated by D.F. Bouchard,

"Nietzsche, genealogy, history", in *Language, Counter-Memory, Practice: Selected Essays and Interviews*, edited by D.F. Bouchard (Ithaca: Cornell University Press, 1977).

26 Deleuze and Guattari, *A Thousand Plateaus*, pp. 172–3.

27 Vladimir Jankovic, *Reading the Skies: A Cultural History of English Weather 1650–1820* (Chicago: University of Chicago Press, 2000); Michael Cook, *A Brief History of the Human Race* (New York: Norton, 2003).

3

"Life as a ride in the métro"
Pierre Bourdieu on biography and space

Hélène Lipstadt

The history of a life is one of those notions that has been smuggled like contraband ... from common sense ... into the world of scholars.... To try to understand a life as a unique and self-sufficient series of successive events with no links other than their association with a "subject" whose constancy is no doubt merely that of a common name, is nearly as absurd as to try to make sense of a ride [*trajet*] in the métro without taking into account the structure of the entire urban transport system, that is the matrix of objective relations between the different stations.[1]

Sentimental Education, that book on which a thousand commentaries have been written, but which has undoubtedly never been truly read, supplied all the tools necessary for its own sociological analysis.[2]

Architectural spaces address mute injunctions directly to the body and, just as surely as court etiquette, obtain from it the reverence and respect born of distance.... Their very invisibility (to analysts themselves ...) undoubtedly make these the most important components of the symbolic order of power and the totally real effects of symbolic power.... One can break with misleading appearances and with the errors inscribed in substantialist thought about place only through a rigorous analysis of the relations between structures of social space and those of physical space.[3]

These days, space has a seemingly exponentially increasing number of friends, and biography, a similarly growing number of less-than-friendly critics. As the epigraphs for this essay suggest, the French sociologist Pierre Bourdieu, considered by many to be the most important sociologist of the second half of the twentieth century, counts as both. In order to use Bourdieu on space for the telling of lives, need we defy his condemnation of biography? If we write biographies, are his insights on space forbidden to us? There is, I argue, no need to choose, for Bourdieu believed that the study of lives is the study of space. Lives should be studied as if they were "a ride in the métro," that is, by taking a "necessary detour through space." After all, "who would think of evoking a voyage without having an understanding of the landscape in which it happened?"[4]

No single text among his 40-odd books and 400 articles[5] explains how this is to be done. His famous analysis of the Berber house of the Kabyle in Algeria and the gendered embodied spatial orientations of its inhabitants does not provide the solution (Figure 3.1). That essay can be transposed to other social and spatial formations, but, Bourdieu warned, only in very specific conditions and then only with a recognition of its shortcomings.[6] The way to the "necessary detour" is through three texts by Bourdieu: his analysis of *Sentimental Education*, Gustave Flaubert's novel about youthful successes and failures in art and love in mid-nineteenth-century Paris (written in 1975[7] and revised in 1992 as "Prologue, Flaubert analyst of Flaubert," it is cited as "Prologue"); his 1986 manifesto for ridding historiography and the social sciences of "The Biographical Illusion" (henceforth, "Illusion") and his 1993 instructions for understanding the "Site Effects" of social suffering and privilege in contemporary society (henceforth, "Site").

All three are needed. "Illusion" identifies the serious epistemological problems biography poses. It offers a solution that, while spatial, leaves the part played by physical space (under which Bourdieu subsumed architectural space) in it unaddressed. "Prologue" accounts for the conditions that

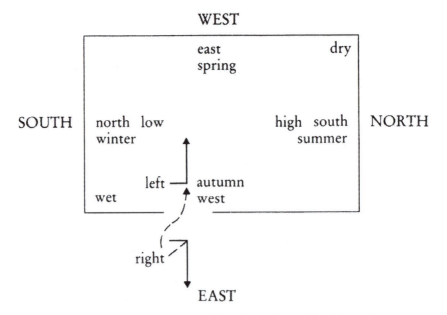

Figure 3.1 The dual spatial orientation of the Kabyle house (the right angles represent the movement of the female and male subjects' bodies), from Pierre Bourdieu, *The Logic of Practice*, 1990 (1980).

made Flaubert's literary innovation possible by reading real historical conditions out of an account of fictional lives lived in real spaces and historical time, but does not explain how to make the spatial component of the analysis available for other readings. "Site" proposes an analytical framework for the reading of contemporary physical space as the homologue of social space, but leaves it to readers to work out the application from accompanying texts – and none of them refer to historical examples.

Metaphorically riding the métro with Bourdieu and observing him struggle to correct current misunderstanding of sites of social differentiation allows us to find our method for the spatial study of lives. It had been "hiding in plain sight," in his reading of Flaubert's reading of his own condition into his account of an aspiring writer in Paris before and after the Revolution of 1848. Following in Bourdieu's footsteps as he follows Flaubert following in the footsteps of the novel's main characters in a specific historic time and space, we arrive at an understanding of how to account for lives lived in space and spaces in lives. More precisely, we come to grasp that both lives and spaces only make sense if dynamically related to other lives and other spaces, for they are constructed by and in those relations.

The understanding is spatial and thus resembles the one that we architectural historians are trained to possess, except it is now rendered more powerfully so. It also serves as an access road to a potentially liberating new self-understanding, an adjustment of the disposition we bring to our study of lives and spaces, or to use Bourdieu's term, our disciplinary habitus.[8] The changes are as timely as they are welcome. The result is a thorough-going reorientation of architectural history that, I will argue in my conclusion, both realizes the internal disciplinary changes that designers and historians of architecture believe the new paradigm of authorship in architecture demands and the external ones sought by the historians who are urging us to go "beyond the boundaries" of architectural history and inviting members of other disciplines to enter ours.[9]

We must first, however, rid ourselves of common misapprehensions about Bourdieu and space. There is no doubt that Bourdieu conceived society as a space.[10] Some students of space go further, claiming that he held that physical or geographic space plays a primary role in shaping social space and in forming the *habitus*, the system of dispositions that orients individuals, or that habitus and habitat, space and disposition, are one and the same.[11] Not surprisingly, the habitus has become one of those words in architecture and planning that attracts serious as well as not-so-serious attention.[12] Emphasizing the habitat narrows our understanding of the habitus.[13] Other places, and especially the school, play an enormous role in the unconscious incorporation of the social and the historical during early socialization, the all-important time for the formation of the habitus. Moreover, that formation is an on-going process. Misconstrue the habitus, and one misses the main objective of Bourdieu's sociology and misses out on his most important achievement. As the philosopher Charles Taylor has explained, the habitus enables Bourdieu to correct the "wrong, intellectualist epistemology [that] has made deep inroads into social science, to ill effect" and thereby to help show philosophy and the social sciences the way out of the "cul-de-sac of monological consciousness."[14]

There is, however, no mistaking Bourdieu's position on biography. A note that his literary executor found attached to the manuscript of *Esquisse pour une auto-analyse*, Bourdieu's *socioanalysis*, his self-reflective social self-analysis of himself, captures his principled opposition to both autobiography and autobiography: "*Ceci n'est pas une autobiographie.* I find it impossible to write one, and not only because of my '*dé(nonciation)*' of biography, my announcing that biography was an illusion and denouncing it for being so. I find the genre profoundly antipathetic."[15] He was referring there to "Illusion."

There is much to be gained in using Bourdieu on space in the place of standard biography. First, in terms of method, as we saw in the first epigraph, Bourdieu insists that a rupture with the commonsensical in ordinary language and the consensual in expert discourse is the necessary first step for the construction of any object of research. Biography is a notion especially susceptible to be taken for granted by non-expert and expert alike, and the spatial study of lives is a new object of research. Second, the aim of Bourdieu's sociology was a kind of emancipation. He sought to generate sufficient understanding in individuals of their social position to free them, as much as possible, from the domination, real and symbolic, to which they are subject. As all students of physical space know, space is complicit in domination, ostentatiously so as representation and surveillance, but also so surreptitiously so that Bourdieu believes it escapes notice, as he asserted in the citation from "Site" with which this essay begins. They therefore have a duty to undertake the kind of analysis that uncovers that complicity at work.

The task is not one to be taken on lightly. Most biographies undertaken by students of space are monographs. The monograph is the genre most prized by academic publishers because, we can presume, it is the genre most read by architectural historians. A reconsideration of biography thus means that architectural historians will be reassessing a mainstay of advancement in the discipline. "Illusion" and "Prologue" were designed to instigate this kind of rethinking. They provoked impassioned discussion in the relevant disciplines.[16] "Site" is a part of *Misère du Monde*. When published, it stimulated broad national debate in France about social inequality.[17]

A review of the core concepts of Bourdieu's sociology that Bourdieu embedded into all three texts will make it easier to keep up with him. The quadriga of *fields, illusio, capital,* and, of course, the *habitus*, together with the study of the dynamic interaction that makes them inseparable from one another, drives all of Bourdieu's sociology. A *field* is a *universe of social relations* constituted by the members of the field in accordance with the field's *logic, stakes, capitals* and *interests*. Overlapping and competing fields – *polit-*

ical, journalistic, juridical (legal), academic, economic, bureaucratic, and the *field of cultural production* – and the overarching and intertwining *field of power* make up society, or *social space.* The *field of power* is constituted by relations between individuals from any field who dominate their particular field and who recognize each other as competitors. The *field of cultural production* is a *market of symbolic goods,* an *up-side-down world* where an *anti-economic* logic of *disinterest* prevails, one that renders that field more autonomous than all others. The *illusio,* most frequently defined as a "belief in the game," is possessed by the player who is invested in – in both the economic and psychoanalytic sense – and committed to the game, even ready to die for stakes whose values are specific to that field and to no other field. *Capitals* are of several types: *economic,* composed of assets and attitudes toward them; *social,* consisting of identities, influence and networks; and *cultural,* constituted by incorporated skills and talents, concrete cultural possessions, and credentials and degrees. The *habitus* is an embodied schema of *perception* and *appreciation* and of *vision and division* that permits improvisation and is capable of transformation. It is not destiny. For example, working with and against the field's highly cherished historic tradition, or its *space of possibles,* makes invention and subversion realizable for those whose habitus is so well adjusted to the field as to detect possibilities undetected by others in that space. On occasion, a member of a field, who possesses the *subversive habitus* of a *misfit* diverges radically from it and launches a *symbolic revolution.*[18]

"The Biographical illusion"

"Illusion" owed its origin to an actual life story. Consulted by a childhood friend from his native village about a dramatic turn of events in his life, Bourdieu had to recognize that while he possessed a full grasp of the facts of the situation, he was incapable of understanding his friend's narrative. Much as if he were William Faulkner, the friend was recounting several different overlaid life stories, with the main narrative serving as the vehicle for telling others in a veiled form. "I realized right there ... the full extent to which the linear life stories with which ethnographers and sociologists are content are artificial.... I was led to bring back ... a whole set of questions that had been repressed concerning biography."[19]

The spatial metaphors of the ride in the métro and the voyage in a landscape clearly invite us to substitute the dynamic matrix of relations between an individual and a field for biography's single focus on the subject. What is less clear is the specifically Bourdieusien motivation for this critique. Given that he is hardly the only one to contest "the atomized, individualistic, pre-Freudian unified self of liberal humanism,"[20] and biography as a "master narrative," we are within our rights in asking what Bourdieu's particular brief against biography is and how his presentation of its deficiencies validates their substitution by space.

Bourdieu holds that biography represents one of those cases where scientific analysis comes dangerously close to the ordinary discourse that describes life as a "path." Biography smuggles "biographical illusions" into the analysis. Phrases like "from the beginning," and "he made his way" bring the presupposition that life is a unified linear progression, while those of "already" and "always" define it as a complete and oriented whole that is, moreover, experienced as a "project," its purposefulness transparent to the subject. In addition, the chronology of a life story introduces the confusion of succession in time with causality, making the chronological appear as the "chrono-logical." Teleology and intentionality are unwittingly taken for granted. In addition, by confusing *states*, or succession in time, with *stages*, successive moves toward success, biography unthinkingly replicates a subject's propensity to be what Bourdieu calls the "ideologist of his or her own life," to offer a selective and flattering narrative of that life. Finally, by replicating the "story line" of the grand narratives of traditional literature, biography compounds these explicitly biographical illusions with a "rhetorical illusion."[21]

As a result, the biographer becomes a colluding partner in the maintaining of this artifice. The "evil twining" of biographer and subject is the unintended consequence of the former's unreflecting pursuit of establishing meaning that comes with, in common parlance, "the job description," or the disciplinary habitus of being a professional of interpretation. In addition, by accepting the life story, biographers join official models of self-presentation in both its blameless form of the official biography and in its disciplinary ones of the official inquiry. They perpetuate everything the state and society invests in making the proper name into the guarantor of the "constancy of the nominal" required by the social order.

What goes missing in biography is as important as what goes wrong, and it is here that time and space are at risk. Time, the variation that comes with each retelling, is effaced by the biographical illusion of the unitary ordered life. Space, especially the relational space of intimacy, is flattened and made unrecognizable. Discourses of the self are normally constructed to be whispered within "protected markets" constituted by familiars and are adjusted to accord with their shared "logic of confidences." Both temporal dynamism and spatial plasticity are lost when these discourses are translated into a "public presentation" of a life.[22]

Bourdieu's solution is the field, with its dynamic ever-shifting relational structure of positions and unfixed boundaries, and the *trajectory* within it. The latter is a "constructed notion, ... a series of positions successively occupied by the same agent (or the same group) in a space which is constantly evolving and subject to ongoing transformations." The trajectory turns biographical events into so many "*locations*" [*placements*] and "*moves*" [*déplacements*] in the field. The meaning of the positions and the moves are defined by their objective relation to all the other positions in the field, the kinds of capitals they require and confer, and the value of those capitals at that particular moment in the history of the field. The trajectory captures the process of *"social ageing,"* which, while it corresponds to biological aging, is not identical with it, and whose full social significance can only be measured by relating it to the trajectories of those agents within the field who define their chances in relation to the same "space of possibles."[23]

So we understand a life to be movement within a field whose meaning is established by the value of the positions in the field held and lost, or never attained at all. Their worth is measured in terms of the amounts and types of capitals that are the coin of the realm in that field, and of the value of the field's currency in the ensemble of fields, or social space. As a constructed notion, a trajectory is neither the trip intentionally taken nor the voyage later selectively recalled by the traveler. Rather, it is an analytical construct (the "ride" or *trajet* in the "métro") established by the sociologically-minded observer who can take into account the "objective," e.g., measurable, "differences" between positions and the internal changes in the field as well as its responses to external pressures that modify the structure and boundaries of the field, and can relate that trajectory to that of others in the field and to the field's history, its successive states.

"Prologue; Flaubert, analyst of Flaubert"

In *The Rules of Art* (1992), "Prologue" frames Bourdieu's historical analysis of the constitution of the *literary field* in mid-nineteenth-century France. Using a traditional internal reading of a classic work of French literature, Bourdieu illustrated the *structural homologies,* or structural mirroring, between the literary field in the early stage of its development that is described in the novel and the one in which Flaubert found himself. He highlighted the novelist's quasi-sociological self-understanding, his imparting to the book those "tools necessary for its own sociological analysis." The novel shows Flaubert possessing, albeit in a masked form, a sociological understanding of the logic that, since his time of and that of his contemporaries, Zola and Manet, orders and energizes fields of literature and art as autonomous fields. This capacity accounts for Flaubert's particular, and particularly important, literary innovation, his symbolic revolution. At the same time, and in a manner that has been overlooked, his analysis of the novel as the story of a set of intersecting lives understood as trajectories within the field of power and within identifiable areas of the city of Paris served as practical demonstration of the conjunction through homology of social and physical space. To make that conjunction clearer, I have mapped a summary of Bourdieu's plot summary onto the map that accompanied his analysis (Figure 3.2).

Frédéric Moreau, the son of a widow from the provinces, comes to Paris to study in 1840, with the vague hope of becoming some kind of artist – a writer, a composer, or a painter. The space of the novel is bounded by and defined against the two social and spatial extremes of Paris, that of the

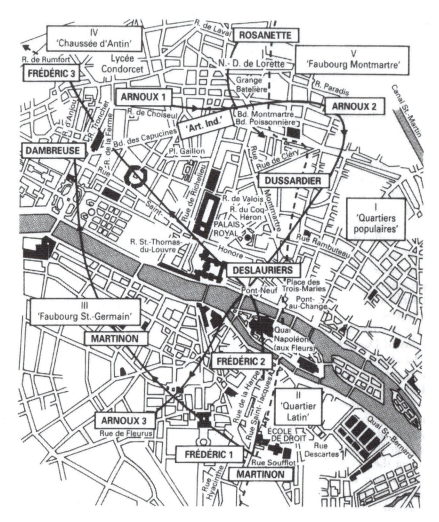

Figure 3.2 The Paris of *Sentimental Education*, from Pierre Bourdieu, *The Rules of Art*, 1996 (1992).

quartiers populaires of the "working classes" (I, the site of his friend Dussardier's office, but otherwise outside the action of the novel, as are the areas of revolutionary armed struggle whose western limit is indicated by the dotted line) and that of the Faubourg St.-Antoine of the old aristocracy (III). Frédéric moves between three groups situated between these two social poles: the "student milieu" (II), "new bourgeoisie" (IV), and the "demi-monde" (V). The student milieu consists of a group of young students from across a spectrum of social backgrounds and of dispositions who gravitate around him, namely, Deslauriers, Sénécal, Dussardier, de Cisy, and

Martinon. They inhabit the Latin Quarter, which is also home to the failed artists of the Latin Quarter. The "new bourgeoisie" is itself subdivided into two poles, that of "politics and business," represented at one end by Monsieur Dambreuse, an aristocrat who has become a banker, his wife and daughter, Cécile, and at the other, that of "art and politics," around the couple of Monsieur Arnoux, an art merchant and owner of an art magazine, and his wife. Each has a salon to which Frédéric hopes to gain entry. The Dambreuses receive well-placed and well-connected politicians, businessmen, and clerics; the Arnoux, aspiring and successful artists and writers, ranging from the aesthetically conservative to the radical. The "demimonde" is the ambit of the actress, Rosanette, who is the mistress of Arnoux. Here, the male denizens of the other spaces meet, and meet sexually available women.[24]

Propelled by an unexpected legacy that makes him very wealthy, Frédéric is able to move from group to group and between each of the women at its center, although he does not lose sight of the young provincial girl (Louise Roque) his mother intends him to marry. Against the background of the Revolution of 1848 and its aftermath, he oscillates between alliances with the women who become his lovers, Madame Dambreuse and Rosanette, all the while maintaining a cult of the pure, and thus unattainable, Madame Arnoux. Some of the students succeed; some do not, Frédéric among them. He eventually returns to the provinces, where, after losing his Mademoiselle Roque and exhausting his legacy, he lives as a petit bourgeois. Madame Arnoux reappears many years later, but only just long enough to tell him that she has shared his love. He is left with memories of his sentimental education, which Bourdieu defines as the experience of *social ageing*, or the process of succeeding and failing in the game of social success.[25]

Like any initiate, Frédéric must make an "inaugural *investment*" in a field by embracing its belief in itself as a game worth playing, its *illusio*. However, he invests in neither the option of art offered to him by the Arnoux nor of business proffered by Dambreuse's circle; nor does he totally reject them by forming a permanent alliance with the demi-monde. Thus, Frédéric's legacy has given him everything but the will to make the proper use of an inheritance. His trajectory, however, is only one of the possible ways of playing the game of a sentimental education, and his moves are inflected by their interaction with those of his fellow students, as they compete for the favor of social power (dispensed by Monsieur Dambreuse) or sexual favors (offered by Rosanette and her friends). Frédéric's sentimental education will consist of learning about the mutual exclusiveness of two forms of love and two forms of art, pure and mercenary, or, put more positively, the need for an "interest in disinterestedness" to succeed in the economically upside-down world of art. It is this world, that of the literary field and the field of cultural production, that was in formation at the time that Flaubert wrote his novel and whose history and theorization is the subject of Bourdieu's book.[26]

Bourdieu describes the social space of the novel as a "field of power," structured by the two salons of the Arnoux and the Dambreuses (Figure 3.3). It is a "true *milieu* in the Newtonian sense, where social forces ... are exercised, and find their phenomenal manifestation in the form of psychological motivations such as love or ambition," and thus a "force-field," as well as a "field of struggles," a game with power at its stake. The trajectories of the group of students in this social space will be conditioned by the relation between the forces at work in the field and the dispositions stemming from their social origins (i.e., the habitus determined by their earliest socialization), which orients but does not determine that trajectory, and the capitals of all sorts that will shape, but not determine, their choices among the possibilities offered to them by the field.[27]

Each of the friends has his own combination of the differing dispositions and capitals needed for success in different arrangements, that, in their ensemble, cover the spectrum of possibilities of social aging, almost as if Flaubert had constructed a controlled experiment of the workings of a field. The narrowness of the social space, which Bourdieu compares to a "crime novel" set in an "isolated manor,"[28] gives an illusion of reality that keeps its nature as a sociological investigation of all the possible trajectories in that space from being visible to the characters, much as the social field remains invisible to individuals in actual social life.

The structure of this social space has a corresponding structure in the physical space of Paris, with the Latin Quarter as its base, the Faubourg Monmartre as its apex, and the Chaussée d'Antin as its westernmost boundary. The social trajectories of the characters are homologous to their movements in physical space. Frédéric (Frédéric move 1) lives in the Latin Quarter on the Left Bank (II). He is received in the Chaussée d'Antin on

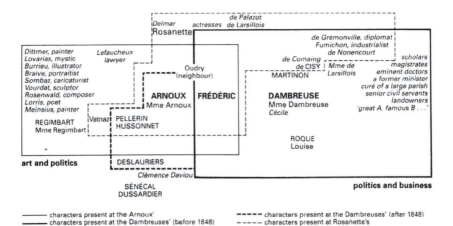

Figure 3.3 The Field of Power according to *Sentimental Education*, from Pierre Bourdieu, *The Rules of Art*, 1996 (1992).

the Right Bank (IV), but will only move there after receiving his legacy (Frédéric move 2). It is a quarter inhabited by the members of the new dominant class (Arnoux 1 and Dambreuse). Rosanette's Faubourg Monmartre (V), to the north and east of the Chaussée d'Antin, is the quarter of successful artists and writers, a kind of shadow of (IV), but one that is much superior to (II), the domain of failed artists. Faubourg Monmartre is the site of Arnoux's gallery and the office of his art magazine (*Art Industriel*) when he is prosperous, and of his home after his bankruptcy (Arnoux move 2). Like social space, the physical space of Paris is *hierarchical* and *structured*, and, as in social space, trajectories in it involve moving to and from positions which are desired or disdained in accordance with the logic of the field. In the novel, all upward trajectories move from south to northwest (Frédéric and his friend Martinon, who will marry Cécile), downward ones from north to the south of true "outsiderdom" (Arnoux move 3), or from west to east (Rosanette), and then to the provinces (Frédéric, whose moves take him off the map to the northwest). The worst is not to move at all (Deslauriers).[29]

Bourdieu's analysis of the correspondence of social space and physical space of the novel does not spell out the role of space in the embodiment that forms the habitus. He hints at the role of space in its incorporation, however, in his analysis of Flaubert's description of Frédéric's working-class friend, Deslauriers' "sense of the social distance which obliged him to keep his distance," and of Frédéric's feminine corporal *hexis*. The hexis[30] is the embodied and durable organization of one's sense of one's place that organizes feeling, thinking, and moving. It is illustrated by Frédéric's tendency to join the women in their space of the salons. Bourdieu's citation of Flaubert's description of Dambreuse's reaction to the overthrow of monarchy by the Revolution of 1848 can also be construed as a description of the kind of dramatic conditions that can transform a habitus, which is, after all, not destiny: "The world was coming to an end! ... He dismissed three servants, sold his horses, bought a soft hat to wear in the street, and even thought of letting his beard grow."[31] Although Bourdieu does not make this point, it seems that when Dambreuse relinquished his horses (in the plural, which suggests he owned a carriage) and opted for a soft hat (which suggests he gave up a banker's top hat), he "down-sized" not only his household but also the sizable figure he had previously cut in physical space ("the street") not only for others, but also for himself. He contemplated modifying the embodied form of his position – he "even thought of letting his beard grow!"

We now understood Frédéric's life as his voyage, his "ride in the métro," having taken into account the "entire urban transport system" of the relations between the literal stations of the salons in the field of power (and those, like Rosanette's outside it), and the objective relations of gender, class, and fractions of class between them. But we have done more, because we have taken in the matrix of objective relations between the spaces occupied by those positions in relation to each other, and in relation to those that actually organized urban and social space, the east and west of the Faubourg Saint-Germain and Faubourg Saint-Antoine, of the aristocracy and the working classes, as well of Paris and the provinces. We are now ready to move from the example to the theory of which it is an instantiation, and to a method that allows us to see the working of structural mirroring between any physical space and any social space.

"Site effects"

"Site" was one of the essays that provided an interpretive framework for the some 60[32] extensive dialogues that make up *The Weight of the World*, Bourdieu and colleagues' 1993 study of the new forms of social suffering among the working class and underclass and of those who provide them with social, educational, and legal services. It was clearly meant to be valid for all spaces. We will show that this is the case by illustrating the propositions he makes there with spatial situations described in "Prologue," which are inserted in our text in italics.

Bourdieu's "Site effects" begins with the necessity of effectuating a rupture with both the commonsensical notions of ordinary discourse about *place* and with the experts' view of place as a direct inscription of the social. For Bourdieu, the notion that everything about a specific place, those observable conditions *"on the ground,"* explains life as lived there exemplifies a *substationalist* error. An explanation of a place will never be found in that specific place, but in the relation between the general structure of all physical spaces and the structure of society, itself a space. Human beings occupy a *site*. If defined absolutely, it is a *localization*, the point in *physical space* where they, like things, are situated. If defined in terms of relations, it is a *position*, the rank that they occupy. When the volume, extent, and surface occupied is taken into account, *site* is *place*, something that has "bulk." Social and physical space resemble each other, inasmuch as both are defined by the inability of individuals to be more than one thing at a time: "mutual exteriority" defines physical space, and "mutual exclusion," or "distinction," defines social space.[33]

Several interdependent conclusions about *physical space* follow:

"The structure of social space shows up as spatial oppositions," enabling inhabited space to function as a "sort of spontaneous symbolization of social space." Hierarchized societies are expressed in hierarchized spaces, which, however, can, by dint of the passage of time, come to look for all that world as if they are facts of nature; they are thus subject to the *naturalization effect. There are spaces in the salons where women naturally gather. They are so identifiably feminine that they establish Frédéric's feminine disposition.* The relation between the social and the spatial is not direct, but rather a "blurred ... translation." Possession of capital endows a power over physical space which appears in that space in one of the three forms that sites take. Each site is constituted by a different type of structured spatial relations between agents and goods and services, private and public, that expresses an agent's position in social space relative to other agents. *Localizations* are either permanent sites of relations such as the home that indicate one's social existence or the temporary ones, like a place on the podium, that denote one's position of rank relative to others. *Positions* express the agent's position determined by outright ownership. *Place*, the amount of space or degree of bulkiness the position consumes, is one of the best manners to express power. *Frédéric's different addresses in Paris; Frédéric's seat assigned by protocol at a dinner at the Dambreuses; Frédéric by virtue of the property he owns; and Dambreuse's ostentatiously powerful appearance in the street before the Revolution of 1848.*[34]

In other words, physical space is social space "reified," that is "physically realized or objectified." Reification appears in the distribution of goods and services and of agents with more or less of the ability to appropriate goods and services as a result of capitals possessed and spatial proximity to those goods. These relations of the distribution of agents and goods, and of agents to goods, endow the reified social space with value or deprive it of value. Reified social spaces are fields, socially bounded universes of relations. *Chaussée d'Antin objectifies the social positions of the spatially translated aristocrat-turned-bourgeois, Dambreuse, and the new bourgeois, Arnoux. The field of power is reified as the triangular space of the Sentimental Education, a space which is itself defined by its relationship to the two reified spaces of the aristocratic and working-class quarters.* Different reified spaces and fields overlap in physical space. Holders of homologous positions in different fields are found in the same spaces, which are at homologously great distances from the addresses of the position holders who, according to the logic of their respective fields, are their opposites. *Arnoux's gallery in IV is close to the residences of successful artists and is far from II.* In the same way as the distinction that a part of Paris confers on those who live there or who aspire to do so only becomes fully analytically comprehensible by virtue of that relation to its opposite, the dominant position in France held by the capital city can only be understood in relation to the provinces. This *site* in *physical space*, which is here the (political) capital, concentrates the poles of all the fields in *social space* that require for their occupation the largest concentrations of all forms of capital and their holders and does so at the cost of the provinces. To be provincial is to lack both the capital and capital. *The Paris of Sentimental Education.* Finally, physical space as a relation of reified and objectified social oppositions is reproduced in language and thought, which are constitutive of mental structures, or the categories of perception and evaluation, of vision and division that make up the habitus. *Frédéric (or any provincial) speaks of "going up" to Paris, independently of the actual geographical position of his provincial town in relation to the city.*[35]

In the societies described in "Site," physical spaces operate as mediators for that conversion of social structure into mental structure by issuing social structure's imperatives in the form of "mute injunctions and silent calls to order." Incorporation takes time – that of continuous or repeated experience of a spatial distance that affirms social distance – and it takes motion in space, the *"displacements and body movements"* by which those silent commands are incorporated. Because they pass through space to the body, it is an imperceptible process whose very imperceptibility causes these social distinctions to be experienced as natural ones, rather than cultural and historical, and thus arbitrary. For example, the value of social ascent or descent and acceptance or exclusion is assigned according to what is really proximate distance to a high-value site. The effect of monumental archi- tecture is to elicit a "respectful demeanor"; the effect of making spatial dis- tinctions such as Left and Right Bank or an East or West End serve in the place of social distinctions is to instigate an equivalent social reverence – silently, imperceptibly. The double inscription of social space in, first, the structure of physical space, and second, in the mental structures that phys- ical space imperceptibly inculcates makes physical space the site *par excel- lence* for the exercise of domination and of *symbolic violence*, a violence all the more insidious for the being masked by its spatial nature. (*Although no example of architecture's symbolic power is cited in Bourdieu's analysis of Sen- timental Education, monuments and museums are often described in these terms in Bourdieu's sociology of culture.*)[36]

Because they are possessed of these qualities, spaces become stakes, and, as stakes, they are the object of *struggles*, both individual and collective. The sites and places of reified social space earn *profits*, according to the nature of the site as *localization, position* or as a *bulky place. Profits of localization* take the form of the benefit of direct proximity to valuable persons or goods, such as valued establishments, public and private; *profits of position* include that of the distinction that comes with possessing a distinctive property; and *profits of occupation* accrue to those sites whose bulk create a distance from unwanted intrusion either through owned private space, or through a public space possessed by one's gaze. Proximity in physical space assures that proximity in social space will be effective and efficient when it generates the opportunities to maximize social capital through encounters of the kind that naturally occur when one is in the right place at all the right times. *Spatial mobility* is the form of the *individual* struggle for space; "moving up," as is well known, allows but also requires moving from one neighbor- hood to another. For an individual to fully appropriate such a space, social and cultural capitals as well as the appropriate habitus are required. Without that habitus, a habitat is not fully inhabited. That said, "if the habitat shapes the habitus, the habitus also shapes the habitat, through the more or less adequate social usages that it tends to make of it." Absent the ability to meet the conditions tacitly laid down by space for its adequate use, one is at risk of being *"out of place"* and deprived of the benefits of the *"club effect"* that comes from having long been in a place that is exclusive and of the *symbolic consecration* that comes from partaking of the accumulation of many agents' capitals in one place.[37]

Every effect present in the exclusive neighborhood is also present in the "problem suburbs," but with, so to speak, the signs reversed. Proximity means distance from valued resources; homogeneity degrades rather than maximizes (or maximizes degradation); proximity and inhabitation produce stigmatization rather than consecration. As the space degrades the individuals, the individuals degrade the place, symbolically and physically. Institutions such as the school that magnify dispossession by offering something other than the excommunication that is the common state of the inhabitants are among the places degraded. As neighborhoods such as these are brought into being through the *political construction of space* – as the result of credit policy, housing policy, and everything that assigns value to land, housing, and social services – the only possible form of struggle is collective, or for the rare individuals who can afford it, flight.[38]

"Site's" compatibility with "Prologue," which is a rewriting of an article of 1975, dispels the (mistaken) impression that the interest in space Bourdieu displayed in the essay on the Kabyle house was not sustained and that space for Bourdieu was only a heuristic and a metaphor.[39] The significance of that recognition lies not in the calming effect it will ideally have on this question, a matter of interest to specialists, but in the changes that it can generate in the practices of students of lives and of space in general, and then for students of architectural space, in particular.

Understanding

Understanding requires embracing Bourdieu's solutions to the problems posed by biography and his propositions about space. To return to Bourdieu's original metaphors of the landscape and the voyage and the "necessary detour," for students of lives to deploy the concepts of *localizations, positions* and *places* in physical space and *spatial mobility* without the corresponding *social space* and *trajectory* is tantamount to describing the "landscape" without the "voyage" that traversed it. When students of social space do the reverse, that is, describe the trajectory through social space without its homology in physical space, they deprive themselves of the full benefit of taking a "detour" through a landscape that is not merely metaphorically spatial.

As for students of architecture, the conditions for entry into this new and powerful understanding are demanding, for they require the same degree of self-reflection that Bourdieu demanded from himself. It begins with a break with one's discipline's "unthought thought." Once we have recognized that splitting biography from space had the effect of keeping architectural history from realizing its natural affinity with the study of social space through the examination of its homologue, physical space, we can look at other aspects of our practice. Let us consider a few of the additional ruptures we will need and the benefits that they offer.

Grappling with the falsely logical "chrono-logical" is a way of confronting the mental constructions that make up the disciplinary habitus of students of architectural space. The establishment of temporal continuity of the logic of the generation of the commission of the design and reconstructing the building campaign is often an architectural historian's primary task. But, as a notion that takes progression for granted, it has every chance of being yet another of those cases in which expert categories reprise the unthought categories of ordinary discourse. How much richer would such analyses be if temporal continuity were to be also conceived as a spatial relation, as a "move forward" that is always and simultaneously a "move against" opposing and designs, designers and, especially, with and against the beckoning and constraining alternatives of the *space of possibles.*

These are practical changes, but they signal a fundamental change in the logic of that practice. We will have recognized that our disciplinary version of biography, the monograph, has kept our disciplinary habitus parked in the "cul-de-sac of monological consciousness" since, well, Vasari's invention of the "life of the artist." But, as Bourdieu told a conference of many, many hundreds of students of space come to discuss the habitus, architecture may be a "very intellectual or intellectualist art," but that habitus does not have to be our destiny.[40]

These practical changes would enable us to realize the promise that Bourdieu held out for any discipline courageous enough to incorporate a sociological dimension. They would help us discover, as Bourdieu did from his study of Baudelaire and Manet, that "that sociology (or social history) that is always accused of being "reductive" and of destroying the creative originality of the writer or artist is in fact capable of doing justice to the singularity of ... great upheavals."[41] How much better would we understand our "misfits," the against-all-odds-but-oh-so-typical trajectories from the provinces to the Veneto or Paris or Berlin that turned a mason into a Palladio, a Jeanneret into a Le Corbusier, a Mies into Mies van der Rohe. The times are propitious for such an endeavor. More and more, architectural historians are grappling with the problematic nature of architectural authorship and architects are celebrating rather than denying architecture's inherently collaborative nature.[42] More than lip service is being paid to cross disciplinarity.[43]

Approaching a life as a constructed trajectory in a field that demands construction and finds its homologues in physical space should have a natural appeal for historians of architecture and urban form, who, after all, are quite at home with the measuring of objective distances and the mapping of urban networks, transport or other. Predisposed to think spatially, students of space and lives will find the detour through Bourdieu's spaces has helped them reach their destination of a specifically spatial way of accounting for lives, and to see the disciplinary promise it contains. The exercise has been spatial, but also temporal. We have accompanied Bourdieu on his "ride" through time, from 1848 to the present, and space, from the historical Paris of the field of power to the troubled suburbs of the disempowered, and through knowledge formations, from the empirical to the

FAITES VOUS MEME VOTRE EDUCATION SENTIMENTALE

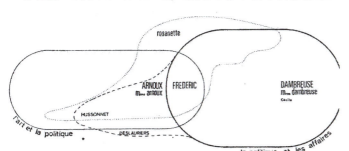

A partir du schéma de la page 72 et sur la base des homologies structurales dégagées par l'analyse, vous pouvez imaginer qui seraient aujourd'hui les personnages principaux de l'Education sentimentale (sans oublier les effets de mai 1968).

Exemple : ARNOUX est (a) directeur d'un hebdomadaire de gauche

(b) directeur d'une galerie d'avant-garde

(c) directeur d'une maison d'édition d'avant-garde

(d) directeur d'une agence de publicité

etc.

Figure 3.4 A board game to "Make your own Sentimental Education," from Pierre Bourdieu, "L'invention de la vie de l'artiste," 1975.

theoretical, without ever falling back into a polarization of one against the other. We have understood national, regional, and urban spaces as the homologue of social space, and neighborhoods and rooms as gendered elements of some of those spaces.

Much has been done, but much also remains to be done. Architecture is notably missing, missing from the analysis, just as architects are, with one exception, missing from Sentimental Education.[44] Bourdieu's exteriors and interiors are spatial without ever being architectural. In this omission, there lies an opportunity for architectural historians to enrich the spatiality of Bourdieu's method of analysis, even as it empowers their own. The effort that Bourdieu never undertook would, I am sure, be welcome. In 1975, Bourdieu designed a board game that allowed readers to "Make Your Own *Sentimental Education*." Using his method of "structural homologies," they were invited to transpose the field of power from the Paris of the epoch of the revolution of February 1848 (Figure 3.4) to that of the student revolt of May 1968.[45]

Students of space, it's our move.

Notes

1 Pierre Bourdieu, "L'illusion bio-graphique," *Actes de la recherche en science sociale* 62/63 (1986): 69. Translated as Pierre Bourdieu, *The Biographical Illusion*, trans. Yves Winkin and Wendy Leeds-Hurwitz, Working Papers and Proceedings of the Center for Psychosocial Studies, n. 14 (Chicago: Center for Psychosocial Studies, 1987). I will be translating from the original French, with the one exception of this citation, which is from Pierre Bourdieu and Loïc J.D. Wacquant, *An Invitation to Reflexive Sociology* (Chicago: University of Chicago Press, 1992), 207, n. 169, translation modified.

2 *The Rules of Art: Genesis and Structure of the Literary Field*, trans. Susan Emanuel (Stanford: Stanford University Press, 1996), 3.

3 Pierre Bourdieu, "Site Effects," in *The Weight of the World: Social Suffering in Contemporary Society*, comp. and ed. Pierre Bourdieu, trans. Priscilla Parkhurst Ferguson *et al.* (Stanford, CA: Stanford University Press, 1999), 126, 123, translation modified.

4 "L'illusion biographique," 71–72.

5 Loïc Wacquant, "The 'total anthropologist': on the works and legacy of Pierre Bourdieu," *American Anthropologist* 105, no. 2 (September 2002): 1.

6 "The Berber House or the world reversed," *Social Science Information* 9, no. 3 (April 1970): 151–70. Bourdieu addresses the "intuitionist" and "structuralist" shortcomings of that essay in *The Logic of Practice*, trans. Richard Nice (Stanford: Stanford University Press, 1990), 316, n. 1. The oft-cited anthologized translation, "The Berber House," in *Rules and Meanings: The Anthropology of Everyday Knowledge*, ed. Mary Douglas (New York: Penguin, 1973), 98–110, is a highly reduced version of the initial version that omits his description of the conditions under which transposition is possible, see Hélène Lipstadt, "'To see, to record, to photograph': rediscovering Pierre Bourdieu's Berber House with Pierre Bourdieu's rediscovered photographs," *Thresholds*, January 2004, 12–17.

7 "L'invention de la vie d'artiste," *Actes de la recherche en sciences sociales*, no. 2 (March 1975): 67–94.

8 Pierre Bourdieu, "The genesis of the concepts of the habitus and the field," *Sociocriticism* 2 (May–June 1985): 15. All technical terms drawn from Bourdieu's sociology are italicized on first usage and are defined at that time. Unless otherwise noted, Bourdieu is the author of the cited text and italics used for emphasis are his.

9 Tim Anstey, Katja Grillner, and Rolf Hughes, Call for papers: architecture and authorship (2005), H-ARTHIST, www.arthist.net and Nancy Stieber, ed., "Learning from interdisciplinarity," *Journal of the Society of Architectural Historians* 64, no. 4 (December 2005): 417–40 and "Learning from architectural history," *Journal of the Society of Architectural Historians* 65, no. 1 (March 2006): 5–25.

10 For interpretations of Bourdieu as a spatial theorist, see Ilana Friedrich Silber, "Space, fields, boundaries: the rise of spatial metaphors in contemporary sociological theory," *Social Research* 62, no. 2 (Summer 1995): 333–38 and Denise L. Lawrence and Setha M. Low, "The built environment and spatial form," *Annual Reviews in Anthropology* 19 (1990): 469–70. For a contrary view, see Joe Painter, "Pierre Bourdieu," in *Thinking Space*, ed. Mike Crang and Nigel Thrift (London: Routledge, 2000), 239–59.

11 John Archer, "Social theory of space: architecture and the production of self, culture and society," *Journal of the Society of Architectural Historians* 64, no. 4 (December 2005): 431, and Jean Hillier and Emma Rooksby, eds., "Introduction," in *Habitus: A Sense of Place*, ed. Jean Hillier and Emma Rooksby (Aldershot: Ashgate, *c*.2002), 5, posit a privileged role for physical space. Ken Dovey, "The silent complicity of architecture," in *Habitus: A Sense of Place*, ed. Jean Hillier and Emma Rooksby (Ashworth, 2002), 269, describes physical space as the direct translation of social space.

12 On the one hand, the international conference "Habitus 2000: A Sense of Place," at Curtin University in Perth, Western Australia, which brought together over 300 speakers and 600 listeners and the University of Hawai'i Press series, "Spatial habitus," and on the other, an architectural firm, http://www.habitus.com.au/philosophy. html and a developers' trademarked brand of tract housing, http://www. habitus.be/fr/over_habitus.html.

13 It is only among groups such as the Kabyle, in which education is not "institutionalized" and "the whole group" exerts "pedagogic action," that "the whole system of objects" informs bodily hexis. Even among the Kabyle, "objects, the house and the village" work alongside other products and practices to inculcate the logic of practice, Pierre Bourdieu, *Logic*, 73–74.

14 "To follow a rule," in *Bourdieu: A Critical Reader*, ed. Richard Shusterman (Oxford: Blackwell Publishers, 1999), 38, 33.

15 *Esquisse pour une auto-analyse* (Paris: Raison d'Agir Editions, 2004), 9, my translation.

16 For sociologists' response to "Illusion," see, among others, Jean-Claude Passeron, "Biographies, flux, itineraries et trajectories," *Revue française de soci-ologie* 31, no. 1 (1990): 6–9; for the reception of "Prologue," see Paul Dirkx, "Réception et récepteurs des *Règles de l'art*," in *Le Symbolique et le social: la réception internationale de la pensée de Pierre Bourdieu*, ed. Jacques Dubois, Pascal Durand, and Yves Winkin (Liège: Sociopolis, Editions de l'Université de Liège, 2005), 195–207.

17 80,000 copies were sold and dialogues were performed as plays, Franck Poupeau and Thierry Discepolo, eds. and comps., "Désenchantment du politique et *Realpolitik* de la raison," in *Interventions, 1961–2001: Science Sociale & Action Politique*, by Pierre Bourdieu (Marseilles: Agone for Contre-feux, 2002), 231.

18 Adapted from Hélène Lipstadt, "Sociology: Bourdieu's bequest," *Journal of the Society of Architectural Historians* 64, no. 4 (December 2005): 433–36.

19 Bourdieu and Wacquant, *An Invitation*, 207.

20 Bridget Fowler, "Mapping the obituary: notes towards a Bourdieusian interpretation," in *Feminism After Bourdieu*, Lisa Adkins and Bev Skeggs (Oxford: Blackwell, 2004), 151.

21 "L'illusion biographique," 69–70.

22 "L'illusion biographique," 70–71.

23 "L'illusion biographique," 71–72.

24 *Rules*, 40–43.

25 *Rules*, 10.

26 *Rules*, 13, 20–21.

27 *Rules*, 9–10.

28 *Rules*, 14.

29 *Rules*, 40–43.

30 Cf. *Logic*, 69.

31 *Rules*, 16, 12, 31.

32 There were 69 dialogues in the original French edition, and 54 in the English language one, of which two were with residents of the inner city "'ghettos'" of Chicago and New York.

33 "Site," 123–24.

34 "Site," 124.

35 "Site," 124–26.

36 "Site," 126.

37 "Site," 127–29.

38 "Site," 128–29.

39 Painter, "Pierre Bourdieu," 253, 255.

40 "Habitus," in *Habitus: A Sense of Place*, ed. Jean Hillier and Emma Rooksby (Ashworth, 2002), 32–33.

41 *Pascalian Meditations*, trans. Richard Nice (Stanford: Stanford University Press, 2000), 86.

42 I address these issues in "'Exoticising the domestic' of new collaborative paradigms: Bourdieu on advance design practices," in *Architecture and Authorship*, ed. Tim Anstey, Katja Grillner, and Rolf Hughes (London: Black Dog Publishing, 2007 [Forthcoming]).

43 For example, the September 2005 conference sponsored by the Society of Architectural Historians (United States) and the Institut national de l'histoire de l'art (France), "Changing Boundaries: Architectural History in Transition," and the special issues of the *Journal of the Society of Architectural Historians*, cited in n. 8.

44 *Rules*, 7.

45 "L'Invention," 93. Make your own *Sentimental Education*. To play the game, overlay the diagram of the Field of Power (Figure 3.3), and, on the basis of the structural homologies established by the analysis in the text, imagine who the principal characters of the *Sentimental Education* would be today (without forgetting the effects of the student revolution of May 1968). For example: M. Arnoux is (a) an editor of a leftist weekly magazine; (b) a director of an avant-garde art gallery; (c) an editor-in-chief of an avant-garde publishing house; (d) a CEO of an advertising agency.

4

'This scarlet intruder'

Biography interrupted in the Dining Room at Tatton Park Mansion

Eleanor Quince

Introduction

The 'scarlet intruder' in the title of this essay refers to a new, red dressing gown purchased by eighteenth-century French philosopher, Denis Diderot, to replace his old, worn out gown. Within his essay 'Regrets sur ma vielle Robe de Chambre',[1] or 'Regrets on parting with my old Dressing Gown',[2] Diderot hypothesised that objects arranged within a space create a biography, or indeed autobiography, of the person who lives within that space, operating as words within a syntax, each word/object relating to the next to create a coherent whole, a life-story. As the life of the resident progresses, the space adapts to reflect a change in circumstances, incorporating new objects, new words, so that the story evolves. Diderot's new red dressing gown was just such a new word, redolent of a change in his circumstances. However, it was also an object which appeared so at odds with the rest of the items in his space that Diderot viewed it not as a continuation of his biography, but as an interruption to the existing story. Taking Diderot's view as a starting point, my focus is the Dining Room at Tatton Park Mansion, Knutsford, Cheshire, a predominantly late-eighteenth-century space which has undergone a series of adjustments to design and layout at the hand of a succession of residents, and which was opened to the public by the National Trust and Cheshire County Council in 1962, and redecorated and re-displayed in the early 1970s. Using Diderot's dressing gown as a conduit, this essay explores the creation of biography within the Dining Room, first through the objects within the current space and then via the written descriptions of the space and how it has changed. Through an identification of the interruptions in the Dining Room and how the curators at Tatton overcome them, my aim is to establish how sites such as Tatton, country houses which are open to the public, create biography within a space and within the information surrounding that space, in order to effectively convey the space to the visitor. I want the story of the

Dining Room at Tatton to unfold slowly, so I am beginning with the room as it is today and working backwards to explain its existence; I hope that by approaching the space in this manner the importance of biography to its coherence, current arrangement and overall impact becomes apparent.

Diderot and his dressing gown

'Regrets sur ma vieille Robe de Chambre', was first published in 1772.[3] In it Diderot described in detail his feelings on replacing his old, worn dressing gown, 'my ragged, humble, comfortable old wrapper' with a new one: 'an article of clothing so precious that I have to bow down to it ... this scarlet intruder in my home'[4] and the subsequent effect that this action had on the room he used as his study. Written against the backdrop of pre-Revolutionary Paris and subtitled 'a warning to those who have more taste than money', the essay cautioned against the dangers of excessive consumerism and was aimed at those who 'go on endlessly heaping up beautiful things'.[5] But Diderot accomplished much more than a simple caveat against over-spending; he employed the example of his new dressing gown, so at odds with himself, his room and his sense of balance and harmony, to explore how we use signs and symbols within our homes, how we identify with the objects that we own and how our sense of aesthetics infiltrates our daily existence. The new dressing gown stood as a catalyst for disorder, disharmony and disunification, an interruption to an otherwise perfect, fluid interior space. My interest in Diderot's new dressing gown lies not with its resonance for those studying eighteenth-century culture, nor with its still pertinent consideration of conspicuous consumption, but rather with Diderot's presentation of it as a word within his biography, or as it should more accurately be referred to in this instance, autobiography.

Diderot's essay begins with a consideration of the qualities which were present within his old dressing gown. Always 'quick to be of service' the old dressing gown served as a duster and a pen-wiper and as a protector against rainwater leaking through the roof and sparks from the open fire.[6] It was an aid to his writing, enabling him to perform the simple tasks, such as unblocking his pen and blotting his paper, with ease. The stains, burns and patches of ink on the dressing gown were a testament to the carelessness with which Diderot treated his homely object. This was all in contrast with his new dressing gown, a stiff, rich scarlet affair that he was almost too afraid to put on, and which he could never envisage cleaning his pen nib on or placing too close to the fire: 'I was master of my old dressing gown, but I have become a slave to my new one.'[7] The new dressing gown, the scarlet intruder, had a devastating effect on Diderot's sense of aesthetics, and subsequently upon his living quarters:

> [m]y old dressing gown was in perfect accord with the rest of the poor bric-a-brac that filled my room. A chair made out of woven straw, a

rough wooden table, a cheap Bergamo tapestry, a pine board that served for a bookshelf, a few grimy engravings without frames, tacked by the corners to the tapestry, and three or four plaster casts that hung between the engravings – all these harmonized with my old dressing gown to make a perfect picture of honest poverty. Now the harmony is destroyed. Now there is no more consistency, no more unity, and no more beauty.[8]

Symbolic of newness and wealth, the 'scarlet intruder' was a sign which pulled all the other signs in the space into question. Alongside the new dressing gown everything else looked shabby, dirty and old, the word did not fit, the syntax was destroyed and the space no longer made sense. Embarrassed by the lack of coherence within his study, Diderot began, much to his own chagrin, to search for replacement items for his space, new objects that would match with the new dressing gown. His Bergamo gave way to a shiny new damask wall covering, his engravings, Poussin's *Shower of Manna in the Wilderness* and *Esther before the Throne of the King of Ahasuerus* were replaced with prints of a Rubens' portrait and Vernet's *After the Storm*. His old straw chair was 'usurped' by a Moroccan leather armchair, Homer, Virgil, Horace and Cicero made their way from the pine board shelf into a new inlaid cabinet and his plaster casts, made for him by a friend, were substituted for a statue of Venus by a 'known maker'. The final object to lose its place in the study was Diderot's 'rough wooden table' hidden under 'a great heap of pamphlets and loose papers piled up helter-skelter' which eventually found their way into the drawers 'of an expensive new desk'.[9] But Diderot's new room was not yet complete: there was a space between the top of the new desk and the Vernet which gained a pendulum clock, bronze with gold inlay; a space in the corner beside the window, which was furnished with a small bureau and above that with two small paintings by La Grenée; and spaces on the remaining wall, filled with framed sketches. 'Thus it was', wrote Diderot, 'that the edifying retreat of a philosopher was transformed into the scandalous likeness of [an] innkeeper's private sitting room.'[10] In writing this, Diderot highlighted the reason for all this change; the money that had allowed him to buy the new dressing gown, that took him away from his previous life as a poverty-stricken writer, money which came from his new patron: Mme. Geoffrin. The study was no longer reflective of Diderot as he viewed himself, but rather of Diderot as he felt he should be, filled with objects, which, though aesthetically pleasing and harmonious in relation to each other, were not the practical items which bore the marks of his profession; if his space had remained biographical then the biography on display was a false one.

Within his essay Diderot acknowledged that change does happen and that change means 'throwing things away, turning things upside down, building something new',[11] in doing so he had destroyed the 'perfect picture of honest poverty'[12] that he had created over the years and replaced it with a new 'luxurious mode of life'[13] created almost instantaneously. For Diderot it took just one object, one interruption, to cause him to want to re-write his autobiography, obliterating rather than acknowledging the past. And yet, in spite of the zealous fashion in which Diderot set about changing his interior space one object remained as a reminder of his 'former modest surroundings'; an old rug. 'Every morning', Diderot wrote, 'when I come into my study, sumptuously robed in scarlet, I shall look down at the floor … [and] it will remind me of what I used to be.'[14] The new objects within what I shall call the second version of Diderot's study, combined to tell the specific story of the new phase in his life, kick-started by the purchase of the new dressing gown, the 'scarlet intruder', his briefest nod to his past life in the form of the rug illustrates that although the story has moved on, Diderot's past is still visible within the space. Diderot once again sees the discordant item as an interruption: 'this pitiable object, I know very well, hardly goes with my other splendid furnishings',[15] but it is an interruption that he welcomes because, as he tells the reader, it reminds him of who he was. In recording this process for us – the carefully created autobiographical space, indicative of Diderot's perception of himself as the humble writer, the interruption to that space and the subsequent creation of an entirely different space, the space of the perceived successful writer – Diderot was able to establish that we relate ourselves to our home and vice versa.[16]

Objects/words/interruptions

Diderot's new dressing gown, the scarlet intruder, did not sit well within his study because the dressing gown was all the things that the study was not; new, sumptuous, expensive, clean, and so on. Diderot's process of change within his study unfolds along a Foucauldian pathway; the old objects taking on different meanings in light of the new, as the present informs the way in which the past is viewed. Diderot's original study was his own space, arrived at by necessity rather than by design, but loved for its physical expression of its inhabitant: his plaster casts were made for him by a friend, his chair was falling to pieces just where he sat on it, his rug threadbare from pacing whilst he thought. The new version of his study is the antithesis of this; each object carefully selected more for its aesthetic appeal than its practicality and is partly removed from Diderot himself. The changing process, as he describes it, happens almost without him: 'I have seen my Bergamo tapestry compelled to give up its place on the wall'; 'this void was filled by a pendulum clock … [a] clock chosen by the wealthy Mme. Geoffrin'.[17] In some ways the changing process within Diderot's study is indicative of the eighteenth-century country house interior space – often designed not by the inhabitant, but by an architect or firm of furniture-makers. The result is also similar, a glamorous, harmonious space, that includes few real 'personal' items, after all the country house was a site of display.[18] When these houses are opened to the public today, the idea of these spaces simply as repositories for fine furniture, fabric and ceramics is tackled head-on by the inclusion of some family objects, portraits, photographs, diaries, clothes, which lift the space from the realm of 'museum' to 'home', reversing the process of Diderot's study, taking the impersonal to the personal. But this process is tempered by what is already in existence, objects which, like Diderot's 'old rug', appear synonymous with the space and which are therefore not removed, but which, when placed alongside the new or the different appear to be entirely out of place.

Consider the photograph of the Dining Room at Tatton Park Mansion (Figure 4.1). If, as a visitor to the house, we know nothing about this space, about the history of architecture or of interior design, if we neglect to read any information about it and we approach it simply as a grand room in a grand house, what exactly do we learn? The space is dominated by a large dining table and twelve dining chairs. The room has wooden floors, covered by a large carpet, red with an intricate pattern. The walls are green with white moulding, and the curtains red. There are other items of furniture within the room besides the dining table and chairs: five further chairs, five further side tables, a carved wooden box and a dumb waiter. At the end of the room, opposite the large window, and not seen in this photograph, is a sideboard suite consisting of a large sideboard, two pedestals (for storing cutlery and crockery) and a cellaret (for keeping the wine chilled). On the other side of the room is a large marble fireplace with carved figures (Figure 4.2) and a fire-screen. Accompanying the furniture is a series of objects:

Figure 4.1 The Dining Room at Tatton, the table is set for Christmas dinner.

Figure 4.2 The fireplace in the Dining Room by Sir Richard Westmacott. Hanging above it is the portrait of Sir Thomas Egerton.

ceramics, glassware, silverware, candelabra, some planters, a chandelier and some portraits. All the objects appear fairly impersonal, this could be a grand dining room in a grand house, more or less anywhere. The portraits are the exception, but even these do not tell us much, if we do not know who the people within the images are. What we learn about this space from simply looking at the photograph, or from going to Tatton and standing in the space as I did, is very little; just that it is a dining room. And yet there is a biography on display here. The portraits are the first indication of that, as is the way in which the room is laid out, suggestive of a possible dinner party, about to take place, evocative of a 'lived-in' space.

For Diderot the inconsistency in the arrangement of the objects in his original study, inspired by the juxtaposition of the new dressing gown, had its roots in an intimate knowledge of his original objects. Consider the photograph again. If we are interested in this space, if we want to know more, then we can look to the history of the room, provided for us by the National Trust and Cheshire County Council.[19] This room was originally designated the Drawing Room, and was designed by Thomas Farnolls Pritchard between 1760 and 1768, who created it in the Rococo style, the moulding of which remains on the walls today. In 1785 the architect Samuel Wyatt was employed at Tatton to make a series of alterations to the existing layout; it was during this programme of rebuilding that the Drawing Room became the Dining Room. Originally it had a bay window, replaced in 1790 by a large tripartite window looking out into the garden. The large white marble fireplace (Figure 4.2), designed by sculptor Richard Westmacott, was added in 1840. In 1887 the house was wired to receive electricity and the electric chandelier added. Thus the room that we see in the photograph is, like much of Tatton and like many country houses currently on display to the public, not a space from one particular historical period, but a space that has been lived in over a much longer period of time and which bears the cumulative marks of its succession of residents. The objects within the space reaffirm this history: the dinner service is from 1859, the silverware and candelabra are from 1809 and 1860; the sideboard suite, the dining table and twelve chairs were added in 1812 and the glassware, by Baccarat, in 1911. The portraits also echo these changes, showing various members of the Egerton family from 1598, when only Tatton 'Old Hall' was in existence, to 1901. This is a space that has been *lived in*. As a 400-year biography the space is full of 'interruptions', objects from disparate eras that do not complement each other. Now, armed with this knowledge, does the space appear disordered, disharmonious and disunified?

The master stroke achieved at the country house is that we do not notice how disunified the space is, unless perhaps we are particularly aesthetically attuned or a connoisseur of interior design. The reason for this is that we are presented with a series of rooms which have at the core a defined purpose, in this instance dining; a purpose which is ultimately related to

people. This is what Martin Heidegger referred to as the 'special hermeneutic of empathy', by offering a space in which the visitor can imagine themselves, by linking the space to an action that they themselves undertake
(eating in this case) the country house curator offers 'the possibility of
understanding the stranger',[20] and by extension the stranger's home and
way of life.

Diderot described the objects within his study as related to the actions
which he undertook within it. His description of his original study referred
to those things which were reflective of himself: objects which were related
to the act of writing, which identified Diderot as a writer. It was the belit-
tling new dressing gown, the scarlet intruder, so stiff that Diderot feels he
cannot sit down in it, so clean that he cannot wipe his pen nib on it, which
destroys his functional space and ultimately undermines Diderot's image of
himself. We can tell that this (Figure 4.1) is a photograph of a dining room
because it is dominated by a large dining table, set for dinner, and twelve
dining chairs, all indicative of the act of dining. As a series of sentences,
created by the existence of objects/words, the room appears coherent, the
objects/words within the space combining to create the story of dining at
the house. The portraits on the walls add a further biographical spin to this
illusion, suggesting that although what we have in this space is 400 years of
historical life, people throughout the ages can be unified by their need to
eat. For the country house which is open to the public, biography is a way
in, but the idea of a 'lived-in' space must then be sustained. The spaces on
display are not real, there is no dinner party about to take place in the
Dining Room at Tatton, but the idea is there for the visitor to buy into. In
a discussion of this type of representation within the theatre, Roland
Barthes draws our attention back to Diderot:

> As is well known, the whole of Diderot's aesthetics rests on the identifi-
> cation of theatrical scene and pictorial tableau: the perfect play is a suc-
> cession of tableaux, that is, a gallery, an exhibition; the stage offers the
> spectator 'as many real tableaux as there are in the action moments
> favourable to the painter'.[21]

The stage set, the film still, the painter's tableau and the carefully staged
country house room, are all contrived to create a false reality, to convey to
the visitor that this is indeed a Dining Room, by presenting objects which
one would expect to find in such a space. In this way interruptions within
the room coming from historically disparate objects are dismissed with ease.
The changes in the Dining Room at Tatton, coupled with the fact that the
room still predates the other interior spaces on display (the rest of the house
dates from 1785 onwards), are explicable with reference to those who lived
in, and altered, the space and with a defined purpose the space itself is
coherent, uninterrupted.

Tatton Park and written biography

Diderot was presenting himself through his space, and to him the interruptions were all too apparent, both on an aesthetic level and because of his intimate knowledge of himself. By virtue of his written explanation we can understand the occurrences within Diderot's life that instigated the changes to his space, and the difficulty he had with his new dressing gown. As with Diderot's study, the display within the Dining Room is consolidated by the existence of a written description of the space, which further explains the 'why' of what we see when we visit: the guide book.

Following the purchase of Tatton Park the National Trust and Cheshire County Council produced a guide book, *Tatton Park*, first published in 1962.[22] Functioning as a story of the house, the guide book provides a concise description of the space and its contents, including the Dining Room. The original guide book is anonymous, but subsequent revised versions, produced between 1963 and 1972, were penned by Gervase Jackson-Stops who wrote many of the National Trust's guide books during that period. The majority of the early National Trust guide books begin with 'the family', and *Tatton Park* is no exception, the first section is entitled: 'Tatton and the Egertons'.[23] A cultural phenomenon in itself, the act of placing the family first points to the need for a biographical explanation of what the visitor will see above all other explanations. In the instance of *Tatton Park* (1972) the biographical explanation is an entire five pages in length, two more pages than are given over to the 'history of the house' (section two). The guide book begins:

> In the Middle ages, the Manor belonged to the Tattons and was held partly under the Barony of Halton and partly under the Priory of St. John of Jerusalem ... Tatton came to the Egerton family in 1598 when on the death of Richard Brereton of Tatton all his estates were settled on his brother-in-law Sir Thomas Egerton.[24]

This reliance upon the Egerton family is not so prominent in the current guide book, produced by Cheshire County Council in 1987 and based upon Gervase Jackson-Stops' 1972 National Trust version. Updated consistently over the last 20 years, this modern guide book starts with an introduction to the house, followed by 'Pedigree of *Egerton of Tatton*'; two family trees, complete with titles and images of those who owned the house at various stages of its existence.[25] In spite of this alternative approach, the introduction to the house is essentially a biography, telling us who owned the house and when and what they did to it, a gentle reworking of Jackson-Stops' original version of events:

> the land was the property of the Brereton family, who had built and occupied the Old Hall near Tatton Mere around 1520 ... The Tatton

property was purchased by Sir Thomas Egerton, who later became Lord Chancellor of England, and was passed on to younger sons of the Egerton family.[26]

The story is slightly different, in this later version Sir Thomas Egerton does not inherit, but purchases the estate, but the inference is the same: biography first.

The way in which the authors of the guide books have dealt with the issue of progress in the various spaces at Tatton Park suggests that our attitude towards the past life of the country house has altered over the years. The 1972 Jackson-Stops' version tells us that

> William Egerton (who married four times) started to build the present house at Tatton but since both he and his architect, Samuel Wyatt, died before their plans could be achieved, it was left to his son Wilbraham Egerton (1781–1856) to bring the building to completion, which he did with the help of the architect Lewis Wyatt, a nephew of Samuel Wyatt.[27]

and this is echoed in the more recent Cheshire County Council edition:

> William Egerton (1749–1806) started to rebuild the house, employing Samuel Wyatt (1737–1807) as his architect for a proposed 'Grand Design' in the Neo-Classical taste. Wilbraham Egerton (1781–1856) employed Samuel Wyatt's nephew, Lewis Wyatt (1777–1853) to complete the mansion on a reduced scale. Wilbraham and his wife, Elizabeth, improved the standard of comfort and elegance in the house with particularly fine furnishings and paintings.[28]

There is more biography present in this later version of the guide book, although details such as William Egerton being 'married four times' are left out. The subsequent additions made to the house by William Tatton Egerton, who 'added an upper floor to the family wing' in the 1860s, by Wilbraham Egerton, 2nd Baron and 1st Earl, who 'designed and had built the forecourt, screen walls and arches, porter's lodge, family entrance hall, smoking room and chapel' during the 1890s, and by Maurice Egerton, who 'built the huge Tenant's Hall' in 1935,[29] highlighted within the new version of the guide book are omitted by Jackson-Stops in the 1972 version, although the individuals themselves are still discussed. Indeed, changes made after 1825 (when Lewis Wyatt is thought to have ceased to work on Tatton) are barely mentioned by Jackson-Stops, and are accompanied by the disclaimer:

> Happily none of the [later] additions marred the pure neo-classical character of the Wyatts' main block and Tatton remains today a

Regency house above all, almost unique in this country for having survived so completely.[30]

If Tatton Park Mansion had remained unchanged following the departure of architect Lewis Wyatt in about 1825, then the Dining Room would not be filled with objects dating from much later in that, and indeed from the next, century. In later versions of the guide book the authors are much more cognisant of the fact that the progress made within the house cannot be denied. Within the description of the Dining Room the authors of the new Cheshire County Council guide book draw our attention to the changes, the interruptions, such as Westmacott's fireplace of 1840: 'a massive white marble chimneypiece ... replacing a simpler eighteenth century predecessor' and to the new(er) objects; the dessert service on the dining table: 'manufactured by Minton in the style of French Sèvres porcelain' from 1859; the glassware: 'by the famous French firm of Baccarat ... dating from 1911'; and the dining table itself: 'supplied by Gillows in the early nineteenth century' (1812).[31] The function of the Dining Room is what draws these items together, the authors of the guide book joyfully reaffirming this with a biographical anecdote:

> One of the most notable occasions of Egerton hospitality was the visit to Tatton on 2nd and 3rd May 1887, when their Royal Highnesses the Prince and Princess of Wales were entertained by Wilbraham, 2nd Baron ... On both evenings twenty-eight guests sat down to dinner.[32]

In the 1972 edition of the guide book, Jackson-Stops draws our attention to the past history of the spaces, rather than to their present display. The Dining Room 'is all that survives of Tatton before the Wyatt remodelling', its rococo decoration 'an extraordinary contrast with the neo-classicism of the rest of the house', the reason for its continued survival being that 'both William and Wilbraham Egerton insisted on preserving this room within their new neo-classical house'.[33] The latter additions made to the space are referred to in a disdainful manner, as if they leave a nasty taste in the mouth: the original bay window, facing the grounds, was 'chopped off by Samuel Wyatt in about 1790'[34] and 'in 1840 ... a large chimney piece by the sculptor Sir Richard Westmacott was inserted ... it cost the comparatively large sum of £815'.[35] Whereas 'saving' the original space, 'eloquent testimony to its beauty',[36] was the result of the residents William and Wilbraham Egerton, the later, unpleasant, changes are undertaken by the architect and the sculptor seemingly on their own recognisance. As with the new guide book, biography is key – this space is here *because* of William and Wilbraham Egerton – but only the biography of those who did not destroy the harmony of the original Dining Room. There is no biographical anecdote to reaffirm the function of the space although some of the eighteenth- and early-nineteenth-century objects within it are mentioned; namely the

Gillows' table, the chairs pushed up against the walls and the vases on the mantelpiece.[37] Whilst Jackson-Stops ignores the newer additions to Tatton, the authors of the new guide book actually go as far as to warn the prospective visitor about the inconsistencies within the interior of the house; 'it is a house which offers contrasting moods and experiences', each room 'quite different from its neighbour'. This is explained with clear reference to biography: the rooms contain the 'furnishings and contents purchased for them by the Egerton family over a period of some 200 years'.[38]

The Dining Room, along with the rest of Tatton, underwent a programme of redecoration during the 1970s, this included repainting the walls in various shades of muted green, re-upholstering some of the chairs and re-hanging the floor-length scarlet curtains.[39] A comparison of the two guide books shows that virtually no other changes were made to the space in the redecoration. The portraits hanging in the room remain the same at Tatton today as in 1972, the earliest is the portrait of Sir Thomas Egerton (the first of the Egertons to live at Tatton) from the early seventeenth century and the latest of Wilbraham Egerton, 2nd Baron and 1st Earl (who made changes to Tatton in the 1890s) painted in 1901. The authors of both guide books list these paintings, but only the later guide book mentions them within the description of the room. The objects in the room are also the same, including a Victorian sabretache or cavalry officer's despatch bag which has been made into a firescreen and an eighteenth-century port table, designed for the serving of port after dinner, objects described in both guide books. There are no photographs of the Dining Room in the 1972 guide book, in fact there is only one interior photograph and it depicts the library, but a series of articles on the house by Arthur Oswald, published in *Country Life* in 1964,[40] provide ample images by which a comparison can be made. The Dining Room today is identical to the one pictured in Oswald's article, right down to the last candelabra. It is not, however, a feature of the article, receiving the briefest of mentions: 'the date of this room is about 1750. The south window, by which it is lighted is an alteration by Samuel Wyatt.'[41] The room is used by Oswald in opposition to the true Tatton, 'begun in the late 1780s'.[42] Although the Dining Room is unchanged, the descriptions offered within the guide books present two quite different spaces. Jackson-Stops' Dining Room is a Rococo space with two unfortunate later architectural additions and a handful of objects, of which only one, the sabretache firescreen, is from after 1812. The Dining Room described in the new guide book is a space incorporating Tatton of 1598 with a portrait of Sir Thomas Egerton 'in the principal position above the fireplace' (Figure 4.2), and the Tatton of 1909, the date when the Cellar Books ceased to record the 'dinners, balls, parties' which took place in the space.[43] By either accounting for, or simply ignoring, possible interruptions, both guide books perform their function: namely to consolidate the biography which is on display.

Conscious display: the country house and biography

Tatton Park as a country estate is rare in that the old Manor House still exists, standing in the grounds of the 'new' Georgian Mansion (Figure 4.3). The Old Hall, built in 1520 and enlarged in the 1580s, is now also open to the public, its interior and that of the Mansion reflecting, as the new guide book tells us, 'the changing usage and lifestyles of its inhabitants over four hundred and forty years of occupation'.[44] As we know, the property was purchased in 1598 by Sir Thomas Egerton (Figure 4.2) and passed down through the family. It was in the late seventeenth century that the land and the Old Hall came to John Egerton who built a new house on the site of the present Mansion. This new house, completed in 1716, was left largely unaltered until Samuel Egerton inherited the property in the 1760s and began his scheme of improvements. Sir William Egerton took over in 1780 and continued the rebuilding, employing architect Samuel Wyatt to create a neo-classical design for a new house to be built over and around the existing property. It is this house, finished by Lewis Wyatt and improved by subsequent members of the Egerton family that is referred to today as Tatton Park Mansion. The existence of the Old Hall in the grounds of the Park amplifies the sense of history at the site, the progress from sixteenth-century Manor to eighteenth-century Mansion is clearly visible. The homes are a rich source for the biographer, not least because the same family, the Egertons, inhabited them for so long. The guide books, the articles in

Figure 4.3 The south front of Tatton Park Mansion viewed from the Italian Gardens.

Country Life, combine to give us a good idea of the various life stories entwined within the lifespan of the houses, and today a room set aside within the Mansion highlights some of the achievements made by members of the Egerton family over the years, bringing biography to the fore.

Working towards a conclusion, I wish to consider the conscious biography on display at Tatton as part of a wider culture of biographical display within country or period houses which are open to the public. My initial premise when starting this investigation was that country or period houses attempt to present life 'as it was then', complete with decoration, furniture, paintings, pots and pans of the period, so that the visitor might be transported back to a time when people lived very different lives. The challenge of conveying a space so much larger than that lived in by the average visitor as having been 'a home' cannot be achieved without some description of those who once lived there. In order to make the 'house as a home' a reality, to bring these houses into the visitor's realm of understanding, those who present them are reliant upon a knowledge of who lived in the house and when, the things that they did there, in order to provide for the visitor an accurate approximation of the past existence of the site, to explain the function of the many rooms and the objects within them. To return briefly to Heidegger's 'special hermeneutic of empathy': we are people and we can understand things through people, biography is a way in.[45] The further challenge is the country house which has continued to be lived in for a long period of time and thus is not just a period site, but a site of several periods all wrapped up in one space. The simple solution is to go back to a chosen period to recreate the house as it was then, to tell the lives of those living in the house during that period alone. But when the marks of time are so clear, for example significant architectural changes, sometimes an action such as this is not possible, and therefore those presenting the house to the public have to try to tell the story of several inhabitants, their lives and the things that they did at the house over a much larger period of time. Occasionally this is successfully achieved through a separation of different parts of the house, for example late Victorian or even Edwardian kitchens, below Georgian 'above stairs' rooms, giving the idea of progression and incorporating some modern objects or partially renovated spaces. However, such a separation is not always achievable, especially if all of the rooms, rather than a select few, bear the marks of progress. This latter instance is that which is experienced at Tatton Park Mansion, with Victorian and later additions made to several of the large social spaces in the house. In this respect the Mansion is inseparable from biography; how else can we make sense of the changes? We need to explore who the owners were in order to provide answers to the alterations made to the house. Thus we have, as we have seen in the Dining Room, a conscious act of biographical display.

As with the two different versions of Diderot's study, the National Trust's infamous stage-set recreations of period rooms are a purposeful act. Unlike Diderot, the National Trust aim to use the interior space to transport us back into the past, to this end what often occurs within these spaces is a formulaic process of display. This is perhaps best summed up by Simon Jenkins in his recent book *England's Thousand Best Houses*. It is in fact in the entry for Tatton Park Mansion that Jenkins describes the formulaic display process with a mixture of praise and recrimination, stating that the rooms below stairs are 'displayed with National Trust thoroughness, with not a speck of dust and every brass pot gleaming'.[46] This comment, applied doubtless as an entertaining aside, aptly describes the hinterland of orderly period design inside the majority of these houses. Is this 'real historical life' which is presented here, or just a sanitised version of it? In alluding to the perfection of National Trust houses, Jenkins recalls Diderot's staged second study, the tableau referred to by Barthes, the false identity created within the space. Jenkins also enters into an ongoing debate regarding the layout of these types of houses epitomised by the decision taken by English Heritage in 1990 to leave another country house, Brodsworth Hall, in the state in which it was found.

Brodsworth Hall, built between 1861 and 1863 by Charles Thellusson, was given to English Heritage in 1990. Unlike Tatton Park Mansion the house had changed little since its creation, although it was in an extremely run-down state. English Heritage embarked upon a five-year conservation, rather than restoration, programme. Controlling humidity, ultra-violet light, drafts and subsidence and halting further deterioration on a series of objects, English Heritage adopted a 'display as found' policy, refusing to restore the house to its former mid-Victorian glory. The wallpaper was left peeling, but stabilised; modern additions, such as washbasins, electric fires, carpets and curtains, were left in place.[47] Thus Brodsworth Hall shows the slow modernisation and then degradation of a home over about 150 years, rather than the snapshot of a home at a particular point in time. I do not want to argue the case for either decision, but rather to point out that in spite of this difference in approach to display this property is still dependent upon biography for an explanation of why the space is as it is. At Tatton the written biography of the house and the staged rooms explain the actions and life-styles of the successive owners, the new guide book tells us that this is the aim: the house is the work of a series of architects and filled with objects purchased 'by the Egerton family over a period of some 200 years'.[48] At Brodsworth all the layers of changes, albeit relatively few, are there for us to see without disguise or pretence, the effects of the various owners and of time are so apparent that we can believe that this property has always been lived in, that the biography is a continuing story, but that does not stop the visitor from wanting to know *why* the space is as it is. The story behind Brodsworth is an interesting one; rumoured to be that used as the basis for the tale of lawyers' greed in Charles Dickens' *Bleak House*.[49] The infamous tontine which saw the vast fortune of Peter Thellusson bypass his living male heirs and be divided, only upon their deaths, between their surviving male heirs, of which Charles Thellusson was one, is an exciting

biographical tale and one which helps to explain the slow, inexorable down-
fall of the grand home. The fortune which Charles would have passed to his
heirs, and which he borrowed against to complete the building, was much
smaller than it would have been had the terms of the will not been contested, and the lawyers' fees not been so high. There was simply no money
left to maintain Brodsworth. It is through an understanding of this story
that we can understand the space as it is today. In the Dining Room at
Tatton the idea is the same, we can make sense of what we see by understanding those who lived in the house and who made it what it is. Ironically
neither house presents anything other than a contrivance, and yet even this
is only understandable via the biographies of those who lived in the space.

Concluding thoughts

Diderot created an autobiography within his study and perceived his new
dressing gown, the scarlet intruder, as the interruption to his story, destroying the harmony of the space and the coherence of the autobiography. In
writing his essay, Diderot consolidated the process of change within his
space, explaining that the interruption led to the creation of a new space
and a new autobiography, even if this second space was in fact telling a false
story. Biography was for Diderot both the reason for the existence of the
space and the explanation for the changes made to it. In the Dining Room
at Tatton we have a comparable chain of events, a space created and then
repeatedly interrupted by the inclusion of new objects and new architectural
features, symbols of progress, with biography ever-present in the portraits
on the walls and in the functional objects within the space, explaining what
we are seeing. The written descriptions of the Dining Room over the years
confirm these changes, but although the staged space that we see today has
remained the same since 1964, the written space has changed constantly.
The use of written biography at Tatton Park has evolved as our tastes,
knowledge, understanding and expectations have evolved, as spaces such as
Brodsworth Hall have led to questions about how we approach the country
house. Although the Dining Room at Tatton has remained thus far immune
to rearrangement, other rooms within the house have developed to answer
the questions of the modern visitor. The recent inclusion of an 'Egerton
Room' in what was previously the Blue Bedroom, is a testament to the
importance of the family to the manner in which the house is presented
today. Four showcases within the space have been 'dedicated to each of the
major owners of the estate',[50] containing personal mementoes, photographs
or miniatures and letters or diaries. At Tatton Park our reading and
experience of the space is dictated by what we know, by what we are shown
or told, as time progresses our reading of the biography, and consequently
the space, will change, perhaps other objects will be added or taken away
from the Dining Room, will cease to be, or become, interruptions, but
biography will remain key to what we see as we struggle to understand

others and the lives that they led within these houses. It is only in asking 'who lived here?' that we can understand the contrived spaces on display within, and only in turning to biography that the curator can hope to create understandable spaces. The 'scarlet intruder' in the Dining Room at Tatton may not be an object so much as the presence of the curator in what we are told about the space and in what we are, and are not, allowed to see.

Acknowledgement

I would like to thank the National Trust and Cheshire County Council for providing the images which accompany this essay.

Notes

1 Denis Diderot, 'Regrets sur ma vielle Robe de Chambre', in *Oeuvres Complètes de Diderot, Miscellanea Philosophie*, vol. IV (Paris: Garnier Frères, 1875), pp. 5–12.

2 This translation is taken from a version of Diderot's *Rameau's Nephew and Other Works*, trans. Jacques Barzun and Ralph H. Bowen (Indianapolis and Cambridge: Hackett, 2001).

3 Denis Diderot, 'Regrets sur ma vielle Robe de Chambre', in *Oeuvres Complètes de Diderot, Miscellanea Philosophie*, vol. IV (Paris: Garnier Frères, 1875), p. 4. Diderot's essay was first published in Paris in 1772.

4 Denis Diderot, 'Regrets on parting with my old dressing-gown', in *Rameau's Nephew and Other Works*, trans. Jacques Barzun and Ralph H. Bowen (Indianapolis and Cambridge: Hackett, 2001), pp. 310–11.

5 Ibid., p. 317.
6 Ibid., p. 309.
7 Ibid., p. 310.
8 Ibid., p. 311.
9 Ibid., p. 312.
10 Ibid., p. 313.
11 Ibid., p. 312.
12 Ibid., p. 311.
13 Ibid., p. 315.
14 Ibid., p. 313.
15 Ibid., p. 313.

16 Since Diderot's essay this idea has continued to be discussed, my reading of Diderot has been influenced by Pierre Bourdieu's *Distinction: A Social Critique of the Judgement of Taste* (London: Routledge, 1984), and by Suzanne Reimer and Deborah Leslie, 'Identity, consumption and the home', in *Home Cultures*, vol. 1: 2, 2004, pp. 187–208.

17 Denis Diderot, 'Regrets on parting with my old dressing-gown', in *Rameau's Nephew and Other Works*, trans. Jacques Barzun and Ralph H. Bowen (Indianapolis and Cambridge: Hackett, 2001), pp. 311, 313.

18 For a fuller discussion of this idea see Dana Arnold, *The Georgian Country House* (Stroud: Sutton, 1998).

19 Over the years the National Trust and Cheshire County Council have produced a series of guide books to Tatton Park; information boards are also provided within the house itself.

20 Martin Heidegger, *Being and Time*, trans. by J. Macquarrie and E. Robinson (Oxford: Oxford University Press, 1962), p. 163.

21 Roland Barthes, *Image Music Text* (London: Fontana Press, 1977), p. 70.

22 The National Trust, *Tatton Park* (London: The National Trust, 1962).

23 The National Trust, *Tatton Park*, revised edition (London: The National Trust, 1972), p. 3.

24 Ibid., p. 5.

25 Cheshire County Council and The National Trust, *Tatton Park: The Mansion* (Crewe: Cheshire County Council, 1992), contents page. The italics are as they appear in the guide book.

26 Ibid., p. 1.

27 The National Trust, *Tatton Park*, revised edition (London: The National Trust, 1972), p. 7.

28 Cheshire County Council and The National Trust, *Tatton Park: The Mansion* (Crewe: Cheshire County Council, 1992), p. 7.

29 Ibid., 1992, p. 7.

30 The National Trust, *Tatton Park* (London: The National Trust, 1972), p. 13.

31 Cheshire County Council and The National Trust, *Tatton Park: The Mansion* (Crewe: Cheshire County Council, 1992), pp. 32–3.

32 Ibid., p. 35.

33 The National Trust, *Tatton Park* (London: The National Trust, 1972), p. 27.

34 Ibid., p. 27.

35 Ibid., p. 28.

36 Ibid., p. 27.

37 Ibid., p. 28.

38 Cheshire County Council and The National Trust, *Tatton Park: The Mansion* (Crewe: Cheshire County Council, 1992), p. 8.

39 This information was kindly provided by staff at Tatton Park Mansion and the Cheshire County Council marketing office.

40 Arthur Oswald, 'Tatton Park, Cheshire – a property of the National Trust', *Country Life*, cxxxvi, 16, 23 July 1964, pp. 162–5, 232–6.

41 Arthur Oswald, 'Tatton Park, Cheshire – a property of the National Trust', *Country Life*, cxxxvi, 16 July, p. 163.

42 Arthur Oswald, 'Tatton Park, Cheshire – a property of the National Trust', *Country Life*, cxxxvi, 16 July, p. 162.

43 Cheshire County Council and The National Trust, *Tatton Park: The Mansion* (Crewe: Cheshire County Council, 1992), pp. 34–5.

44 Cheshire County Council and The National Trust, *Tatton Park: The Mansion* (Crewe: Cheshire County Council, 1992), p. 1.

45 Martin Heidegger, *Being and Time*, trans. by J. Macquarrie and E. Robinson (Oxford: Oxford University Press, 1962), p. 163.

46 Simon Jenkins, *England's Thousand Best Houses* (Harmondsworth: Penguin, 2004), p. 90.

47 Liz Hollinshead and Karen Wilcox, *Brodsworth Hall* (Colchester: Palladian Press, 2002), pp. 1–8.

48 Cheshire County Council and The National Trust, *Tatton Park: The Mansion* (Crewe: Cheshire County Council, 1992), p. 8.

49 Liz Hollinshead and Karen Wilcox, *Brodsworth Hall* (Colchester: Palladian Press, 2002), p. 1.

50 Cheshire County Council and The National Trust, *Tatton Park: The Mansion* (Crewe: Cheshire County Council, 1992), p. 55.

5

Amsterdam eternal and fleeting
The individual and representations of urban space

Nancy Stieber

> Gather up the fragments that remain that nothing be lost.
> (John 6:13)[1]

Visual representations of the industrialized metropolis around 1900 were inextricably interwoven with conceptions of time. The city's inhabitants confronted the rapid transformations of their social and economic milieu with a variety of strategies that both embraced and repulsed the onslaught of urban fragmentation and renewal, both celebrated and lamented the city's past and future. While much has been written about representations of the alienating streetscape or about the picturesque cityscape, particularly those depicted by well-known painters and photographers, we know relatively little about the ways that individual "ordinary" observers of these mutating cities encountered those changes or about their visualizations of the city and the notion of time inherent to them. This essay will examine two responses by members of the metropolitan elite.

In September 1888, Sheldon Thompson Viele (1847–1916) returned from a nine-day stay in the Netherlands with 34 albumin photographs documenting his trip. He had the luxurious cabinet-size photos mounted in a handsome leather-bound album along with a handwritten list identifying each one. Viele's album exemplifies a touristic practice common before the advent of the postcard or portable Kodak camera. Travelers with sufficient funds would visit photographic studios and select images of the sites they had visited taken by professional photographers. The places represented in Viele's album – Amsterdam, the Hague, Scheveningen, Rotterdam, Hoorn, Dordrecht – comprise a general tour of North and South Holland. Without any further evidence, we would simply classify this album as a souvenir of the standard American tour to the Netherlands as it had developed after the introduction of steamboat passage from New York in 1872. The new ease of transportation had spawned a series of guidebooks and descriptions of the Netherlands touting picturesque charms already familiar to Americans from stereoscope images and popular literature. At first glance, the album simply provides the usual warrant of visits to pre-conceived places along pre-scripted itineraries.[2]

However, Viele's album presents an unusual opportunity to penetrate beyond the stereotypes of tourism to understand how photographic imagery performed in the creation of geographic imaginaries animated by individual biography. Evidence about the man and the context for his voyage will make it possible to see the album through his eyes and thus increase our understanding of the way that perceptions of time and space around 1900 resonated with identity formation. The views of Amsterdam in Viele's photo album are standard prints of well-known sites. But the very ordinariness of the album taken in conjunction with Viele's biography begins to reveal relationships between the construction of self and the perception of a city and its history. Viele's visit to the Netherlands in general and to Amsterdam in particular provides an occasion to explore the processes through which one individual encountering the complexities of modern urban society made use of space to fulfill needs generated from his biographical conditions. His album will be compared with a scrapbook of Amsterdam images compiled by the Dutchman John Anthony Jochems (1836–1920). The aim will be to situate urban representation within a biographical context, to demonstrate the specificity of each individual's confrontation with modern space in order to suggest patterns in the imbrication of history, space, and identity.

The reification of heritage: an American encounter with Old Amsterdam

By the 1880s travel to Europe had become a common prerogative of the American elite. Newspapers printed the names and addresses of Americans staying in Paris. *Social Registers* noted individuals' arrival and departure dates to and from Europe.[3] Viele himself was known as a frequent traveler to Europe; he had visited the ruins of Rome by the time he was 13 and as an adult had made at least four trips to the Netherlands before 1900.[4] Of those, his trip in 1888 was exceptional because he traveled as a member of the Holland Society of New York on a tour organized by the society's founder George West Van Siclen.

The Holland Society took its place alongside other elite clubs and associations in New York, such as the Union, Century, and Knickerbocker, formed in the nineteenth century by New Yorkers who were constructing a distinct and self-conscious identity in the face of the changing social and physical complexion of the city. Beckert tells us that "By the 1880s bourgeois New Yorkers had forged a shared class culture, along with social networks and institutions, that held their world together."[5] Girding themselves with shared historical links, the members of ancestral societies often reinforced existing connections within the elite already established via clubs whose basis was social, athletic, philanthropic, or cultural. Ancestral societies like the Holland Society or the Sons of the American Revolution and the Daughters of the American Revolution, established in 1885, 1889, and 1890 respectively, allowed their members to build histories that lauded the first European settlers and attribute to them the foundations of civilized life in America in order to establish their own patriotic identity.

Roosevelts and others qualified for membership in the Holland Society as descendants "in the direct male line of a Dutchman who was a native or resident of New York or of the American Colonies prior to the year 1675."[6] Among the stated aims of the Holland Society was "to collect and preserve information respecting the early history and settlement of the City and State of New York by the Dutch..." and "to perpetuate the memory and foster and promote the principles and virtues of the Dutch ancestors of its members..."[7] The values of the society, reflected in its many published speeches and yearbooks, expressed a peculiarly American amalgam of democratic and republican ideology combined with pro-Orange monarchist proclivities. They read John Lothrop Motley's version of Dutch history[8] to find parallels between the Dutch struggle for independence against Spain and the American battle for independence from England. Indeed, the tendency of the society's members to wax eloquent at their annual dinners about the precedents set by their Dutch forebears was gently ridiculed in one newspaper article in 1888: "There will be a wealth of oratory and it will be solemnly shown that from Holland came the public school system, the name of the 'United States,' the design of the Stars and Stripes, religious liberty, all the arts, laws, science, and everything that is good and great and well fitted for after dinner speeches."[9] Dutch ancestry was used to forge a national history that defined what it meant to be American. At the annual dinner in 1890 Theodore Roosevelt, in response to the toast "The Hollander as American," argued that the new immigrants to the United States should emulate the Dutch in becoming thoroughly American in language and values.[10]

While such sentiments displayed attitudes fine-tuned to the political challenges of late-nineteenth-century New York, they evinced no particular contemporary understanding of the Netherlands. The Holland Society exhibited a highly selective interest in things Dutch. They had patriotic poems and songs translated; they published their menus in Dutch on orange paper; they chose a Dutch motto for their seal. But aside from an enthusiastic embrace of the reigning Dutch royal family – due to its association with the historic House of Orange – contemporary conditions in the Netherlands were rarely referenced.[11] Their eyes were riveted on the past. This is made visually evident by the design of the membership certificate introduced in January 1888[12] (Figure 5.1). It depicts scenes of "Old

Figure 5.1 Membership certificate of the Holland Society, 1888. From *Year Book of the Holland Society of New-York* (1888–1889). From the collection of the author.

Amsterdam" and "New Amsterdam." The view of Old Amsterdam shows a canal running past a building vaguely reminiscent of the 1648 City Hall, but representing no precise location in the city; the faulty depiction of Amsterdam's architecture indicates the artist's unfamiliarity with it. A contemporary movement to invent "Old New York" as "a haven that affirmed elites' identity and their role as guardians of American heritage" corresponds with the Holland Society's visual invocation of "Old Amsterdam" as the imagined origin of the forefathers who settled "New Amsterdam."[13]

In a period in which an elite was paying increasing heed to colonial descent as a means to secure a distinctive identity, historical consciousness had become integral to family identity for Sheldon Thompson Viele[14] (Figure 5.2). A Yale-educated Buffalo lawyer, he had in 1884 written a short biography of his maternal grandfather Sheldon Thompson, the first elected mayor of the city, an important shipping magnate on Lake Erie, and descendant of a Revolutionary War officer.[15] On his father's side, Viele was linked to both the Vieles and the Knickerbockers, early Dutch settlers of upstate New York. His grandmother, Cathalyntje Knickerbocker, was sister to the friend of Washington Irving whom Irving called his "Diedrich Knickerbocker" – the pseudonymous author of Irving's 1809 satirical history of the New York Dutch which gave rise to the association of the name "Knickerbocker" with Old New York.[16] Viele's first cousin Kathlyne

Figure 5.2 Sheldon T. Viele as Dean of the Saturn Club, 1888. From Frederic Almy, *Forty Years 1885–1925* (Buffalo: The Saturn Club, 1925), 56. From the collection of the author.

compiled the family history of the Vieles and Knickerbockers, stating her purpose in terms much related to the historic and patriotic values and attitudes of the Holland Society:

> my desire was to give general interest to the task by putting on record an average Dutch family which would exemplify the courage, the virtue, the industry, and the power of endurance of those early pioneers who represent the bone and sinew of our national strength.[17]

Viele not only identified with the Holland Society's interest in genealogy, he was also an energetic participant in the kinds of social rituals that constituted the activities of such an organization: its meetings, banquets, toasts, speeches, and songs. At his preparatory school, he wrote to his parents with great gusto about the banquets of his club which were juvenile exercises for later membership in the associational institutions central to the social life of the elite.[18] At Yale, he joined the debating society Linonia, won a poetry prize in his sophomore year, and wrote the Parting Ode for the Class of 1868. Established in Buffalo, he became an active member in clubs and societies related to ancestry, religion, culture, politics, socializing, and charitable work. In the year of his 1888 trip to the Netherlands, he belonged to a variety of civic and social clubs and associations as vestryman of St. Paul's Church, curator of the Buffalo Library, Dean of the Saturn Club, Vice President of the Holland Society for Western New York, president of the Delta Kappa Epsilon Association of Western New York, member of the executive committee of the Civil Service Reform Association in Buffalo, and trustee of the Charity Organization Society, the first such district committee in the United States and one he helped found in 1879.[19]

Experienced clubman and avid historian of his family, Viele was well prepared to join the band of travelers who set off for the Netherlands in July 1888 under the auspices of the Holland Society. George W. Van Siclen, who traveled frequently to the Netherlands and maintained close ties there, had proposed the journey two years after the founding of the society. He envisioned a trip unfettered by business interests, a sentimental "pilgrimage" to the fatherland.[20] As announced in the pages of the *New Amsterdam Gazette*, a newspaper catering to Americans with Dutch ancestry, the trip was touted as an opportunity to trace one's genealogy at cut rates.[21] From the outset, the trip was thus justified by what it could contribute to the members' identification with the Netherlands based on their historic link. Van Siclen prepared a rigorous nine-day tour through North and South Holland, Zeeland, Utrecht, Friesland, Groningen, and Gelderland, viewing the chief sights noted in the current Baedeker guide.[22] He planned a thorough documentation of the trip for posterity, anticipating the daily publication of log on a portable press and expecting the travelers to bring along small cameras to record the journey photographically.

Thirty members of the Holland Society accompanied by 17 family

members and a special correspondent from the *New York Herald* sailed on
the steamship "Amsterdam" on 28 July, reaching Rotterdam on 9 August.
The men were for the most part professionals: lawyers, doctors, ministers.
Few of the group had known each other previously[23] and the social events
and meetings organized on board the ship were important means of forging
relations. The culture of the bourgeois club was re-created. A choral group
was formed and comic lyrics written for general entertainment. A mock trial
was held. Meetings were convened to organize the group. At one of those,
Viele was elected "historiographer" of the trip, while John van Duyn was
elected "pictoriographer" and a three-dollar assessment was levied on the
members for the purchase of photographic supplies so that the visual record
of the journey could be deposited in the archives of the society.[24] Viele's
account of the trip was published in the 1888–1889 *Year Book of the
Holland Society* and also in a private edition he financed himself in 1890.[25]
One hundred and thirty-one glass slides were made from Van Duyn's
photographs.[26]

Van Siclen's ambitious plans for the nine days were modified by arrangements made by the Dutch. Upon their arrival in the Netherlands, the party
was welcomed by a series of local reception committees that surprised the
group with lavish treatment. The recently appointed American Minister,
Robert Branwell Roosevelt, himself a founding member of the Holland
Society, reported to the Secretary of State on the extraordinary reception of
the Americans.[27] A royal train carriage was provided for the ladies on their
trip from Rotterdam to Amsterdam. Arriving in Amsterdam, with a cheering populace along the way, they were whisked by carriages to the Doelen
Hotel, erected in 1882 on the site of a recently demolished tower that had
served as the assembly hall for the seventeenth-century militia that commissioned Rembrandt's *Night Watch*. The mayor received them the next day at
the town hall, where an exhibit of historical documents connecting Old and
New Amsterdam had been prepared. At the University Library another
historical exhibition presented books and documents related to the early
Dutch settlement of New Amsterdam, including the Washington Irving
account. The director of the famed Amsterdam zoo treated them to lunch.
Amsterdam hosted a boat trip to the island of Marken and to the city of
Hoorn, accompanied by the mayor of Amsterdam. And a gala reception was
held at the most luxurious of the city's hotels, where the toasts and decora-
tions followed rituals familiar to the Americans. The Amsterdam reception
committee, composed of bankers, businessmen, newspaper editors, and professionals such as lawyers, comparable to the band from the Holland
Society, spent over 2000 guilders on the festivities.[28] From Amsterdam, the
group traveled to Leiden, Rotterdam, the Hague, and Scheveningen, everywhere treated as visiting dignitaries. No reception was more enthusiastic
than that in Leiden, where they paraded through throngs of cheering
inhabitants and were welcomed by the members of a sister organization to
which many members of the Holland Society already belonged: the Third

of October Society which had been founded two years before to commemorate the liberation of Leiden from Spanish rule.[29] It is evident that the travelers were recognized as belonging to the equivalent class as their hosts in Amsterdam and elsewhere. One of the participants comments in his journal: "We had to buy high hats, that being a caste necessity."[30]

To the surprise of the Americans, their visit became a national event – followed closely in the major Dutch newspapers and even the subject of a friendly political cartoon in the *Nederlandsche Spectator* with the caption "See the sons returning to the motherland...."[31] Other editorials in Dutch newspapers underscored the shared republican nature of the two governments and their mutual love of freedom.[32] Such high-flown rhetoric not only echoed the positions represented in the toasts and speeches at the Holland Society, which had not gone unnoticed in the Dutch newspapers, they were in tune with the current Liberal domination of Dutch politics. The Americans, however, did not appear to be aware of the particularities of contemporary Dutch politics, indeed committing the occasional gaffe,[33] but dwelled as in the United States on shared principles of liberty, free instruction, and free religion. As Reverend Suydam put it: "so long as the desire for liberty shall dwell with the breasts of man anywhere throughout the world ... so long must Old Holland be cherished in the memory."[34]

That invented "Old Holland" was the focus of their travels. While the Netherlands was experiencing an economic upturn that reversed its long decline since the heights of the seventeenth century, the travels of the Holland Society were largely organized around two aims: contact with the equivalent elite and contact with the remnants of "Old Holland," the historical documents, commemorative statues, buildings, and sites that underscored the importance of Dutch culture in the period when the visitors' ancestors made the trek to the New World. The group, which had spent the first three days onboard ship comparing genealogies,[35] took a personal interest when confronted with remains of that past, seeking connections to their own family histories. They responded to Rembrandt's *Night Watch*, the most renowned painting in the recently constructed Rijksmuseum, by taking pleasure at finding their own family names represented there and in other group portraits of the militia companies.[36] The personal connection to the Netherlands had been underscored during the journey to the Netherlands when the *Herald* reporter had asked each member to supply stories of his Dutch ancestors.[37] Viele not only provided the Knickerbocker and Viele links, but traced the family back to relatives of no less a figure than William the Silent.[38]

In Viele's published account of the trip, most of the text is given over to transcribing the many speeches, toasts, and songs composed for the occasion, providing ample opportunity for reciting the historical links between Dutch and American principles of liberty. Viele returned to the United States his luggage filled with portfolios of material,[39] and indeed the *Year Book* includes original documentation in the form of invitations, tickets, guidebooks, and maps pasted in. Having fully documented the trip's social events, however, he leaves out the description of the standard tourist sights that he could presume his audience already knew from reading popular accounts. Viele shared with that audience assumptions about the character of Old Amsterdam. For instance, when the group sees the Schreiers Tower in Amsterdam, Viele finds it sufficient to refer it as "so beautifully described by De Amicis" – a well-known guide.[40] Viele clings to an image of Dutch society based on stereotypes of the staid burger. His midnight visit to the Kalverstraat, a street ablaze with activity, elicits the comment that "it certainly was a scene strange to American eyes, and one not entirely consonant with our ideas of Dutch phlegm and decorum."[41] While he compares the view of new districts arising on the outskirts of Amsterdam to those visible in New York[42] and while he comments briefly on the evident vibrancy of the Dutch economy,[43] Viele pays little attention to contemporary Dutch conditions, which play no role in the pre-conceived vision. Instead he provides a faithful rendition of the group's activities in viewing the historic remains and socializing with its Dutch peers.

His account is paralleled in the photographs taken by Van Duyn which largely follow the activities of the group. Over half of Van Duyn's images chronicle the journey on board ship with numerous pictures of the crew and the travelers, including humorous shots of the mock trial. Once in the Netherlands, Van Duyn photographed the events of the journey: the reception in Leiden, the boat ride to Marken. His five views of Amsterdam are those of an amateur with unsteady hand. Two depict landmarks, the Oude Kerk and Montelbaanstoren, and three show street and canal life (Figure 5.3). While the Kodak camera had been introduced to the market in May 1888 just months before the departure of the Holland Society, Van Duyn used another camera, which produced rectangular photos rather than the Kodak's circular ones, although the immediate fame of the Kodak's stringpull mechanism influenced Viele's ditty on Van Duyn's photographic efforts:

Now Doc. Van Duyn, he pulls the twine,
Drops a nickel in the slot,
And photographs the fleeting grin
Instanter – on the spot.[44]

The immediacy and spontaneity that Viele comments upon is visible in the askew compositions that reflect the handheld camera. Van Duyn shoots the present movement around him – be it the crowd in the Jewish flea market, children at play on a day off, or fellow pedestrians whose heads appear inadvertently in his shot of a shopping street. Through his concentration on the present moment, Van Duyn's images reveal something of the active world around him.

His lively views contrast sharply with the vision of Amsterdam represented in the photographs Viele chose to place in his own souvenir album.

Figure 5.3 "Shops, centre Amsterdam," photo by Dr John van Duyn, 1888.

Viele very likely ordered a set of the photographs taken by Van Duyn and had them mounted separately. Several were incorporated into his published account of the journey. A printed list of all 131 photographs by Van Duyn was placed in his souvenir album, yet he decided to supplement that record with professional photographs. His selection of 12 images for Amsterdam include highly recognizable landmarks and picturesque canals frequently depicted in photographs for the tourist trade (Figure 5.4). Ten represent "Old Amsterdam": the Montelbaanstoren, the St. Antoniespoort, the Munt, the Dam, the Binnen-Amstel, the Rokin, the Kolkje, the Pijpen-markt, the Town Hall of 1648, and a view of the Prinsengracht taken from the tower of the Westerkerk. Only one shows a recent building, the Rijksmuseum completed only three years before, and that one was built to hold and celebrate Dutch national treasures of art and history, thus conso-nant with Viele's focus on the past. The photographs present a staid and proud city contrasting with the lively, commercial vigor revealed in Van Duyn's views. Aside from the horse-drawn trams in the Dam, there is no sign in these photographs of the renewed economic activity of a growing metropolis. Advertisements are missing; the bustle of the street is not in evidence. Instead, this set of photographs captures what for Viele and the others was the essence of a historic past, the idealized Old Amsterdam that remained untouched by the ephemeral shifts of time, forever caught in a

Figure 5.4 Page from the album of Sheldon T. Viele: Montelbaanstoren (above); Kolkje (below). From the collection of the author.

museum gaze that disregards the present. Indeed, one of the photographs depicts the still and reflecting waters of the Nieuwezijds Voorburgwal, a canal that had been filled four years before the trip in order to provide a street that was presumed needed for increasing traffic. Viele's inclusion of a view that had disappeared suggests his pre-occupation with an Amsterdam that did not exist and never existed, with an Amsterdam of gracious canals rather than the city of metropolitan growth.[45]

The stillness of Amsterdam in the photographs Viele selected for himself and to show his family on his return to Buffalo also contrast sharply with the representation of Amsterdam in the guidebook specially prepared for the Holland Society pilgrims by their hosts. There the only visual image is a map of the North Sea Canal, completed in 1876 and critical to the renewed commercial activity in Amsterdam's harbor. Alongside the museums and older landmarks, the Amsterdammers included in their recommended sights contemporary institutions such as the Exchange, the Law Courts, the Institute for the Blind, the jail, the cavalry, naval yards, orphanages, naval school, and the newly constructed Commercial Quay (Handelskade).[46] But for Viele and the other members of the Holland Society, the trip was intended as a journey to the past, not a survey of current accomplishments. Viele's photographs, more than those of Van Duyn who was chronicling the events of the trip, capture that imagined past visually. They enable Viele's construction of an Amsterdam presumably unchanged from the seventeenth century, pre-conceived as the unaltered place associated with the forefathers who anchored his American identity, yet bearing little resemblance to the thriving and active city of that era.

For most American travelers to the Netherlands around 1900, "Holland" was a carefully edited journey to the past.[47] Their encounter with the actuality of the country was highly selective: geographical fragments left over by history. But Viele's trip was something beyond the ordinary tourist's; it was a self-conscious pilgrimage to the place which gave his identity status. His self-definition as an American of Dutch descent required the construction of an idealized Old Amsterdam and the photographs in his album became, like the Old Amsterdam on his membership certificate for the Holland Society, a visual warrant of his identity. In his album Amsterdam appears as if time had stopped, without evidence of movement, all signs of economic renewal erased or overlooked. This picture was appropriate to the interests of the Holland Society travelers. What they needed was the visual counterpart to their ideological reduction of Dutch history as the precursor to the American republic.

The melting city: a Dutch encounter with changing Amsterdam

The menu and program for the annual dinner of the Holland Society held in January 1890, at which Theodore Roosevelt had spoken, was decorated with a reproduction of a Frans Hals painting showing a group of dining militia officers.[48] The parallel being drawn between the hearty Dutchmen of the seventeenth century and the jolly American clubmen of the Holland Society was evident. But the reproduction of the militia scene also attracted the interest of a contemporary Dutchman. A few weeks after the annual dinner, the Holland Society received an inquiry from the captain-adjutant of the Amsterdam militia, John Anthony Jochems, asking for a copy of the program with the reproduced painting. The current president of the society, Robert B. Roosevelt, sent it to him along with descriptions of the evening from the *New York Herald* and the *New Amsterdam Gazette*.[49] In return, Jochems donated to the society's library a catalogue he had compiled of printed works on the militia[50] and several months later, he donated three more books on the history of the militia.[51] This event was considered sufficiently newsworthy that the *New Amsterdam Gazette* published Jochems' letter to Roosevelt.

John Anthony Jochems (Figure 5.5) was born in Amsterdam, son of the head of the Merchant Marine Academy (Kweekschool voor de Zeevaart)

Figure 5.5 John Anthony Jochems, 1899.

there.[52] After he ended a career in the army in 1882, he joined the Amsterdam municipal civic guard in 1883 and remained in it until his retirement.

The Amsterdam municipal civic guard (*schutterij*) originated from medieval guilds organized to defend the city. By the seventeenth century the officers, drawn from patrician families at the height of their mercantile power, had formed fraternities whose purpose was as much social as military. Their gatherings, documented in extraordinary group portraits by Rembrandt, Van der Helst, Hals, and others, reflected and produced Amsterdam's glory; by the nineteenth century the paintings had become among the most important symbols of Dutch nationalism. Rembrandt's *Night Watch* and Van der Helst's *Celebration of the Peace of Munster (Schuttersmaaltijd)* were enshrined in the Rijksmuseum. At the same time, however, the citizen militia itself, long supplanted by a standing army, had outgrown its military function and was increasingly the butt of ridicule, viewed as an outmoded organization clinging to an aura long dissipated.[53] Even as the memory of the historic militia grew in prestige, respect for the current citizen militia declined.[54] In 1900 the government decided to suspend the nation-wide system of municipal militias by 1907.

Aware of the declining contemporary import of the citizen militia but convinced of its historic significance, in 1884 Jochems established a collection of memorabilia, largely uniforms and printed material, associated with its long history. He did so in collaboration with his colleague first lieutenant Jan Eduard van Someren Brand (1856–1904), son of the commandant.[55] As their collection grew, they began to issue catalogues of their holdings, meticulously compiled and annotated. Jochems took charge of the printed material, while Van Someren Brand oversaw the collection of uniforms and paraphernalia. Jochem's catalogues reveal a catholic interest in all related to the militia, including the contemporary political cartoons and commentary that ridiculed the present state of the institution. That his reach extended to ephemera such as the dinner program of an American club indicates the nature of the collecting mentality at work: one in which historic sensation predominates without disciplinary perspective. All fragments of the civil guard's history were considered equally worthy as means to create contact with the past.

Eventually, when Van Someren Brand was appointed first curator of the newly founded municipal (Stedelijk) museum in Amsterdam, the collection found a home in several rooms there alongside another antiquarian collection. Van Someren Brand had fashioned historic style rooms from the legacy of the museum's founding donator Sophia Augusta Lopez Suasso and from the interiors of rooms he had salvaged from homes being destroyed in 1895 for the construction of the Raadhuisstraat.[56] When the exhibition of the historical collection of the militia moved to the new museum in 1896, Jochems and Van Someren Brand led Queens Emma and Wilhelmina through it.[57] That official recognition of their efforts contrasted dramatically with the ridicule of cultural critics who found laughable the effort to enshrine an obsolete institution and for whom the dolls dressed in regalia represented an outdated approach.

Jochems' historical activities can be understood as typical of late-nineteenth-century antiquarian collecting in the Netherlands and resulted from several factors. His father had ambitions as a historian, writing two unpublished manuscripts which his dutiful son placed in the Amsterdam municipal archives. Jochems fulfilled his father's hopes by himself publishing works of historical scholarship. One put out in the year of the Holland Society's visit completed documentation of the Amsterdam militia begun by the great eighteenth-century chronicler of the city Jan Wagenaar. Jochems' interest in the history of the militia was motivated by his own participation in the institution and the quality of belonging that such club-like groups instill. Larger patterns of contemporary historical consciousness also contributed to his and Van Someren Brand's project. An increased interest in the history of seventeenth-century Holland was characteristic of national identity formation at the end of the nineteenth century.[58] The militia not only represented vaunted values of the bourgeois society of Old Amsterdam, reconceived as harbingers of the liberal bourgeois society of the present, they embodied in the form of the group portraits that aspect of cultural achievement that was enduring when Dutch economic hegemony was only a memory. The entirety of the militia's history, including its recent past, was musealized, incorporated into a seamless continuum valorized by its earlier glory, its preservation made urgent by the anticipated disappearance of the institution.

The forging of Dutch nationalism at the end of the nineteenth century did not encounter the challenge of immigrant diversity as in the United States; rather, internal diversity in the form of emergent Catholic, Orthodox protestant, and working-class identities made a shared identity problematic. As others have shown, bourgeois liberals threatened by the imminent political organization of these disparate groups turned to cultural and historic constructs in order to suggest shared national identity.[59] Here, new rituals involving the House of Orange were exploited, particularly after the death of Willem III; and other cultural expressions were given national import that overlooked sectarian difference. Folkloric costumes, Dutch Renaissance architectural forms, the genius of Rembrandt were tapped to sustain a new construction of national identity stripped of actual ideological divisions. Jochems' collaborator Van Someren Brand played a central role in one such cultural configuration when, as curator of the Stedelijk Museum, he oversaw two exhibitions during the celebration of Queen Wilhelmina's coronation in 1898. Continuing the interest in costume he already displayed in his work for the historic collection of the militia, he curated an exhibition of folk costumes from throughout the Netherlands. The Stedelijk also hosted an extensive exhibition of Rembrandt's work. These two contrasting sources, representing popular and high culture, the regional and historical, craft and art, the nameless creator and the genius, were manipulated as symbols of national unity, associated with a royal patronage intended to indicate a position above partisanship. When Viele and his son visited the two exhibitions on their trip to witness the coronation in 1898, they took these symbols of Dutchness as self-evident and transparent.[60]

The musealization of art, customs, and history was integral to this phase of antiquarianism.[61] While the folk costume exhibition, the new style rooms at the Stedelijk, and the installation of the militia memorabilia was attacked in the intellectual press, they participated in the wider creation of popular historical consciousness and the construction of institutions which in the next decades would be supervised under professional notions of curatorship and the historical discipline. Amateur collectors played an important role in forming historical collections and documentation at this time.[62] Following loosely in the seventeenth-century tradition of compiling topographical atlases related to Amsterdam, a figure like A.T. Hartkamp (1848–1924) collected newspaper clippings related to events as they occurred in the city. From 1887, J.E. van Someren Brand participated in the committee for the Atlas Amsterdam of the Royal Antiquarian Society, which in addition to rare prints and photographs, also collected plates from contemporary periodicals.[63] In 1900, the newly founded society Amstelodamum, "a society for the advancement of knowledge of the present and past of Amsterdam," planned the project of collecting press clippings of important Amsterdam images and events in order to publish "contemporary history" (*hedendaagsche geschiedenis*).[64] Jochems himself, after his retirement from the militia, began to collect material about the history of Amsterdam. A carefully compiled collection of such clippings appears in a scrapbook that he assembled between 1911 and 1916; it is unclear if it is one in a series. It consists of clippings from newspapers and magazines, postcards, photos, and other ephemera accompanied by Jochems' own carefully handwritten annotations. Together these provide a minute account of physical changes taking place in the city. The bound volume has embossed on its spine the title *Amsterdam van Vroeger* (Bygone Amsterdam).

In the scrapbook, Jochems records the disappearance of one building after the other over the course of his life, but primarily those of the previous decade[65] (Figure 5.6). The age of the building matters little to Jochems; he gives those built in the nineteenth century the same attention he gives to those from the seventeenth century. His interest is consistent: he shows only the building that has been demolished, never the building that comes in its place. The scrapbook thus represents a record of disappearing Amsterdam, a series of erasures. We get the impression of time obliterating history: there is an awareness of change taking place, but the perspective presented here allows us only to see a gradual dismantling of the familiar. In only one instance does Jochems record the takeover of a building rather than its demolition when he narrates without reference to himself the abandonment of the headquarters of the citizen militia on 30 July 1907 and its subsequent adoption by the police. Only once does he turn his attention to

Figure 5.6 Pages from the scrapbook of J.A. Jochems, *Amsterdam van Vroeger*.

restoration: in the case of the reconstruction of the Rembrandt House in 1911.[66] Otherwise, the scrapbook represents the relentless charting of destruction, the disappearance of buildings one by one.

Jochems' method is simple: he cuts out illustrations and articles related to the demolition from printed sources and to these he adds in clear script additional information about the history of the building. He draws from major daily newspapers such as the *Nieuws van de Dag* and from popular illustrated magazines such as *De Prins*. Frequently he selects reproductions of eighteenth-and nineteenth-century prints, but he is just as ready to use new photographs and postcards. The aim is not encyclopedic; for the most part Jochems leaves out reference to the filling of canals and demolition of bridges, which were major contributors to the changing landscape of the city. No attempt is made to organize the demolition reports chronologically; instead he brings together images and texts on the topic of one building to form an independent chapter.

The cumulative narrative these chapters tell about the place of Amsterdam in time is clear. Unlike Viele's album of a city eternally occupying the past, the vision of Amsterdam that emerges from Jochems' scrapbook is that of a city in motion through time. However, we are only made aware of the destructive force of that movement. For the man whose primary experience at the prime of his life had been participation in an institution that had lost its meaning in the modern world, Jochems' orientation facing the past rather than the future can be understood as self-referential. In its obsessive observance of a constantly mutable present, it is a position that is the product of modernity, though its failure to welcome change and celebrate the new marks it with conservatism. Yet there is no nostalgic dwelling on an idealized city consisting of fragments that remain from the past as with Viele; Jochems' Amsterdam consists entirely of buildings that no longer exist. Like Viele's it is an imaginary city, but one produced through the ravages of time, one in which history is never still, but whose future cannot be grasped. Jochems translates for us the anxiety of the individual experiencing continuous urban change, so traumatized by that cavalcade of demolitions that he cannot focus on what is being built anew. It is the result of profound insecurity anchored in an identification with what has become obsolete in the modern world.

Jochems' scrapbook contrasts with other contemporary accounts of the changing city such as that of J.H. Rössing the drama critic whose newspaper series with the title "Disappearing 'Old-Amsterdam'" (*Het Verdwijnend "Oud-Amsterdam"*) was followed with a book of the same title in 1916.[67] Rössing wrote, "As one can see, the Old Amsterdam that holds the memory of centuries is coming to an end. Extensions to the city, change and increase of traffic, the requirements of health and well-being, have made and still make it necessary that old houses tumble, that entire neighborhoods disappear with the sacrifice of much that is beautiful and characteristic."[68] But Jochems makes no comment on the beautiful and the characteristic. He simply observes the departure of the familiar, be it a cigar store or the post office. The militia he had served had lost its usefulness and was gone; the buildings he documented were gone. Jochems records these disappearances with the same dry recital of facts that graced his catalogues of the historic collection he founded, but the intensity of his passion is evident from the painstaking effort he makes to document his losses in minute detail.

The eternal and fleeting city

Viele and Jochems, the visitor from afar and the inhabitant, the tourist and the antiquarian collector, the Dutch descendant and the native Amsterdammer, each looked at Amsterdam and saw something different. For Viele the unfamiliar realities of contemporary Amsterdam were insignificant; he visited a city whose past he could reconstrue to sustain his own identity in the present. The images he chose for his album translated buildings that still existed into the representation of an imagined and unchanging past. Jochems, on the other hand, demonstrated his intimate familiarity with the city by assembling a meticulous visual account of what he was currently losing. His scrapbook depicts a fleeting city, one disappearing before his eyes. For neither of these men was the aesthetic perception of urban space a key factor. Rather, a temporal perception prevailed. The visual records of the city that each of them compiled reveal contrasting notions of time constructed in relation to needs arising from their biographical circumstances. Viele's nostalgic vision recovers an invented home, necessary to sustain his Dutch-American identity. Jochems' focus on continual erasure mirrors his identification with loss, his connection to a dissolved institution that linked him to Amsterdam's "glorious" history. Jochems' scrapbook provides a valorization of what has ceased to be useful to the present whereas Viele's photographs make useful to the present something that never existed in the past.

Neither created the visual images he used to construct his fragmentary description of Amsterdam. Instead, each developed a vision of the city in time by assembling existing images into a personal memento. While Viele's vision was a synthetic one that optimistically sustained his identification with the rise of American power, and Jochems' was a pessimistic vision of disintegration through which he associated his identity with the eclipse of Dutch power, each produced a physical object that reflected and constituted identity. As Susan Stewart has suggested, "Because of its connection to biography, its place in constituting the notion of the individual life, the memento becomes emblematic of the worth of that life and of the self's capacity to generate worthiness."[69]

Both Viele and Jochems were engaged in similar mental projects of bringing time, space, and identity together. Such a project in imagined geographies was typical of a period in which individuals confronted the changing metropolis. However, these two very specific examples of urban representation crafted in relation to individual identity by no means exhaust the repertoire of ways that modern individuals read time into the city. Privileged men in their respective societies, Viele and Jochems shared a historical consciousness that found differing expressions in their visual ego-documents. Their perceptions of the essentialist and transitory nature of the city make evident the need to probe how other individuals facing modern urban change perceived and represented time in space to construct identity.

Notes

I am grateful to Sheldon T. Viele and Rob Joghems, descendants of Viele and Jochems respectively, for their generous assistance. I also wish to acknowledge the help of Patricia Virgil of the Buffalo and Erie County Historical Society and E.M. Donner of the Koninklijk Oudheidkundig Genootschap.

1 Epigraph on title page of Kathlyne Knickerbocker Viele, *Viele 1859–1909: Two Hundred and Fifty Years with a Dutch Family of New York* (New York: Tobias B. Wright, 1909).

2 On the relationship of photography and travel in the nineteenth century, see Joan M. Schwartz, "*The Geography Lesson*: photographs and the construction of imaginative geographies," *Journal of Historical Geography*, vol. 22, 1 (1996), 16–45, and especially 31–33.

3 The Buffalo *Social Register*, for instance, included a section reporting

individuals' European arrivals and departures.

4 Viele traveled to Europe in 1882 (with his wife), 1886, 1888 (with the Holland Society), 1894 (with daughter Grace), and 1898 (with son Dorr).

5 Svan Beckert, *The Monied Metropolis: New York City and the Consolidation of the American Bourgeoisie, 1850–1896* (Cambridge, UK: Cambridge University Press, 2001), 271. See also pages 237, 246, 263, 270. For another account of the role played by the social clubs of New York, see David C. Hammock, *Power and Society: Greater New York at the Turn of the Century* (New York: Russell Sage Foundation, 1982), 72–77. The *Social Register of New York* began publication in 1887.

6 "Constitution and by-laws of the Holland Society" (1886), 18–19. This was in contrast with the St. Nicolas Society, established in 1835, which admitted descendants of any nationality whose ancestors were residents of New York City or New York State prior to 1785. Willem Frijhoff discusses the founding of the Holland Society in the context of American definitions of Dutchness in "Reinventing an old fatherland: The management of Dutch identity in early modern America," in Regina Bendix and Herman Roodenburg, eds., *Managing Ethnicity; Perspectives from Folklore Studies, History and Anthropology* (Amsterdam: Het Spinhuis, 2000), 125–127.

7 "Constitution and by-laws of the Holland Society" (1886), 10. On the history of the Holland Society, see David William Voorhees, *The Holland Society: A Centennial History 1885–1985* (New York: The Holland Society of New York, 1985). Alice P. Kenney provides historical context to its founding in *Stubborn for Liberty: The Dutch in New York* (Syracuse:

Syracuse University Press, 1975), 239–240.

8 John Lothrop Motley, *The Rise of the Dutch Republic: A History* (New York: Harper and Brothers, 1856).

9 Newspaper article 7 January 1888 in New York Historical Society BV Robert B. Roosevelt Collection, Volume 23. After-dinner speeches at the Annual Dinner of the Holland Society in 1889 expressed a confluence of patriotism, historical mythologizing, and contemporary ideology in the manner predicted by the newspaper article. William Waldorf Astor stated, "The Dutch established for all mankind the principles of religious tolerance and constitutional government." Rev. Henry van Dyke proclaimed, "I do not believe in those societies which are intended to perpetuate class distinctions, arouse enmities in this country of ours, and split up the broad continent of national feeling into little islands of unnaturalized foreigners, but I do believe in a society which emphasizes the honor of pure republican descent, and reminds us that we are bound of all men to defend against anarchists, against aristocrats, and against socialists, those laws and liberties which were established on the shores of this New World by the free spirit and daring courage of our Dutch forefathers," Annual Dinner of the Holland Society of New-York, 8 January 1889, *Year Book of the Holland Society of New-York 1888–1889*, 185, 189.

10 Theodore Roosevelt, quoted in *New Amsterdam Gazette*, vol. 6, no. 5, 3–4. On varying attitudes of the New York elite to recent immigrants, see Beckert, 270–271. The New York Genealogical and Biographical Society was established in 1869, the Huguenot Society of America in 1883.

11 Morris Coster established the *New Amsterdam Gazette* in 1883 to report

on the history of New York's Dutch founders while supplying them with current news of the Netherlands, but so little was the interest in that endeavor that within a few years the newspaper had largely become the outlet for reporting club activity of the various ancestral societies of New York.

12 The model of the certificate of membership adopted by the society was presented at the annual dinner of the Holland Society on 10 January 1888 and was reported to be "a great work of art. It represents scenes of Old Amsterdam and a number of others copied from scenes in New Amsterdam in its earliest days," *New Amsterdam Gazette*, vol. 5, no. 1 (2 to 31 January 1888).

13 Clifton Hood, "Journeying to 'Old New York:' elite New Yorkers and their invention of an idealized city history in the late nineteenth and early twentieth centuries," *Journal of Urban History*, vol. 28, no. 6 (6 September 2002), 699–719. Hood notes that "some late-nineteenth century historians invented an imagined city known as 'Old New-York' that idealized colonial New York" and that "the attraction of patrician histories of New York City was largely that they constituted a community of feeling that was locally based and delimited by class and heritage." Hood, 699.

14 Short biographies of Viele are available in Henry P. Wright, ed., *The Biographical Record of the Class of 1868, Yale College, 1868–1893* (New Haven: Tuttle, Morehouse & Taylor, 1894), 133–134; *A History of the City of Buffalo, Its Men and Institutions; Biographical Sketches of Leading Citizens* (Buffalo: Buffalo Evening News, 1908), 215–216; Truman C. White, ed., *Our County and its People, a Descriptive Work on Erie County, New York* (Boston: Boston History Co., 1898), 497–498.

15 Sheldon Thompson Viele, *Biography of Sheldon Thompson* (Buffalo, 1884).

16 On Washington Irving's references to the Knickerbockers of Schaghticoke, family home of Sheldon's grandmother, see Chase Viele, *The Knickerbockers of Upstate New York* (New York: Holland Society of New York, 1973), 9.

17 Kathlyne Knickerbocker Viele, *Viele*, p. 8. See also her *Sketches of Allied Families Knickerbacker-Viele, Historical and Genealogical, to which is added an Appendix Containing Family Data* (New York: T.A. Wright, 1916).

18 Sheldon T. Viele to his parents, letter of 19 February 1861, Buffalo and Erie County Historical Society, Viele Family Papers, Viele Box 1, Folder Sheldon T. Viele to parents 1860–1894.

19 In the 1890s Viele established the University Club in Buffalo, became president of the Buffalo Association of the Sons of the American Revolution, and was president of the Yale Alumni Association of Western New York.

20 Despite repeated pronouncements by Van Siclen that the trip was a pilgrimage for pleasure and sentiment without any business associations, its disinterestedness was questioned in the Dutch press because of the prominent advertisements of the Holland Trust Company at the time of the journey. The Holland Trust Company started business on 1 April 1888, several months before the trip, and was managed according to financial schemes devised by Van Siclen, founder of the Holland Society and initiator of the trip. The American Minister to the Netherlands, Robert Barnwell Roosevelt, prominent member of the Holland Society, had been elected president of the Holland Trust Company. A letter dated 7 January 1888 from Roosevelt to Hooper C. Van Horst, founding

president of the Holland Society, indicates clearly the strong links between the two organizations. Van Vorst had presided over the meeting that elected Roosevelt president of the trust company and in his letter Roosevelt asks his assistance in raising subscriptions to the trust at the upcoming annual dinner of the Holland Society. New York Historical Society, BV Robert B. Roosevelt Collection, Volume 23. The Dutch ancestry of members of the board of directors is discussed at length in "The Holland Trust Company," *New Amsterdam Gazette*, vol. 5, no. 6 (2 July–31 July 1888), 6–7. Van Siclen resigned his post as secretary of the trust company in 1891 because of several episodes that had caused negative publicity. At the time of his resignation it was reported that "the interests which became identified with the trust company were largely the same as those represented by the society." *New York Times* (22 October 1891), 3. Whatever may have been Van Siclen and Roosevelt's business interests during the 1888 trip, fellow passengers like Viele were not involved.

21 "This excursion will also give the visitors an opportunity to learn more of their ancestors and pedigrees in the Fatherland, and at twice a lower figure than they would be able to become informed of by enquiries made by letters and other means for the purpose," *New Amsterdam Gazette*, vol. 5 no. 3 (14 March–14 April 1888), 2.

22 "Naar de bakermat hunner voorouders," *Nieuws van de Dag*, Derde Blad, 30 July 1888. In his diary of the trip, Charles Lydecker states, "We are not clear as to what plans may have been made for us when we arrive, but we have a set of plans laid our for ourselves which compromises Amsterdam, The Hague and Scheveningen,

Haarlem, some islands of the Zuyder Zee, Delft, Utrecht, Middelburg & other places in South Holland." Holland Society Archives, transcript of Charles Edward Lydecker diary, 2. In the end, after the larger group left for the United States on 19 August, only four members stayed on to visit Friesland, Groningen, Arnhem, Utrecht, Middelburg. The account of their journey is found in J. Howard Suydam, "Narrative of the visit of the Holland Society of New-York to the Netherlands, Part II," *Year Book of the Holland Society of New-York* (1888–1889), 125–171.

23 Sheldon T. Viele, "The Narrative of the Visit of the Holland Society to the Netherlands, Part 1," *Year Book of the Holland Society of New-York* (1888–1889), 7.

24 Viele, *Year Book*, 15.

25 Sheldon Thompson Viele, *A Glimpse of Holland in 1888; A Journal-Narrative of the visit of the Holland Society to the Netherlands* (New York: De Vinne Press, 1890).

26 Of those, 100 survive at the Holland Society in a wooden box labeled "Glass plate negatives of a trip to Holland before 1900 (1888)." A complete list of captions for all 131 slides was printed, a copy of which was placed in the Viele photo album. A complete album with photos made from all the Van Duyn slides exists in the Lydecker Archives.

27 Roosevelt reported to Secretary of State Thomas F. Bayard about "the remarkable evidences of good-will which have lately been evoked by a visit of members of the Holland Society of New York to the Netherlands. This Society is composed of descendants in the direct male line of Hollanders who were residents of America early in the seventeenth century having emigrated from Holland as settlers of the New World.

Desiring to visit the land of their ancestors they, to the number of almost forty members, chartered one of the steamships of the Netherlands line for a trip which was to be one of pleasure and sentiment solely. They were received in the same spirit and with unprecedented enthusiasm and were everywhere treated with the greatest attention, people turning out almost en masse to welcome them. I felt it my duty to be present on several of these occasions and was impressed by the pronounced friendliness of feeling which actuates all classes, high and low, rich and poor, in the Netherlands towards the people of our country." Robert Barnwell Roosevelt to Secretary of State Thomas F. Bayard, 24 August 1888, Record Group 59, Dispatches, Netherlands, Department of State Archives.

28 Municipal Archives Amsterdam, 395/3010: Archief van het Koninklijk Zoölogisch Genootschap Natura Artis Magistra, Dossier der ontvangst der leden van de "Holland Society" of New York, 1888–1889.

29 The account by Sheldon T. Viele in the Holland Society *Year Book* of 1888–1889 is the main source for an account of the journey. In addition, there are three other known first-hand accounts of the trip: the Charles Edward Lydecker diary (transcript at the Holland Society; original in the Lydecker Archives) and published accounts by Judah B. Voorhees, *New Amsterdam Gazette*, vol. 5, no. 10 (17 December 1888 to 18 January 1889), 4–5 and Warner van Norden, "How we Dutch took Holland in August, 1888," *New Amsterdam Gazette* vol. 6, no. 9 (2 June till 15 July 1890), 7. The *New Amsterdam Gazette* reported extensively on the trip: *New Amsterdam Gazette*, vol. 5, no. 6 (2 July to 31 July 1888), 1; vol. 5, no. 7 (1 August to 8 September 1888), 12–14;

New Amsterdam Gazette, vol. 5, no. 6 (2 July to 31 July 1888), 1; vol. 5, no. 8 (17 September–31 October 1888), 2–10. The *New York Herald* published reports of the journey on 29 July 1888, 7; 10 August 1888, 5; 21 August 1888, 4. The *New York Times* reported on the trip on 29 July, 1888. A folder of press clippings from Dutch newspapers such as the *Algemeen Handelsblad, Nieuws van de Dag*, and *De Amsterdammer* is in the Amsterdam Municipal Archives, 395/3010: Archief van het Koninklijk Zoölogisch Genootschap Natura Artis Magistra, Dossier der ontvangst der leden van de "Holland Society" of New York, 1888–1889 and in the Persverzameling. The trip is described in Voorhees, 32–38; in George Harinck, "Homeward bound: New Yorker's quest for Amsterdam at the end of the nineteenth century," in George Harinck and Hans Krabbendam, *Amsterdam-New York: Transatlantic Relations and Urban Identities Since 1653* (Amsterdam: VU Uitgeverij, 2005), 154; and briefly in Annette Stott, *Holland Mania: The Unknown Dutch Period in American Art and Culture* (Woodstock: Overlook Press, 1998), 138.

30 Charles Edward Lydecker diary, 6.

31 In a cartoon entitled "Van éenen stam," the personification of Holland cordially greets the personification of the United States with a caption quoted from Da Costa "Ziet tot het moederland de zonen wederkeeren." In the same issue, the visit of the Holland Society is noted and the Netherlands is identified as the origin their "mighty republic." Flanor, "Vlugmaren," *De Nederlandsche Spectator*, no. 32 (11 August 1888), 267.

32 *De Amsterdammer,* 12 August 1888.

33 "An American's Awkward Toast," *New York Herald*, 2 September 1888, 7.

34 Viele, *Year Book*, 53, 73.

35 Viele, *Year Book*, 12.

36 Viele, *Year Book*, 59. Charles Edward Lydecker diary, 7. Lydecker also tried to find a namesake in Amsterdam and writes that "A genealogist has sent word that he has a most charming history of the Lydeckers and wants an order." Charles Edward Lydecker diary, 8.

37 Viele, *Year Book*, 13.

38 "Dutch raiders: descendants of the Patroons in the land of their ancestors," *New York Herald* (21 August 1888), 4.

39 *New Amsterdam Gazette*, vol. 5, no. 8 (17 September to 31 October 1888), 8.

40 Viele, *Year Book*, 86. The reference is to Edmondo De Amicis, *Holland and Its People* (New York: G.P. Putnam's Sons, The Knickerbocker Press, 1887).

41 Viele, *Year Book*, 45.

42 Viele, *Year Book*, 44.

43 Viele, *Year Book*, 59.

44 Viele, *Year Book*, 18.

45 I have written elsewhere on the invention of a picturesque Old Amsterdam: "Postcards and the Invention of Old Amsterdam around 1900," in Jordana Mendelson and David Prochaska, eds., *Postcards: Ephemeral Histories of Modernity* (Penn State University Press, forthcoming, 2008).

46 "A Guide through Amsterdam offered to the members of the Holland Society of New-York on the occasion of their visit to this city" (August 1888), 13.

47 On American travel to the Netherlands at the end of the nineteenth century, see Stott, 120–151.

48 Program of the Fifth Annual Dinner of The Holland Society of New-York, 10 January, 1890, Koninklijk Oudheidkundig Genootschap, Historische Verzameling der Schutterij, Box 60. The program is illustrated with a reproduction of the painting by Frans Hals, "The Banquet of the Officers of the St. George Civic Guard, 1627," which is given the title "A Holland Dinner, A.D. 1627." In 1935, the Holland Society established its own Burgher Guard and published lists of those who joined it, e.g. R.H. Amerman, ed., *Who's Who in the Burgher Guard* (New York: Holland Society, 1939).

49 Letter from Robert B. Roosevelt to J.A. Jochems, 10 February 1890, Koninklijk Oudheidkundig Genootschap, Historische Verzameling der Schutterij, Box 60.

50 Receipt signed by George W. Van Siclen, 1 March 1890, Koninklijk Oudheidkundig Genootschap, Historische Verzameling der Schutterij, Box 60.

51 Translation of letter from J.A. Jochems to Robert B. Roosevelt, 7 June 1890 published in "Some valuable books presented to the Holland Society of New York," *New Amsterdam Gazette*, vol. 6, no. 10 (1 August to 12 September 1890), 7–8. Jochems writes that he has sent two of his own works: *Amsterdam's Oude Burgervendels* (Amsterdam: Van Looy, 1888) and *Gewapende Burgermacht Te Amsterdam* (Amsterdam: Stads-drukkerij, 1890).

52 For the biography of Jochems, see R. Joghems, "John Anthony Jochems, Kapitein Adjutant, Eén van de twee oprichters van de Historische Verzameling der Schutterij te Amsterdam," *Gens Nostra*, vol. 55, no. 8 (September 2000), pp. 448–462; A.J.J. Haas, "J.A. Jochems," *Maandblad Amstelodamum*, vol. 7 (1920), 14–15; obituaries in various newspapers, Municipal Archives Amsterdam, Perverzameling personalia "J.A. Jochems."

53 On the history of the *schutterij*, see C. te Lintum, *Onze Schutter-Vendels en Schutterijen van Vroeger en Later Tijd, 1550–1908* (The Hague: W.P. van Stockum & Zoon, 1909).

54 By the 1880s and 1890s the militia was frequently ridiculed in the press. For a contemporary, if biased, account of a

citizen's frustration with his service in the militia, see Jan Kalf, *Schutterlijke zeden* (Amsterdam: Scheltema & Holkema, 1900).

55 On Van Someren Brand, see "Mr. J.E. van Someren Brand," *Maandblad Amstelodamum*, vol. 22, no. 8 (October 1935), 101–104. E.W. Moes, "Levensbericht van Mr. J.E. van Someren Brand," *Levensberichten van de Maatschappij der Nederlandsche Letterkunde te Leiden*, 1905–1906, 1–21.

56 Moes, p. 12. J.E. Van Someren Brand, "De Sophia-Augusta Stichting," *Elsevier's Geïllustreerd Maandblad*, vol. 12 (1901), 251.

57 On the history of the collection, see Koen Kleijn, " 'Equipementstukken van vervallen model': De Historische Verzameling der Schutterij te Amsterdam," in *Voor Nederland Bewaard: de verzamelingen van het Koninklijk Oudheidkundig Genootschap in het Rijksmuseum, Leids Kunsthistorisch Jaarboek*, vol. 10 (1995), 391–410. I am grateful to Rob Joghems for allowing me to read his unpublished manuscript, "Het laatste Schuttersstuk ofwel de historie van de Historische Verzameling der Schutterij te Amsterdam."

58 N.C.F. Sas, "Dutch Nationality in the Shadow of the Golden Age: National Culture and the Nation's Past, 1780–1914," in Frans Grijzenhout and Henk van Veen, eds., *The Golden Age of Dutch Painting in Historical Perspective* (Cambridge: Cambridge University Press, 1999), 49–68.

59 On the cultural means used to define Dutch nationalism around 1900, see, for example, J.T.M. Bank, *Het roemrijk Vaderland: Cultureel nationalisme in Nederland in de negentiende eeuw* (The Hague: SDU Uitgeverij, 1990); H. te Velde, *Gemeenschapszin en plichtsbesef: Liberalisme en nationalisme in Nederland 1870–1918* (The Hague: SDU Uitgeverij, 1992), 121–162.

60 Dorr Viele, [diary of trip to the Netherlands, August–September 1898], Buffalo and Erie County Historical Society, Viele Family Papers, Box 4, Folder Dorr European trip journal.

61 Ad de Jong, *De diregenten van de herinnering; Musealisering en nationalisering van de volkscultuur in Nederland 1815–1940* (Nijmegen: Uitgeverij SUN, 2001), *passim*.

62 On the formation of the individual collector and of her relationship to historic sensation, see Susan A. Crane, *Collecting and Historical Consciousness in Early Nineteenth-Century Germany* (Ithaca: Cornell University Press, 2000).

63 On the Altas Amsterdam, see Bert Gerlagh and J.F. Heijbroek, "De Atlas Amsterdam," in *Voor Nederland Bewaard*, 199–220.

64 Municipal Archives Amsterdam 499/48: Archief van het Genootschap Amstelodamum, manuscript memorandum, May 1900.

65 For example, the Haringspakkertoren (1829), the Westermarkt Waag (1857), the Leidsche Poort (1862), Swyght Utrecht (1872), the Haarlemmerpoort Station (1879), Post Office (1892), the Exchange by Zocher (1902), the Old Headquarters of the Militia (1902), the Nieuew Zijds Kapel (1909), the Boomkerk (1911), the Beurspoortje (1912), the Commandantshuis (1912), the Parkschouwburg (1912), Zeemanshoop (1914), the Hof van Holland (1916).

66 J.A. Jochems, *Amsterdam van Vroeger*, mss., 74–75.

67 J.H. Rössing, *Het Verdwijnend "Oud-Amsterdam"* (Amsterdam: Bernard Houthakker, 1916).

68 Rössing, 5. "Het loopt met Amsterdam, gelijk men ziet, ten einde. Met oud-Amsterdam, dat heugenis draagt van vele eeuwen. Uitbreiding der stad, verandering en toeneming van verkeer, eischen van welstand en gezondheid, hebben het noodzakelijk gemaakt en

maken het nog steeds noodzadelijk, dat oude huizen vallen, geheele buurten verdwijnen met opoffering van veel schoons en karakteristieks."

69 Susan Stewart, *On Longing: Narratives of the Miniature, the Gigantic, the Souvenir, the Collection* (Baltimore: Johns Hopkins University Press, 1984), 139.

6

Turner

Space, persona, authority

Sam Smiles

Given the volume of critical theory of the last 50 years questioning the primacy of authorship, it is perhaps remarkable that the biography is still an important constituent of arts publishing. In its desire to locate the well-springs of creativity, artistic biography carries with it a number of assumptions that are redolent of its nineteenth-century hey-day.[1] Biography unites what may often be a heterogeneous life's work under the unitary sign of one individual, giving authorship a pre-eminent position and circumscribing a professional career with the outline of the life itself. The biographical narrative moves in a relatively narrow compass, from the artist to his/her social and professional circle, giving the 'outside world', at best, the function of a *mise-en-scène*, providing a loose context for creativity, or using it to explain any sudden violation of the organic world of artistic production, normally restricted to domestic and collegial spaces. Art works, on this model, are ultimately expressive of their maker, irrespective of their imbrication in a variety of social and ideological contexts; artists and their motives are prioritised over works and their effects. The implication is that knowledge of an artist's birth, upbringing and daily life, the familial and social spaces in which s/he works, makes an important, perhaps an essential contribution to any serious engagement with their artistic production. To that extent, biography can be distinguished from a critical study of an artist's achievement, where authorship is at least balanced by wider contextual understandings.

To talk about biography and J.M.W. Turner is immediately to confront a major problem of evidence or, rather, the seeming inadequacy of the evidence we have to constitute a fully rounded biography. No matter how diligent our researches, the explanatory force of biography seems much weaker in Turner's case than it does in many of his contemporaries. Our knowledge of the artist is skewed by archival gaps, notably the destruction of his correspondence with some of his closest friends, yet even granting the inevitably distorted picture resulting from that loss, the widely accepted image of Turner as 'mysterious', especially towards the close of his life, has some basis in fact. Many of the reminiscences garnered by Walter Thornbury to produce the first biography of the artist in 1862 tend towards the portrayal of a secretive individual, guarding his private life from even his closest acquaintances, withholding his private address, and constantly attempting to throw off those who would track him down. Turner's behaviour in this regard seems eccentric, even obsessional and it has struck most subsequent observers as problematic. An artist who in his closing years lived in deliberate obscurity under an assumed name seems to show every sign of resistance or opposition to biographical scrutiny.

Irrespective of Turner's own reticence, his achievement as a painter has occasioned such a volume of critical responses and individual studies that a critical biography, at the very least, would seem essential to those who like their artists whole. Turner's admirers have censured the inadequacies of Thornbury's approach and particularly regret his willingness to chronicle the more wayward traits of the artist's personality, which helped produce an image of the artist as a curmudgeonly loner. Over the last 70 years there have been four major attempts to amplify and refine Thornbury's account.[2] The cumulative effect of this work has been to fill in some of the biographical gaps, to dispel what for Thornbury was often an impenetrable fog and to secure a more certain understanding of the artist as an individual. Certainly these biographies have made a valuable contribution to any understanding of the artist's achievement, but we may be too ready to congratulate ourselves on having 'revealed' Turner, penetrating his defences to expose the man whose mature behaviour had attempted to frustrate such personal enquiries. For all our success in having uncovered more exactly Turner's behaviour with his parents and his patrons, his relationships with women, his illegitimate daughters, his friendships, enmities, financial affairs and the like, the question begged by all this information concerns its value. Much of what has been added to the stock of knowledge is what one would expect to find of any artist; there is little in these discoveries that was worth concealing. Moreover, we seem to be no closer to having available for Turner what has been revealed for others of his contemporaries. For example, although over 350 letters, or fragments of letters, by Turner are still extant, they do not provide the ample resource supplied by Constable's correspondence, which has allowed the interpretation of his work to make reference to his expressed motives and intentions.[3] Indeed, Constable's repeated recourse to autobiographical material, when talking about his art, makes a significant part of his output seem almost confessional when compared to Turner's seeming reticence.

Yet, from the viewpoint of a man born in the late eighteenth century Turner had little to hide; if he chose, especially in his maturity, to withhold his private life from public scrutiny that choice might be better understood as strategic. What I mean by this is that it may be worthwhile to examine Turner's seemingly obstructive behaviour as a deliberate check on any complacent notions of art as primarily the product of a gifted private individual. In the rest of this essay I will argue that Turner's reluctance to allow his domestic circumstances to become part of the stock of knowledge about him was occasioned by a view of the art world and the artist that closes down the space normally occupied by biography. The artist's biography works on the premise that such a life is intrinsically interesting, and that knowledge of it allows us to penetrate a little further towards the centre of the creative matrix, to the point of origin of works of art. Turner's modus operandi, on the other hand, and especially his use of differentiated spaces, articulated a view of art that emphasised instead its public position and its social meaning.

From the mid-1790s until his death in 1851 Turner was accepted as a force in the art world of his day. His technical innovations and imaginative reach, so unlike most of his contemporaries, ensured that his exhibited work elicited a critical response, whether in praise or censure. Yet while the works occupied the centre of the British art world, the painter who produced them discouraged intrusions into his domestic life, promoting his professional persona instead. His reluctance to be portrayed underlines his resistance to scrutiny. Although a number of portrait likenesses of the artist were taken in the 1790s, Turner's early self-portrait of about 1799 is the last reliable picture we have of him, until some hasty and surreptitious sketches of him were made in his maturity.[4] His enjoyment of anonymity, when away from his professional world, is caught by an anecdote relating to the 1840s. From late 1847 to 1849 Turner was a frequent visitor to the London studio of the photographer J.J.E. Mayall who took at least four daguerreotype portraits of him (now lost). Mayall's testimony reveals that Turner was fascinated by the whole photographic process, trying out different effects of light for himself, and discussing light, chemistry and the spectrum with the photographer. In all of this, however, Turner let Mayall believe that he was a Master in Chancery and his identity was only revealed at a Royal Society soirée which both attended. When a mutual acquaintance informed Mayall that his 'Mr Turner' was '*the* Turner', Mayall immediately offered to conduct experiments on light and shade for the benefit of Turner's art and parted on the understanding that the artist would call on him. Turner never visited Mayall's studio again.[5]

For a painter otherwise so insistent on guarding his reputation, capable of producing paintings that seem to have been deliberately intended to trump his rivals, alive or dead, this reluctance to be known by his appearance sets up a curious disjunction between the works and their author. We might consider it as a spatial separation, insofar as biography can be understood as a form of topography. As already indicated, in their ability to map a career, to outline the boundaries of a creative life, the spaces of biography are predicated on understandings of authorship and the location of the work of art as the product of a particular individual. The spaces thus configured are orientated to the logic of a matrix in which the self and subjectivity determine its co-ordinates. But these areas of biographical concern compete with other spatial possibilities, spaces in which the artist and the work of art perform their roles dialogically with their spectators. Instead of biographical space, predicated on the creative individual, we may turn to the public spaces in which reputations are negotiated and where assumptions concerning creative practice are debated. For it is here that an artist's project meets public perception and where the idea of the artist is constituted. Turner's resistance to personal scrutiny may therefore represent not diffidence or cussedness but a tactical separation of his domestic life from these other public spaces.

At the risk of inevitable over-reduction, the public spaces available to artists might be described as of three generic kinds and all of them, to varying extents, provide contexts in which the artist's identity is enacted or realised in a performative sense. First there are physical spaces, comprising public exhibition rooms (primarily the Royal Academy and the British Institution, in Turner's case), but also the town and country residences of patrons and collectors (sometimes opened to the public) and the artist's own gallery and painting rooms (opened with varying degrees of access to artists, patrons and members of the public). From early in his career Turner took steps to manipulate the exhibition spaces available to him, the better to control the circumstances attending the display of his work. At the Royal Academy, he adjusted paintings in terms of the opportunities afforded by Varnishing Days from as early as 1798, and could on occasion upstage his rivals by doing so, as Constable and Clarkson Stanfield found to their cost.[6] In 1804 he had a picture gallery constructed to his own design at his central London address and replaced it with another in 1816, to show his work in optimal conditions. All of this activity could be seen as impressing Turner's professional personality on the spaces his pictures were to inhabit.

Next are discursive spaces, such as art criticism, biography and art historical accounts, all of which might be said to establish a position for the critical estimation of the artist, irrespective of the consumer's ability to visit the physical spaces of exhibition or display. Although Turner claimed to Ruskin that he never responded to art criticism, he clearly took an active interest in it, as suggested by remarks in his letters and elsewhere, and it is conceivable that he was privy to the writing of the two anonymous *Catalogue Raisonnés*, published in 1815 and 1816, which attacked the British Institution and defended Turner from critical attack.[7] The remarks on the history of art, especially landscape painting, in the Perspective Lectures Turner gave at the Royal Academy from 1811 suggest a very clear understanding of the quality and value of the artists he discusses.

Finally, there are creative spaces existing within both physical and discursive spaces where the artist's professional behaviour and his/her fictive representations can suggest an ideal spatial situation for artistic activity. Professional behaviour was brought to a pitch of intensity in Turner's activities on Varnishing Days at the Royal Academy and the British Institution. Varnishing Days were introduced in the late 1790s to allow artists to adjust their paintings in respect of their position in the room and the pictures adjacent to them, acknowledging, in effect, that they were not isolated statements but part of a bigger colloquy. From the 1830s Turner used this opportunity to hypostasise the act of painting, offering audacious demonstrations to his fellow artists of how finished pictures could be elaborated from little more than lay-ins in a matter of hours. He was also ready to help improve his colleagues' work, when requested, resolving technical problems with a much admired economy of means. Turner's virtuoso performance of his artistic identity on these occasions was very much orientated to his creative prowess and it can be compared with his fictive representations of artists and the painter's world, which will be discussed below.

These public spaces are particularly significant insofar as they can be understood as operating within a relatively new historical context, responsive to the recent florescence of professional and bourgeois interests in British society. Jürgen Habermas has theoretised the development of new forms of social space in the eighteenth and nineteenth centuries as a constituent of this development. For Habermas, the salon in France, and its equivalents in England and Germany, are instances of a newly emerging bourgeois sphere midway between the private space of the home and the public sphere of politics. In these spaces, Habermas argues, the free play of creative thought becomes possible: social status is replaced by professional ability and opinion becomes emancipated from patronage. Fundamentally the salon is a place where ideas can be freely exchanged and legitimised within a critical, yet supportive context.[8] We can extend Habermas' analysis to the developing world of professional arts practice in London. The Royal Academy, although ostensibly benefiting from the patronage of the Crown, presided over its own affairs and sought the promotion of the visual arts through its training and exhibition policies. It offered, in short, a social space in which the individual artist could make common cause with fellow professionals to advance a view of the arts that insisted on their public relevance. As Turner declared to the students of the Royal Academy: '... never mind what anybody else calls you. When you become members of this institution you must fight in a phalanx – no splits – no quarrelling – one mind – one object – the good of the Arts and the Royal Academy.'[9] Thus, against the stereotype of the Romantic artist as an isolated genius, whose art is fundamentally an expression of individual thoughts and feelings, we can posit the idea of the artist as effectively engaged in conversation with contemporaries and with tradition in the public space of the exhibition and the professional arts organisation of the Academy.

If we accept the idea of Turner's commitment to the public sphere then his opposition to personal enquiry has less to do with personal squeamishness and much more to do with his understanding of the role of the artist in society. As so often with Turner, this emphasis on art's utility as a public discourse, as opposed to a private expression, is an eighteenth-century inheritance. For all his embracing the new material and political culture of the nineteenth century, his intellectual habits seem closer to Sir Joshua Reynolds, still President of the Royal Academy when Turner was admitted as a student to the Royal Academy Schools, than to many of his contemporaries. He maintained a respect for history painting throughout his career, produced numerous historical and mythological subjects and, even in works seemingly orientated to topography, would include details which, when attended to, suggested social, political or historical readings of the image. Characteristically, then, much of his art is turned outwards and invites its consumers to respond to its seriousness: its ability to comment on contemporary events, to meditate on history, to anatomise the social and technological world of the nineteenth century.

If this sounds like an educator's programme we should recall that Turner actively contributed to teaching in the Royal Academy. He acted as Visitor in the Life Academy eight times between 1812 and 1838, and was considered to be highly effective in that role. He was elected Professor of Perspective in 1807 and began delivering his lectures on that subject from 1811. Although a failure as a public speaker, Turner nevertheless took inordinate pains to improve his presentation, especially in the production of visual exemplifications of his topic. To these didactic activities we should add the production of his *Liber Studiorum*, a part-work produced between 1807 and 1819, which offered its subscribers a visual demonstration of the modes of landscape painting employed in Turner's art. Turner's willingness to use his art as an educational device is telling, for it can be seen as recapitulating the educational role of the Royal Academy, as seen especially in its various lecture series and inaugurated so successfully with Reynolds' *Discourses*. And if Turner can also be regarded as using his art to communicate ideas, so, too, the social spaces available to him become places of education, and his pictures are complicated by their participation in that role. Rather than appearing as unique utterances of the individual artist, they can be understood as contributions to a dialogue with his fellow artists, with the great masters of the past, with history and with society: they become exchanges in a relay, nodes within a network.

But are we forced to conclude from this that Turner selflessly allowed his own artistic personality to become dissipated in this network? At one level, the answer is obvious. The singularity of Turner's achievement is marked: it is difficult to confuse his work with any other artist's. Moreover, there is evidence in his attitude to the old masters and to his contemporaries that he was competitive enough to deliberately suggest comparisons between his work and theirs, comparisons that would not only position his achievement within art history but might also suggest that he surpassed any rival. Here, surely, the link between work and author is tangible. Turner's overall vision is coherent in its development from pedestrian apprenticeship to accomplished complexity; his artistic 'personality' is easily legible insofar as his mature work is so emphatically distinctive. Yet it is also clear that it is from the work and the work alone that the author is to be inferred. Turner's 'biography', in other words, is inscribed in his activities as an artist and, rather than requiring knowledge of his personal circumstances to comprehend his achievement, his professional practice finds its validation in its position vis-à-vis artistic tradition and contemporary society. These are the spaces in which the artist is to be found and it is there that his biography is constructed.

Turner's treatment of the old masters provides a clue about his understanding of the social role of the artist. Between 1820 and 1841, he painted six pictures of his predecessors in the history of art and through these imaginary 'portraits' he indicated something about the appropriate spaces for the artist to inhabit. Only one of them, *Rembrandt's Daughter* (1827) (Figure 6.1), attempts to show something of the domestic space of the artist, participating in the fashionable genre of depicting incidents from artists'

Figure 6.1 J.M.W. Turner, *Rembrandt's Daughter*, 1827, oil on canvas, 121.92 × 89.54 cm, Harvard University Art Museums, Fogg Art Museum. Gift of Edward W. Forbes, 1917.214.

lives. Rembrandt's pose owes much to his self-portraits; he is dressed for the studio and holds the implements of his profession, a palette and brushes. The fact that Rembrandt brings his painting equipment into an otherwise intimate setting positions him ambiguously between the spaces of the household and the painting room, the domestic and the professional spheres. All the attention, however, is on his young daughter in the foreground, bathed in light next to an ornate bed and reading a letter, which, in the tradition of Dutch genre, we may presume to have come from a suitor. The title, to that extent, is somewhat beside the point and the artist's achievements, like his shadowy presence, are secondary to his daughter's. It has been speculated that Turner ventured an autobiographical comment here, insofar as his own daughters were illegitimate, but although Rembrandt's daughter Cornelia was indeed born to Hendrickje Stoffels in 1654, this fact was not discovered until the 1860s. For unknown reasons, Turner simply invented a daughter for Rembrandt.[10] If an autobiographical meaning were intended, knowing Turner's penchant for referring to his pictures as his children, we might speculate that he was playing on the tension between two different sorts of progeny: the biological and the artistic.

Although Turner painted a genre scene of *An Artist's Colourman's Workshop* (*c*.1807), his decision not to exhibit it suggests that his interest in depicting the activities of painting was chiefly motivated by the dignity of his profession, selecting the luminaries of art and presenting them in public situations, as opposed to recording the paraphernalia of the work-room. Indeed, there is only one occasion when an artist in his studio is depicted. This is the sketch *The Artist's Studio* (*c*.1808) (Figure 6.2), which uses the squalid surroundings of an indigent artist's home to send up his pretensions to genius.[11] Painted at roughly the same time as the oil painting *The Garreteer's Petition* (exhibited in the Royal Academy in 1809), which lampooned the underside of the literary life, such images can only de described as squibs in the Rowlandson mode. *The Artist's Studio* was not worked up into a finished picture and may best be considered as a private memorandum produced at the same time that Turner was preparing his Perspective lecture series for the Royal Academy in which he made frequent remarks on the need for sound training and the limitations of genius as the basis for a successful career.[12] The artist's failure in this satirical sketch is summed up precisely by the fact that his domestic circumstances constitute his creative world. Deluded by the idea that genius is all that is required to make effective art, and thus incapable of making a public contribution through his practice, he is trapped within the narrow confines of his lodgings.

We might compare the domestic location of failure in *The Artist's Studio* with Turner's other images of artists at work. As we have seen, his 1827 painting of *Rembrandt's Daughter* was one of six homages to his predecessors.[13] The remaining five are concerned with the public reputations of art and artists. The first of these was exhibited in 1820 to coincide with the 300th anniversary of the death of Raphael: *Rome from the Vatican.*

Figure 6.2 J.M.W. Turner, *The Artist's Studio, c.*1808, pen, ink and watercolour on
     paper, 185 × 302 mm.

*Raffaelle, accompanied by La Fornarina, preparing his pictures for the deco-
ration of the loggia.* The artist is presented reviewing his creations (and
others, like the landscape, he was believed to have painted) in a deliberately
anachronistic setting, with Bernini's colonnade perhaps completing what
Raphael's own architectural plans had initiated. Raphael presides over a
public space, whose perspectival representation encourages the spectator to
enter it. It is not Raphael's life but his creations that we are invited to
explore, in architecture, wall painting and easel pictures. La Fornarina, who
might otherwise be a genre-like reminder of domestic affairs, is positioned
next to the *Madonna della Sedia*, as though asserting Raphael's ability to
transform a matter of personal erotic intimacy into a powerful religious
image for public consumption.

Watteau study by Fresnoy's Rules (Figure 6.3), exhibited in 1831, extends
this idea of the public artist but now in an educative role. Watteau is surrounded by attentive onlookers in an interior containing two of his more
famous works, *Les Plaisirs du Bal* and *La Lorgneuse*, both of which were in
London collections at the time. Turner's picture is designed to demonstrate
Fresnoy's analysis of how white pigment, depending on its adjacent colour,
can make forms seem to advance or recede. Watteau himself seems, equally,
to be painting as a demonstration to those attending him and doing so in a
public space. In effect it offers an ideal image of the artist and his
responsibilities, using his art to share his insights with a broader public. But
compared to Turner's own routine this picture is a fantasy, for Turner's

Figure 6.3 J.M.W. Turner, *Watteau study by Fresnoy's Rules*, exhibited 1831, oil on oak panel, 400 × 692 mm.

habitual procedure was to work in private; with the exception of Varnishing Days he very rarely allowed others to witness him at work. The same contrast between an idealised presentation of the artist and Turner's own practice is caught in his record of painters at work at Petworth, which also positions the activity of painting as a public or semi-public performance. Three of his Petworth sketches, made in 1827, show artists using the Old Library as a studio open to public scrutiny.[14] Turner, in contrast, painted with the door to his temporary studio locked and allowed no one but Lord Egremont himself to enter.[15]

The anomalies in Turner's next homage, *Bridge of Sighs, Ducal Palace and Custom House, Venice; Canaletti painting* of 1833, perhaps bear on these concerns. Canaletto is visible in the bottom left of the picture, painting on a wooden platform above the water and hemmed in by barges on one of which a couple of figures observe his work. The easel on which his picture is placed faces the wall and, in any case, the barges occlude the view across the canal to the sunlit facades beyond. The fact that the canvas on which he is painting is framed suggests that Canaletto, rather than attempting to paint the view he cannot properly see, is touching an already completed picture to help it harmonise with its surroundings. But if Canaletto is adjusting the tonality of his painting, then his spectators are not witnessing the creative act, nor sharing the intimacy of a painter's work-place, but are merely observing the picture's necessary accommodation to the circumstances of its public exhibition.

Van Goyen looking out for a subject (1833), again, takes the artist out of his studio to position him in a sailing craft on the busy waters of the Scheldt, with Antwerp in the distance. The diminutive figure of the artist, helpfully identified by the 'Van G' painted on the boat's stern is, like Canaletto, placed amidst the subject of his art, sharing the same element as the boats and their crews. It is an image of the artist as an active agent, finding his subject in the phenomenal world. The picture was painted at the same time as Turner produced three paintings of van Goyen's contemporary, the great Dutch admiral Marteen Harpertzoon Tromp: *Admiral Van Tromp's Barge at the Entrance of the Texel, 1645* (1831), *Van Tromp's Shallop, at the Entrance of the Scheldt* (1832) and *Van Tromp returning after the Battle of Dogger Bank* (1833). Van Goyen's placement on the same waters and amidst similar craft seems to assert that the artist's contribution to the life of the nation is as important as any other's.

The final homage Turner painted was a picture exhibited at the Royal Academy in 1841: *Depositing of John Bellini's three pictures in la Chiesa Redentore, Venice*. Turner shows a procession of gondolas approaching the church; in the leading boat are three paintings of the Madonna from the Redentore's sacristy, which were believed to be by Giovanni Bellini at the time.[16] Here the figure of the artist is absent, but his work stands in for him. Turner was 66 in 1841 and had been drawing up his will in a bid to secure the best possible use of his estate. The honour afforded Bellini in this picture might be read as a reflection on the contrast between the Italian Renaissance and modern Britain. In the 1830s the artistic legacies of two former Presidents of the Royal Academy, Benjamin West and Thomas Lawrence, had failed in their purpose: to invigorate the study of art by leaving a substantial collection of works for public edification. Unlike the honour paid to Bellini, the modern artist's situation offered no guarantees that his achievement would be maintained for public inspection. Turner's own will was intended to ensure that 'Turner's Gallery' was established on a proper financial basis to protect it from the perils of inadequate public patronage, to ensure that his work, too, would be properly deposited in a space that kept it on permanent public display.

While Turner may have been emulous of others' achievements and mindful of his own reputation (as, for example, his bequeathing two works to hang alongside two Claudes in the National Gallery), what we can infer from these five pictures is the idea of the artist as a professional working in the public realm, perhaps even for the public good. These paintings do not dwell on the personal circumstances of artists but on their professional achievements and, more particularly, the locations of those activities in public view. We need to remind ourselves how curious these homages actually are. Turner's own working practices, with the signal exception of his activity on Varnishing Days, privileged solitary work in the studio as the place where the creative act took place, distilling and refining the raw material of observation. Yet none of his treatments of his predecessors attempt the depiction of these creative spaces; he is much more concerned to show them outside the studio in the realm where their art would have its impact. For it is at this point, where a picture's public reception supersedes the physical labour of painting, that an image ceases to be the artist's creature and becomes the property of its viewers. And because it is also the place where the artist engages with his public in his professional persona, we might also say that it is the place where the business of being an artist is validated.

If homages such as these suggest something of Turner's understanding of the social position of some of his predecessors, what hints did he provide about his own role and status? Even granted the loss of so much intimate correspondence, which may well have provided a counter-weight to the emphasis on the practising artist seen in Turner's spoken or written remarks, there is evidence that Turner adopted a creative strategy that stressed above all his professional identity, perhaps even constructing the idea of the public figure or persona 'Turner' as a vehicle for his artistic production.[17]

It is noteworthy in this respect that Turner is unique among British artists in his posthumous presentation by surname and initials alone. The use of all three initials in his signature has the effect of blocking the route to biographical intimacy offered by a first name and although at the outset of his career, from the late 1780s to the early 1800s, 'W. Turner' is the characteristic choice of signature, 'J.M.W. Turner' begins to appear in the mid-1790s, with 'RA' (Royal Academician) and, on a couple of occasions, 'PP' (Professor of Perspective) added as these distinctions came his way. At first sight the inclusion of academic honours seems to be no more than canny marketing, but it is debatable whether any potential patron needed reminding of Turner's professional affiliation or achievements. These inscriptions serve more to assert Turner's adherence to a particular institution, his belief in its traditions and values, than anything else.

One category of self-inscription, however, is more obviously autobiographical than these and asserts Turner's presence as insistently as any signature. The repeated use of a child's hoop in the foreground of many of his paintings may function as some sort of rebus (from its turning motion), as may the water bird taking off (mallard for Mallord, his middle name), which occurs in a few images and as a signature in a letter to Augustus Wall Callcott.[18] While these devices would not have been easily decoded by many spectators, at the outset of his career Turner was also capable of entirely unambiguous self-referencing. On two occasions he inscribed his identity in a pictorial field of obvious national significance: in a 1796 watercolour of Westminster Abbey, *St Erasmus in Bishop Islip's Chapel*, he included on a tomb-slab in the foreground the lettering, 'William Turner Natus 1775;' the following year the same device was employed to add 'Turner. Sarum' to a watercolour of the *Choir of Salisbury Cathedral*. These inscriptions not only mark a moment in time, the artist's coming of age in 1796 as well as the first year in which he exhibited an oil painting at the Royal Academy, but also an attachment to place, as though Turner were melding his identity with the historical legacy vested in these national monuments.

With these rebuses and inscriptions we have moved beyond signature, with its demonstration of authorship, to something much closer to identification, asserting not merely Turner's origination of the painting, but somehow also his inhabitancy of the image. The artist, on this reckoning, does not merely produce a topographical record; he takes possession of the visual field. In placing surrogates for himself within the image, Turner declares that the scene in view is subject to his authority. If such a manoeuvre is suggestive of vanity, we should remind ourselves of the lowly status of landscape art in Britain when Turner's generation began work, with many connoisseurs agreeing that it lacked the capacity to elicit the intellectual responses associated with history painting. For Turner's contemporaries, what distinguished creative art from servile imitation was precisely the artist's ability to transform the mundane. Most topographical paintings, the vehicle for Turner's early reputation, were therefore subject to attack for their unassuming representation and were denied serious consideration as works of art. Given this context, we may consider Turner's self-inscriptions as reminders to the viewer that the picture they consume is unarguably a work of art, not a tame and unthinking copy of reality. More than any signature, the authorial devices contained within the image suggest the mediating presence of the artist.

In this connection, it is interesting to observe how Turner inserts a painter's portable sketching equipment in the foreground of a watercolour produced some time between 1820 and 1825 of the Thames from Richmond Hill (Figure 6.4). The watercolour shows the same view as an oil exhibited in 1819, *England: Richmond Hill on the Prince Regent's Birthday*. Given that the Prince Regent's birthday was often celebrated on St George's Day, 23 April, it is tempting to see the watercolour as a representation of the same date, especially as Turner claimed that he, too, was born on 23 April, which is also Shakespeare's birthday as well as the national saint's day.[19] (No records have ever been found to corroborate Turner's assertion.) The vantage point was equally resonant. James Thomson, one of Turner's favourite authors, had described the view from Richmond Hill as a microcosm of Britain:

> Heavens! What a goodly prospect spreads around,
> Of hills, and dales, and woods, and lawns, and spires,
> And glittering towns, and gilded streams, till all
> The stretching landscape into smoke decays!
> Happy Britannia! Where the Queen of Arts,
> Inspiring vigour, Liberty, abroad
> Walks unconfined even to thy farthest cots,
> And scatters plenty with unsparing hand.[20]

In this image, then, with the painter's equipment standing in for the absent artist, it is possible that Turner is allying his biography with the central

Figure 6.4 J.M.W. Turner, *Richmond Hill*, *c.*1820–25, watercolour and bodycolour on paper, 297 × 489 mm.

definitions of the nation's identity. We should note, however, that if this equipment stands for Turner, his presence in this place is achieved not insistently and unambiguously, as it had been in the 1790s with inscribed texts, but is manifested through the trappings of the generic artist. Turner's identity in this image, for all its assertions of authority, is not simply that of his biographical self; through its lack of specificity it incorporates an eponym in whose presentation is crystallised the profession of the artist in England.

How then can Turner's biography be spatially situated? I have argued that he effectively elaborated the idea of the professional sphere as the only significant location for his identity, letting his art perform in public on his behalf and himself undertaking an educator's role, through his paintings, his lecturing, his demonstrative activities on Varnishing Days and in the terms of his bequest. I have also suggested that Turner was prepared to elaborate a professional persona, capable of inscription within the national identity of the country, both in time and place. It is important to emphasise that all of these spaces necessarily invoke a sense of the public as a complement to artistic activity, that ultimately every one of them positions art practice within a social nexus. The identity, even the personality of the artist, is produced within these spaces in dialogue with the spectator. As opposed to somehow lying behind the activities of painting and exhibition, the artist might be better understood as coming into definition in the public and semi-public spaces available to him or her.

When 60 of Turner's watercolours were exhibited in 1819 in Grosvenor Place, at the London residence of his patron Walter Fawkes, a contemporary witness caught something of how Turner could, in effect, exhibit himself as pure professional artist.

Turner generally came alone, and while he leaned on the centre table in the great room, or slowly worked his rough way through the mass, he attracted every eye in the brilliant crowd, and seemed to me like a victorious Roman General, the principal figure in his own triumph.[21]

Turner's triumph, among other things, was to have preserved the idea of the public responsibility of the professional artist into the new century. Outside those public spaces there was no worthwhile biography to be had.

Notes

1 See Julie F. Codell, *The Victorian Artist: Artists' Lifewritings in Britain, ca. 1870–1910*, Cambridge: Cambridge University Press, 2003.

2 See, in particular, Walter Thornbury, *The Life of J.M.W. Turner* [1862] second edition, London: Chatto and Windus, 1877; A.J. Finberg, *The Life of J.M.W. Turner, R.A.*, [1939] second edition, Oxford: Clarendon Press, 1961; Jack Lindsay, *J.M.W. Turner His Life & Work: A Critical Biography*, London: Cory, Adams & Mackay, 1966; Anthony Bailey, *Standing in the Sun: A Life of J.M.W. Turner*, London: Sinclair-Stevenson, 1997; James Hamilton, *Turner: A Life*, London: Sceptre, 1997.

3 See John Gage (ed.), *Collected Correspondence of JMW Turner*, Oxford: Oxford University Press, 1980 and 'Further correspondence of J.M.W. Turner', *Turner Studies*, vol. 6, no. 1 (Summer 1986), pp. 2–9. For Constable see R.B. Beckett (ed.), *John Constable's Correspondence* (six volumes), Ipswich: Suffolk Records Society, 1962–8, and Leslie Parris and Conal Shields (eds), *John Constable: Further Documents and Correspondence*, Ipswich: Suffolk Records Society, 1975.

4 See Richard Walker, 'The portraits of J.M.W. Turner: a check-list', *Turner Studies*, vol. 3, no. 1 (Summer 1983), pp. 21–32.

5 Walter Thornbury, *The Life and Correspondence of J.M.W. Turner* (second revised edition), London: Chatto and Windus, 1877, pp. 349–352.

6 Constable and Turner clashed over Constable's rehanging of the Royal Academy exhibition in 1831 to his advantage and at Turner's expense and again in the following year when Turner used the Varnishing Days to alter his *Helvoetsluys* to the detriment of Constable's *Opening of Waterloo Bridge*. In 1833 Turner apparently painted *Bridge of Sighs, Ducal Palace and Custom House, Venice: Canaletti painting* as a riposte to Clarkson Stanfield, who had recently received a commission from Lord Lansdowne for a series of Venetian scenes.

7 Some have proposed that Turner's patron, the radical Whig Walter Fawkes, wrote the *Catalogue Raisonnés*. But Shee, Smirke, Reinagle and Landseer have also been suggested, as well as James Perry of the *Morning Chronicle*.

8 See especially Jürgen Habermas (translated by Thomas Burger with the assistance of Frederick Lawrence), *The Structural Transformation of the Public Sphere: An Inquiry into a Category of Bourgeois Society*, Cambridge: Polity, 1989.

9 Recalled in W.P. Frith, *My Autobiography; and reminiscences*, London: Richard Bentley, 1888, pp. 98–99.

10 For the link between Turner's and

Rembrandt's illegitimate children, suggested by Evan Maurer, see Martin Butlin and Evelyn Joll, *The Paintings of J.M.W. Turner*, New Haven and London: Yale University Press (revised edition), 1984, p. 147. Michael Kitson has suggested that Turner may have known of a portrait in the Dresden Picture Gallery, now presumed to be of Saskia, which was listed as *Rembrandt's Daughter* in an illustrated catalogue of 1753, this ascription being repeated in two unillustrated French catalogues of the collection, published in 1782 and 1817. It seems more likely, however, that Turner simply made the incident up. See Michael Kitson, 'Turner and Rembrandt', *Turner Studies*, vol. 8, no. 1 (Summer 1988), p. 12.

11 TB CXXI-B. On the verso of this sheet are verses satirising the painter's pretensions: 'Pleas[d] with his Work he views it o'er and o'er/And finds fresh beauties never seen before/The Tyro mind another feast controuls/The Master loves his art, the Tyro butter'd rolls.' See Andrew Wilton, *Painting and Poetry: Turner's 'Verse Book' and his Work of 1804–1812*, London: Tate Gallery Publications, 1990, pp. 40–41.

12 See, for example, British Library Add. MS. 46151 K ff. 4–4r and Add. MS. 46151 AA f. 26v.

13 In addition there are paintings whose styles emulated his predecessors, including Claude, Rembrandt, Titian, Van de Velde and Cuyp, as well as the allusively titled paintings *Port Ruysdael* (1827) and *Fishing-Boats bringing a Disabled Ship into Port Ruysdael* (1844).

14 TB CCXLIV 20,103 and 102 show respectively: (probably) Sir William Beechey, seated before his portrait of *Mrs. Hester as Flora*, an unidentified artist painting a large upright canvas with another figure beside him and an unidentified artist painting an upright canvas with three women looking on.

The last of these is often known as 'An Artist and his Admirers', with the supposition that it is autobiographical, but this contradicts what is known of Turner's behaviour at Petworth.

15 Turner's artistic presence at Petworth was manifested not by painting in public but by having his finished works on public display; 14 oil paintings purchased 1802–12, four landscapes painted for the Carved Room *c*.1828–30 and two further paintings added to the collection in 1827 and 1830. Egremont's purchase of *Tabley, Cheshire* (1808) from Sir John Leicester's collection in 1827, insofar as it did not involve the artist, needs to be distinguished from the remaining 19 paintings which were all direct purchases or commissions.

16 Now attributed to Andrea da Murano, Francesco Bissolo and Alvise Vivarini.

17 Thornbury's biography relied on the reminiscences of many witnesses, including those who had been Turner's friend, colleague or patron. From these recollections it is clear that Turner was known to most of his contemporaries chiefly in his professional persona.

18 The bird accompanies a signature of 'Willm Turner'. See John Gage (ed.), *Collected Correspondence of JMW Turner*, Oxford: Oxford University Press, 1980, no. 329, p. 231. The letter is undated.

19 The 1832 codicil to Turner's will assigned his residuary estate to the Royal Academy and stipulated, among other things, that his birthday be commemorated with an annual dinner on 23 April, 'my birthday'.

20 'Summer' (first published 1727) from *The Seasons* (revised 1746), lines 1438–1445.

21 William Carey, *Some Memoirs of the Patronage and Progress of the Fine Arts in England and Ireland*, London: Saunders and Ottley, 1826, p. 147.

7

Mapping the 'bios' in two graphic systems with gender in mind

Reading Van Gogh through Charlotte Salomon and vice versa

Griselda Pollock

Writing in Paris in 1932 in his *Berlin Chronicle*, Walter Benjamin proposed that:

> Reminiscences, even extensive ones, do not always amount to an auto-biography ... For autobiography has to do with time, with sequence and what makes up the continuous flow of life. *Here, I am talking of space, of moments and of discontinuities.*
>
> (my emphasis)[1]

For Benjamin, the city of his childhood, Berlin, contained in its varied places and spaces a snapshot history of his becoming that included his childhood walks, his education, youth movements and political affiliations, sexual initiation, love affairs and funerals. He imagined these memories not as narratives but as points on a map.

> I have long, indeed for years, played with the idea of setting out the sphere of life – bios – graphically on a map. First I envisaged an ordinary map, but now I would incline to a general staff's map of a city centre, if such a thing existed. Doubtless it does not, because of ignorance of the theatre of future wars. I have evolved a system of signs, and on the grey background of such maps they would make a colourful show if I clearly marked in the houses of my friends and girlfriends, the assembly halls of various collectives, from the 'debating chambers' of the Youth Movement to the gathering places of Communist youth, the hotel and brothel rooms that I knew for one night, the decisive benches in the Tiergarten, the ways to different schools and the graves that I saw filled, the sites of prestigious cafés whose long forgotten names

daily passed our lips, the tennis courts where empty apartment houses stand today, and the halls emblazoned with gold and stucco that the terrors of dancing classes made almost the equal of gymnasiums. And even without this map, I have the encouragement provided by an illustrious precursor, the Frenchman Léon Daudet, exemplary at least in the title to his work, which exactly encompasses the best that I might achieve here: *Paris vécu*. 'Lived Berlin' does not sound so good but is as real.[2]

The question of *bios* – that is lived, social life as opposed to *zoë*, bare life – and its graphic inscription in/as art has tended to collapse, in art history, however, into simplistic biographism. Based on reflexivity, a presumption of direct expression between the author and his/her representations is rife in art history. Art thereby becomes implicitly narrative because it always has an anterior starting point outside/before its own performance. Hence it is always read in retrospect from work back to its supposed prior origin and cause in the artist-subject, rather being read as a momentary poïesis: an unforeseen creative event reliant intertextually on its both signifying and material specificities and 'play' in a world of signs and subjects.

Nowhere has this been more persistent than in the case of Vincent van Gogh (1853–1890).[3] Perhaps the epitome of the expressionist biographical fantasy of art as pure and direct expressivity, Van Gogh's literary and artistic works have been read for the unmediated revelation of his subjectivity deposited in his letters and images. This same tendency, but with even more injurious consequences, is also widespread in the art historical writing on artists who are women.[4] Walter Benjamin's reflections on *bios* (*social living mediated by memory*) graphically (*mediated by rhetorical and semiotic systems*) inscribed through space (*remembered, subjectifying, imagined and artistically re-created*) will enable me both to challenge this tendency and to pose an alternative 'frame' of viewing two artists: Vincent van Gogh (1857–1890) and Charlotte Salomon (1917–1943) whose works I wish to read through each other's uses of space as a device for the creation of the very memory traces that Benjamin fantasised about mapping.

Since her major surviving work *Leben? oder Theater?* 1941–1942 (1325 gouaches paintings and overlays conceived and presented as a musical play in image, music and text, now held at the Jewish Historical Museum in Amsterdam) was first brought to public attention in 1961, Charlotte Salomon has been framed within a predominantly autobiographical reading of this her major surviving art work as a painted life story or diary.[5] To disarticulate this tendency, I invoke Benjamin's fine distinction between autobiography based on sequential time, on the one hand, and discontinuity plotted through the spacing (différance) of memories on the other. Salomon's work may be read as a painterly enactment of Benjamin's concept of the bio-graphic as the spatially imag(in)ed, the projected revisualisation of life as fragments of memories – not all hers, when paralleled with those of Van Gogh will equally displace the biographical reductionism in that archive.

In the following I intend to break the rule of historical writing which usually flows from past to present. Instead, I intend to read Van Gogh back through a possible legacy of his spatial inscriptions of subjectivity in the work of the later artist, Charlotte Salomon. It is the relay created by this virtual encounter that breaks the biographical reductionism to allow us to contemplate the specific ways in which modernist spatialities sustained innovative ways to produce the kind of bio-graphic mapping to which Walter Benjamin alluded. This is not to suggest the simplicities of influence. Rather reading Charlotte Salomon *through* a Van Gogh thereby reframed *by* her belated reading of his legacy, enables me to explain the ways we can advance our studies of modernism beyond the limitations of canonical chronologies of style and movement figured around the biographically known individual.

Part I   Charlotte Salomon: staging a memory of an other's becoming and unbecoming[6]

On a single page, harmonised by an overall tonality of pale blue, a series of vignettes are strikingly interwoven to create at once a functioning and unified composition and a multi-part, narrativised space that we must *read* to produce its effective proposition (Figure 7.1).

At the top right, there is a troop train bulging with its khaki passengers while other orderlies rush down the platform with the wounded. At one window we can just detect the figure of a slender woman elegantly dressed in blue saying a tearful farewell to a man leaning out of the carriage. In a second diagonal band on the left-hand side, that slips under the space of the scene of tender parting on the right, the same train whooshes out of the station; the woman in blue stands almost alone still waving to the departing lover. Moving to the centre of the painting, she then reappears as if coming up the incline under the bridge now formed by the overlapping bands that remind us of European stations where the passageways for access lie beneath the platforms. She walks, an action signified in a still image by repetition, towards an elderly couple. She stands momentarily centred in the painting conversing with them. Separation – or rather a parting of the ways is now signified by the fact that she moves in one direction and they in another, a movement that repeats the directions of the bands above and a division underlined by the triangulation of this space by the two bands of the platform departure.

Movement is signalled by the repeating figure of the woman in blue who crosses the drawn boundary of the central 'frame' – one is tempted to use cinematic terms here – to move downwards towards a new space, a lobby before the entrance to an apartment which she, now increased in size, approaches alone and prepares to enter with her key in a counter movement that takes her into its promised space.

Figure 7.1 Charlotte Salomon, *Leben? oder Theater?* 1941–2, gouache on paper, 32.5 × 25 cm, JHM 4167 (Departure 1917). Jewish Historical Museum, Amsterdam, Charlotte Salomon Foundation.

The complete painting is, therefore, made up of several compartments of space each with a discrete semantic load. For analytical purposes, I can disassemble them into painted compartments. In doing this, the remarkable feature of how the whole coheres visually as a painting disappears. Only when bound into their constructed interrelations, bonded onto the surface of their supporting paper, does the work appear before us in its aesthetic effectiveness where its integration of spaces sustains a narrative of disjunctions: departure and separation, togetherness and aloneness, integration and independence. For this to happen and for this painting's meanings to work, the artist must have had knowledge of a range of visualities and visual narratives that could be called upon from nineteenth-century children's illustrated books to medieval manuscripts, from Persian miniatures to stained glass. At the same time, the painting claims the freedoms of more recent modernisms such as those of Marc Chagall and the Cubist legacy with their radicalisation of space, rewriting of composition, and restructuring of pictorial unity through colour and the imprimatur of singular stylisation.

Knowingly, yet with apparently naïve disregard for any one system, modernism's daring reconceptualisation of the possibilities of painting and painting as space-creating are unequivocally deployed. Unified by the overall harmony of the blue tonality, yet toughened up by the strong Manetian browns and blacks, the scene also makes this space support the emergence into view of a feminine subjectivity centred by the painting on the multiple incarnations of the woman in blue. Almost unnoticed at the upper registers, she slowly emerges into view to take her place first as a subordinate in a father-dominated family group that is at the centre of the painting, only to insist on her separation and her own new space in her own home marked by crossing the boundary where her figure grows in scale to enact the final, significant gesture towards which the painting has *visually* led us: unlocking the door to an unseen space: her future. This painting could be called a kind of *bios-graphy*, only if understood as a 'writing' – in this case a painting – of an emerging/crystallising subjecthood of the represented woman in blue as a figure of a historically and geo-culturally specific, modern femininity through the spatialisation of its subject across the field of the imagined event. This painting, therefore, does not illustrate a life narrative of the real-life referent of the woman in blue anymore than it calls into view the life or subjectivity of the artist who painted the picture. Painting the picture – creating its pictorial place brings into view a subjectivity, itself invisible and relational, that is signified rather than experienced. That subjectivity inscribed into space is not the artist's, nor is what we see the mere retelling of a story known to her. Like and unlike Benjamin's own writings about the city of Berlin as the space of his becoming at the turn of the twentieth century, this painting makes us see a modernist moment of decision imagined, however, for a feminine subject whose experiences at this moment in 1916 were unknown to the artist, born in 1917, who, in painting, imaginatively created the scene in her exile in France in 1941.

The next painting in the sequence to which this work belongs opens the door, into which the key is inserted, onto another complex configuration of space: the apartment where the woman in blue will now live her new life (Figure 7.2). The viewpoint, however, is no longer that of the woman. It is a third-person viewpoint, as if we had taken the roof off a doll's house to

Figure 7.2 Charlotte Salomon, *Leben? oder Theater?* 1941–2, gouache on paper, 32.5 × 25 cm, JHM 4168 (Apartment). Jewish Historical Museum, Amsterdam, Charlotte Salomon Foundation.

see the pattern of rooms within. Neither architectural nor topographical, the painting recreates the interior of a Berlin apartment home, as a patchwork of spaces, divided in ways that are colour-coded to signify familial, domestic, sexual and social relations that will be formally staged within, and by, these lived spaces that signify their surrogate subjects: space as bios.

The blue salon in the upper left with its elegant sparseness and large piano will be the space of the lady of the house. There is a gloomily serious dining room to the right and a passageway off which we see the bodily rooms: a kitchen that comes complete with attendant maid/cook, Augusta, and the bathroom. Bright and hygienically white, these spaces are linked colouristically to the prospective baby's nursery on the other side of the corridor, and to the places for sleeping. In a slightly darker set of grey-whites and reds there is the parental bedroom, the visual highlight of the painting, and almost lost, at the lower edge, is the maid's little bedroom. Without indication of its access, the earnestly sombre left-hand part of the apartment is designated the doctor's study and consulting room in tones which vary from a green-based darkness to a reassuring pale hospital green. Gender and class are instantly visible in their spatial inscriptions. So too are the functions of work and sex: work represented by Augusta in her kitchen and the doctor's consulting room; sex marked by the bedroom – primal space of origin and the begetting of the artist who will create this image from memory 25 years after the moment it enshrines in 1916.

Procreation takes place – it was imagined in a cinematic representation of frames of a celluloid film slipping through the gate showing the parents on their honeymoon night in a hotel before the farewell at the station (JHM 4166).[7] The painting (JHM 4169) following the overview of the apartment presents the woman in blue – her colour throughout the work – watching at the window; she is pregnant. The following paintings imagine the early years of an enraptured motherhood spent at home and in a variety of holiday resorts.

Suddenly, however, the *jouissant* scenes darken. A painting composed of three registers, the upper one itself doubly subdivided into many tiny scenes marks the psychic disintegration of the woman in blue who is once again found seated at the window, in more melancholic reverie, her daughter in identical pose yet drawing (Figure 7.3). Drenched in blood red or paled into ghostly desolation in the lowest register, the melancholic woman looms up along the whole of the left side of the painting rendering the scenes then detailed beside her as visualised projections of her own darkening state of mind that leads to an attempt to poison herself. Two paintings later, vigilance is momentarily suspended and the desperate woman rises from her bed where she is painted in the pose of the figure of sleep quoted from Michelangelo's Medici tombs. As a diminutive figure she approaches a window set within the painting's field. The painting, however, repeats this frame at its lower edges, gaping horribly and placing the viewer, suspended outside, as a witness only to the trailing naked foot – the poignant sign of this woman's *unwitnessed* suicide (JHM 4179).

Mediated by one more painting (JHM 4180), the viewer is placed street-side (JHM 4180) and forced into a single-spaced, but un-localised confrontation with the broken body, its skull crushed and bleeding onto the heedless ground. The drama which the paintings are restaging occurs in

Figure 7.3 Charlotte Salomon, *Leben? oder Theater?* 1941–2, gouache on paper, 32.5 × 25 cm, JHM 4176 (Franciska's Pain Collection). Jewish Historical Museum, Amsterdam, Charlotte Salomon Foundation.

imagined memory; the artist did not know of, or see this event. Thus the imagined memory of another's psychological disintegration and death finds its force precisely in the choreography of another subject's inner vision plotted onto paper, and in the capacity to create and sustain complex spatialities that inscribe aspects of a woman's subjectivity, her inner life and psychic breakdown from the multi-scened social emplacement to the monumental confrontation with the irreducible fact of solitary, self-inflicted death.

The overall structure of *Leben? oder Theater?* finally comprising 769 paintings is not narrative in a linear sense. In fact, it concludes with its own genesis: the final painting (JHM 4925) shows a modern young woman in mermaid pose, poised to begin to paint the work as she submerges herself in a Duffyian Mediterranean scene, embracing not the dark German expressionist mode of the paintings we have discussed so far, but *jouissant* in the French, post-impressionist faith in the creative force of Southern sun and sea. The blue of the sea also signifies the cleansing beauty of nature in contrast to the faecal horror of the concentration camp from which this woman in a bathing-suit was released in July 1940 – the camp invisibly functioning as the traumatic void of the degree zero of the fascist Real against which this massive visualisation was produced. The blue also re-invokes the remembered maternal presence of the woman in blue; a chance apparition of a face rises out of the sea created by the movement of the loaded brush.

The blue mother, whose terrible death is confronted so shockingly in the painted work, is traced as a coloured thread of reconnective feminine memory – dangerous yet also solacing, forming part of the doubled ground on which this unique epic of contemporary history and diverse memories would be produced as the record of a deep philosophical and psychological enquiry into the conditions of living or dying in such catastrophic historical and tragic personal circumstances.

At the beginning of the second act of the Prelude ('Act Two: 30 January 1933') of *Leben? oder Theater?* the events of 1933 impinge upon its cast of German-Jewish characters. Militarised masculinity fills the urban space like a faecal flood; the artist reverses their swastikas back to the Hindu symbol of peace yet they still tumble suffocatingly down the walls of her apartment, filling interior space while the Nazi shouts resound in its air. She declares she will not return to such a school where racist reclassification renders her less than a person. Charlotte Kann decides to learn to draw. She declares her intention in terms that suggest a knowledge of Julius Meier-Graefe's novel *Vincent* (1922). She says: 'I will learn to draw – that is a profession that God made for everyone – why not me?' (JHM 4320). This declaration has distinctive Van Goghian overtones as if art is a calling available to anyone to take up. We should note how, in signing this painting with her enigmatic initials, *CS*, that veil both the artist's gender and ethnicity, the intersection of the letters and the architectural border produces a visual pun on the very swastika that invades her life.

Despite the anti-Jewish laws proscribing Jewish students, or limiting them to a minute quota, in 1935 she is allowed into the State School of Free and Applied Arts from which Oscar Schlemmer had recently been expelled as one of its teachers. In an environment both filled with SA students in brown uniforms but also now known for its anti-Nazi staff and students, she paints a modernist manifesto (Figure 7.4).

Using the repeating figure of the young blonde woman drawing on a Chagallian flat blue field – the field of art – drawings, chairs, flowers, pots, dolls, clothes, apples, shoes and a guitar seemingly float on a cloth of flowered blue. In the upper left-hand corner, the young woman works diligently

Figure 7.4 Charlotte Salomon, *Leben? oder Theater?* 1941–2, gouache on paper, 32.5 × 25 cm, JHM 4351 (A Modernist Manifesto). Jewish Historical Museum, Amsterdam, Charlotte Salomon Foundation.

on her drawings surrounded by the delicately budded sprigs of flowering trees that seem to reappear in the finely drawn and traditional fairy tale illustrations on the left. The second incarnation of the drawing woman leans towards a different jumble of artistic resources and motifs. The centrally positioned third incarnation of the art student in blue, turned more towards the viewer, seems to confront much more significant signs of her artistic interest that fill the right-hand side and lower part of the painting; they are represented in a different, boldly painted and colourist manner. These are calculated inclusions: a pair of workman's boots and a large sunflower connote a knowledge of and reference to the work of Vincent van Gogh while the heavily distorted and phallic jug placed above a bowl of apples and pears initiates a chain of association with Paul Cézanne.

In the context of its implied dating, painted in 1941 but picturing a moment in 1936, by an isolated Jewish woman art student in Nazi Berlin, such adamant invocations of Modernist painters like Van Gogh and Cézanne as counter forces to the original artistic environment of her study under anti-fascist Professor Ludwig Bartning who trained his students on German fairytales and illustration, is a declaration both brave and foolish. From 1933 Modernist works were in process of being de-accessioned from German public collections while advocates of their modernism fled into exile. In 1937–8 the National Socialist regime's cultural police collected all remaining examples of modernism into one exhibition under the same rubric that disemancipated this young woman: degeneracy. *Entartete Kunst*, Degenerate Art, was an exhibition constructed to humiliate and decry the corrupting, Jewish-Bolshevik excesses of modernist art. Starting in Munich in 1937, the exhibition came to Berlin between 26 February and 8 May 1938.[8]

Paradoxically, this vast retrospective of the masters of early twentieth-century modernism would be Hitler's gift to young artists of the Third Reich like Charlotte Salomon.[9] Surreptitiously visiting the exhibition during its many months in Berlin in 1938, shielded by her blond hair and blue eyes from visible racist typology, she, like many other young artists, knew this was her last chance to drink at this particular fountain, to take nourishment from an exhibition in which the most comprehensive retrospective of modernist visualities of the last 30 years were assembled in a chaotic, ridiculing but (negatively) didactic display.

Both in Salomon's painting's (Figure 7.4) bold invocation of French and Dutch modernists, and in her developmental momentum from upper left to lower right that places Van Gogh's ebullient sunflower and Cézanne's erotic jug and fruit in the forefront as the signs of her advancing direction in art, Charlotte Salomon's artistic manifesto declared a counter, anti-fascist aesthetic of enrichment in nature and celebration of the human imagination in colours and forms. The boots of Van Gogh, the addendum to Heidegger's 1935–6 lecture 'On the Origin of the Work of Art', almost touch the artist – suggesting a more specific knowledge of the emerging legend in which these boots, identified as surrogates for the ever-dislocated artist, signify the modern artist as a figure of both social degradation and exile, a deep resource in her own moment of internal exile as a Jewish art student in a fascist state.

There were Van Gogh exhibitions in Berlin during the 1920s including an extensive showing at the Nationalgalerie of the holdings of Mrs Kroeller-Mueller, now the collection of the Rijksmuseum Kroeller-Mueller assembled for the said patron by her perspicacious adviser H.P. Bremmer who cherry-picked from the artist's surviving estate. Charlotte Salomon's father was an art lover and collector – although his taste was for Persian miniatures, Oriental carpets and Baroque paintings. Listening to the testimonies of many German–Jewish refugees, and following the researches of Peter Paret and Vera Grodzinski into the specific cultural correlations between social subject positions in modernity of the German–Jewish bourgeoisie and the ethos, as Meyer Schapiro calls it, of Impressionist modernism, it is more than probable that Charlotte Salomon had seen and furthermore knew, in colour illustration, some of the works by Van Gogh.

Her manifesto painting becomes one more important index of the multifarious ways in which Van Gogh's work itself and the evolving legend of Van Gogh's outsider status and willed decision to make himself an artist could function as a supporting narrative for a young woman in a radically different situation. Appropriating both means and mantra, she makes herself not only an identity. She becomes in practice an active reader of Van Gogh's art work, translating it to reveal something perhaps not visible without her use of it. She uses this translation to claim permission for a radical play with invested, narrative, subjectivising space. Van Gogh's eccentric position vis-à-vis modernism's more rigorous and anti-romantic engagement with pictorial structure and specifically flatness held open a space for a none the less modernist exploration of subjectivity through pictorial spacing – not in terms of the expressionist stylisation of extremity – but by means of what I call a theatre of memory that articulates narrative, space and oblique inscriptions of many modern and gendered subjectivities.

Part II   Van Gogh: housing memory and the discontinuities of space

On 22 July 1878, a Dutchman of unfixed abode and a history of professional failures, wrote to his brother from a small village in Brabant in which he had grown up as the second son of a Reformed Protestant pastor Theodorus and his wife Anna Cornelia. The letter is atypical, at least according to the later image of the writer once he had begun to refashion himself as the artist we now know as Vincent van Gogh. It is a joyful letter about a trip he and his father had just made to explore training schools in evangelism for the former trainee art dealer, bookseller and theology student, then aspiring to follow the paternal example into religious service through evangelism. On their return from Brussels, father and son had walked through the twilight. The letter describes the scene lyrically in terms indicative of the writer's extensive know-ledge of the paintings of Daubigny, Dupré and Rousseau: 'the sun setting red behind the pine trees and the evening sky reflected in the pools; the heath yellow and white and grey sand were so full of harmony and sentiment – see there are moments in life when everything, within us too, is full of peace and sentiment, and our whole life seems to be a *path through the heath*; but it is not always so.' He then reports that he spent the next morning with his younger brother Cornelius, collecting heather for rabbits. They sat in a pine wood and sketched a map of Etten in its surroundings with all its paths through the heaths. Cor had written on the drawing: 'Vincent and I did this in the pinewood – Cor – and I must go to bed. Goodnight' (Figure 7.5).

This 1878 map, drawn in artistic innocence with his younger brother at a moment of relative peace with his family and its familial or even natal

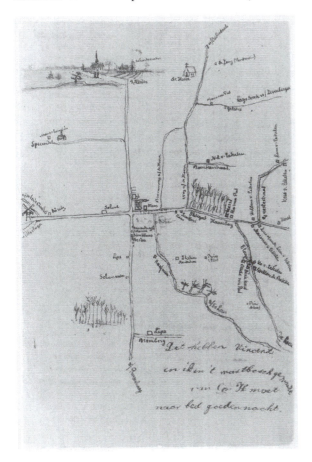

Figure 7.5 Vincent van Gogh, Map enclosed in Letter to Theo, LT, 123, 22 July 1878. Rijksmuseum Vincent van Gogh, Amsterdam.

location in rural Brabant, takes on a kind of emblematic significance. Only a long traverse of what came later can bring this drawing into its significance as a symptomatic anticipation of what was to come which would, in fact, be its recapitulation otherwise and elsewhere. We need only to juxtapose this map with this famous passage from Van Gogh's literary works to catch something of the oddity of his thought about travel, time and space:

> For my part I know nothing whatsoever about it, but looking at stars always makes me dream, as simply as I dream over the black and white dots representing towns and villages on a map. Why, I ask myself, should the shining dots of the sky not be as accessible as the black dots on the map of France? Just as we take a train to get to Tarascon or Rouen, we take death to reach a star. One thing undoubtedly true in this reasoning is that we *cannot* get to a star while we are alive, any more than we can take a train while we are dead.
>
> (LT 506)

Cornelius and Vincent van Gogh's drawing is a map that works simultaneously on the axis of planar projections as if seen directly from above and perspectival vignettes seen from ground level. Even in this strange juxtaposition I detect a defining feature of this body of work, that marks off its singularity from the rest of the modernists. Yet the peculiarities of space practised by the later artist Van Gogh introduced into modernism an extraordinary breakthrough in terms of how a picture can imagine psychological or phenomenological space that other artists, better equipped than he, would be able to exploit precisely because modern thought would demand other modes of visualisation of subjectivity and place.

The ground of the drawing is marked by lines that form roads as a network of pathways through a blank territory otherwise not registered as flat or ribbed. Supplemented, the drawing also includes tiny renderings of buildings and tree plantations, although there is no indication of the precise location of the pinewood from which this drawing was made. Indeed the map is not at all a projection from a point in material or geographical space. The vantage point would need to be a star. Without that possibility of aerial overflying, we know that we are looking at a conceptual projection of a world as if imagined from on high – a vantage point already projected in dreams and, therefore, a mapping from memory inscribing in the arrangement, not an external viewpoint, but a centring, spatialising of a subject: a bios-graphic writing.

The buildings represented are of two kinds: churches and associated dwellings such as the rectory – in this case the drawing boys' parental home (Figure 7.6). At the upper left is one church. It will travel in memory to be recalled or travelled to by star, as it were, in the second of Van Gogh's attempted master works, the landscape titled *Starry Night* completed in June 1889 (Figure 7.7). Some suggest that the village shown in this painting is

Figure 7.6 Vincent van Gogh, *Vicarage and Church at Etten* (Juvenilia XXI), April 1876, 9 × 17.3 cm. Rijksmuseum Vincent van Gogh, Amsterdam.

Figure 7.7 Vincent van Gogh, *Starry Night*, F 612, June 1889, oil on canvas, 73 × 92 cm. Museum of Modern Art, New York.

Figure 7.8 Vincent van Gogh, *View of a Town (St. Rémy) with a Spire,* F 1541verso, summer 1889, pen, pencil and wash, 16.5 × 30.1 cm. Rijksmuseum Vincent van Gogh, Amsterdam.

that of the Provençal town, St. Rémy seen from the window of the hospital in which the painter then resided. I would like to suggest another, time-reversing possibility. A montage of the details of the churches seen in the painting, related drawings (Figure 7.8) and this map confirm the thread of memory that underpins *Starry Night.* By tracing the lines between the drawings of a church embedded in the drawing and the painting, the sketch of the church in St. Rémy (Figure 7.7), and this tiny register of a childhood landmark (Figure 7.5) I want to make the proposition that Van Gogh's oeuvre is structured through what I have recently theorised as natal memory which is the deep memory of the landscape childhood becoming. It is also a socially significant phenomenon of that first modernist generation so many of whom were born in the country and became metropolitans as the condition of their professions. Bridging the two worlds of city and country, the new urban culture is infused with nostalgia and fantasy focused on an imaginary countryside that psychically screens an even deeper maternal memory of home.

At the central crossroads of the 1878 map, however, the brothers drew another large church and a house which we can recognise from a drawing of Vincent the previous year, April 1877, of the *Vicarage and Church at Etten* (Figure 7.6). This drawing again marks what will become through repetition – always psychologically significant as an index of both emotional investment and neurotic cathexis – Van Gogh's parallel fascination with the representations of spired churches and of his homes that will form a significant repeating motif across his migratory work tracing into each new version the deeper layers of memory that is the structuring trope of his oeuvre and its historical significance as a discourse on the relations between location/dislocation and unconscious memory.

When he returned to Brabant in 1883–5, Van Gogh portrayed this home – I use the term portray rather than represent advisedly, as we are led to wonder if these works are not better read as indirect self and other portraits for which the poetics of the house that can be both father-sign (rectory) and mother-sign (maternal body) might substitute. In Nuenen in 1884–5, Van Gogh painted the considerable mansion in which the bourgeois Protestant pastor was housed by his tiny community (compared to the large Catholic church glimpsed in a drawing from the vicarage garden, March 1884). Van Gogh's peculiar take on space will imprint upon this view the vital substance of the house, stretching and leaning beyond the rigid solidity that the photograph captures. Van Gogh will also picture this house from its backyard, from the private garden, looking at its rear entrances off which lies the shed he renovated and made into a studio – out of view of the street and the public because of the way his, the pastor's eldest son's rough dressing and defiant identification with the catholic poor might shame his family. Identifying with the back, the rear and the lowly, Van Gogh makes his window visible in the gloom.

Yet never again, it seemed, would this artist be able to imagine himself or his family, as is inscribed in the map of 1878, at the centre of the spatial universe. The power of this motif as the sign of memory is precisely underlined by its contradiction when Van Gogh the artist becomes a tourist and an exile in the hybrid spaces of modernity in which he attempts to situate himself and his elective practice as a painter of the modern world, first in the Hague, then Paris and then, most perplexingly in Arles.

In 1882 shortly after his arrival in the Hague, Van Gogh made a drawing (Figure 7.9). It is a drawing of his house at the edge of the city. Across the vast stretch of empty ground, we see some newly built houses on the very outskirts of the city of the Hague to which, as a result of familial dissension after the failure of his evangelical mission, Van Gogh moved to begin his career as an artist in the centre of the Dutch avant-garde in December 1881. The drawing registers a precarious location on a new estate just emerging in that between space that is neither city or country; the edge of the city. This scene is perceived across from the other side of the canal that runs beside the main street leading into the still rural fields surrounding the city. What makes it a Van Gogh drawing, or what creates that which we will appropriate in reading it and responding to it as a singularity we name 'Van Gogh-ness', is the fact that it contains and holds multiple points of view. Although the space is not compartmentalised, it is multiple and held together by a force of will imposing itself upon the viewer with its not easily discerned novelty.

Figure 7.9 Vincent van Gogh, *Group of Houses*, F 915, pencil, chalk and sepia on paper,
40 × 69 cm.

The drawing seems to be constructed from the point of an orthogonal,
opening out the space to left and right of this viewing position. We also
look deeply into receding space marked by the canal at the right. Yet we
appear to be seeing the houses from a position directly in front of them. A
lot of this is a result of the fact that perspective is just plain difficult and
requires mathematical or mechanical calculation rather than perceptual
description. It is an abstract system of projections that has the effect of centring the viewing position. As with much of what makes Van Gogh's work
interesting, it is his incompetence and lack of skill that introduces under the
pressure of sheer will power into the sphere of art, something that other
artists will find liberating and useful in his re-assembling of space under
multiple positionalities.

Lured rather than repulsed by this estrangement, we then look across
rough ground, perhaps marked out for market gardens or new plots of
houses. A cross street has barely begun to form with five houses on its left
and two different buildings on the right. Fencing suggests the next plot to
be developed. The drawing is desolately empty, with no signs of the
inhabitants of the ghost town of the new estate. The lowering sky and the
chosen range of inks and pencil create a sombre even sinister effect that will
be resumed by both Hopper and Hitchcock. The house with its upstairs
window illuminated is the residence of Vincent van Gogh. The view from
the window at the back of the houses, however, opens onto the open
country. This juxtaposition underlines the hybrid, becoming and changing
space that Van Gogh transgressively made the subject of his first major commission in the Hague.

I want to bring together these two levels that I have been plotting out: the habit of drawing emotionally invested as well as socially indexical place, on the one hand, and on the other, the habits of the ways these drawings construct pictorially lived (*erlebte*) space. We can then link these early projects with ones more classically identified as the post-Paris Van Gogh to reveal not the usual narrative of early regional beginnings and modernist maturity but a different kind of continuity shaped precisely by discontinuity of place. After the difficulties and failures of his two years in Paris, 1886–88, Van Gogh rented perhaps his most famous home, the *Yellow House* (Figure 7.10). Juxtaposing the two images of his Hague and Arlesian homes relieves the usual nonsense written about Van Gogh's later work and draws us back to register a recurrent habit of inscribing the self obliquely in space by creating an image of a spatial location for the self, mirrored not by a spectral double as in the self-portrait but by its housing, its emplacement that in its visual representation from outside equally signifies a radical displacement or dislocation.

For all its more glorious and saturated colour, the painting of the Yellow House rehearses what we have learned to see by our study of Van Gogh's drawings in the Hague. The strange painting opens out, almost fans out before us without making it at all clear what the viewing position is. In fact

Figure 7.10 Vincent van Gogh, *The Yellow House*, F 464, 1888, oil on canvas, 76 × 94 cm. Rijksmuseum Vincent van Gogh, Amsterdam.

the painting is re-assembled from several positions of the artist's wandering eye and adjusted body position. He looks directly to his left to see the curve of the road over the hump of road-working debris. A favourite motif marks the extreme edge of the painting: a street lamp. We are looking down this road to the station buildings beyond. We then look as if we were standing on that pavement across to the frontage of a café with its pink awning. The sidewalk begins to slither down to the right as the next directly viewed frontage is added on and the level of the ground seems to suggest an incline. In fact according to the scrupulous reconstructions for the Van Gogh/Gauguin catalogue, there is an angle here but the opposite one: that is to say rather than sloping down and towards us, the angle should be recessive into the space of the image. The sidewalk is further stretched to allow us to feel its expanse as if we were looking down onto it rather than seeing it as a mere plane marked by its lip in receding space. From that spillage into space, it does recede and we look down its length to a hooded café space where people sit at tables. The angle necessary to allow us to feel as if we are looking in is then shifted to create a long and open gaze down the road at the right that leads into the space that passes under the two bridges and beyond. This road is marked by two women strolling with a child in tow and a curiously dressed almost toy figure. They are seen from behind in a direct view that is not consistent with the angle of the road on which they walk.

The whole picture is composed of these varied and mobile positions and yet conceived as if looking from a low point at the lower right of the painting when all the protocols of urban painting suggest that a high view point allowing recession to the lowest point of the horizon is the best way to generate a sense of space (Figure 7.11). The height of the virtual horizon line is masked by the railway bridge with its own introduction of movement and implied travel that runs across the plane of the painting. What causes some of the disturbance in the field of vision is Van Gogh's disarming habit of setting up a canvas and painting its main contents from one level only to find he has an empty foreground. This he fills in by painting in what lies between his feet and his eye line, creating these yawning foregrounds that literally fan open this space, creating the double V effects that I identified above.

What Van Gogh put into the history of art through his particular refusals of the orthodoxies of composition and equally the emerging canons of the counter, modernist visualities was this complex of simultaneously inhabited and experienced space. We can do this best in relation to the scene in the interior of the Yellow House which is, extraordinarily, a self-portrait by means of the image not of the artist's studio but his bedroom, the intimate place of sleep and dreams (Figure 7.12). Again the space almost flows out of the painting in this V, opening to encompass the posited viewer. The bed on the other zooms into the space driving it backwards. The chairs stand ready to receive a sitter – titled up to show the space they offer rather than

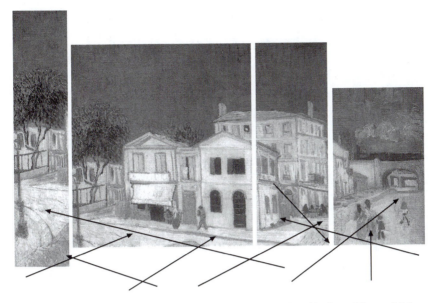

Figure 7.11 Vincent van Gogh, *The Yellow House*, sectioned and indicated lines of sight.

compressed to conform to their perspectival presence. Lived space, remembered from all the countless experiences and varied positions adopted within it, is thus embodied space, and embodied space is psychically invested since the ego is a body ego and the body only an instrument through these endless transactions within a world that surrounds the subject. Merleau-Ponty wrote of the entwining of vision and movement as the hallmark of the situated subject seeing and seen by the active visuality of the world. The density of Cézanne's coloured field worlds captures what Merleau-Ponty theorised philosophically. Lacking Cézanne's subtlety, Van Gogh none the less registers this phenomenological dimension archaically in an adamant literality that becomes extraordinarily compelling.

I have used the term failure several times. It will probably sound heretical as we are trained in reverence for the great masters. Being a pupil of Sigmund Freud in this matter, I have argued in my recent book on *Differencing the Canon* that we need to distinguish between the narcissistic fantasies that create hero-worship and fascination with artistic biography so structural in what passes for art history and analytical work on what art works actually do. The idealisation of the artist as hero achieved a kind of negative apogee in the creation of the legend of Van Gogh as tortured suffering genius. As Rilke said, any excessive fascination with the artist overshadows analytical engagement with the painter, or with painting itself as a mode of thought and an articulation of experience semiotically that is both poetic and aesthetic, creative of meaning and affecting – but is also a form of critical reflection and unconscious inscription. I mean no disrespect to

Figure 7.12 Vincent van Gogh, Bedroom, F 482, oil on canvas, 72 × 90 cm.

the complexity of art and the need for us all to acquire the most extensive tools and theoretical resources with which to attempt readings of what is inscribed into culture through literary, visual and cinematic practices. I do not need the concept of the individual genius to see significant things happening knowingly or unconsciously in art works. Indeed in a number of cases, especially in the field of modernist studies, the very incapacity that arises from lack of academic disciplining of the would-be painter generated new possibilities for painting and indeed the counter-discourse of skilled non-competence has come to be almost central to the field of modernist practice.

What was the legacy of Van Gogh mediated through the prism of his appropriation by German expressionism and utopian socialist writing? How differently did his work signify for a young Jewish woman choosing art as a means of self-defence and self-realisation in a moment of radical depersonalisation and political terror? That an artist, Charlotte Salomon, we otherwise find hard to locate in art history could appropriate as a possible position for her own creative defiance not only the mad inventiveness of Van Gogh's multiple spaces, but also the tenacious restaging of remembered places figured through an untrained but intuitively creative freedom with colour and drawing, helps us create different questions to ask of modernist painting and to map out different pathways through its many

Figure 7.13 Charlotte Salomon, *Leben? oder Theater?* 1941–2, gouache on paper, 32.5 × 25 cm, JHM 4177 (The terrible news Collection). Jewish Historical Museum, Amsterdam, Charlotte Salomon Foundation.

possibilities. Charlotte Salomon appears to have been a thoughtful reader of Van Gogh, and my *a posteriori* proposition of an affiliation reflects back to confirm my proposition about the discontinuity of moment in Van Gogh but the persistence of the spaces of memory as the core structuration of his oeuvre. Thus reading a canonical 'modernist master' through an uncanonical 'young mistress' opens the space of art's multiple histories while allowing us beyond the policing censorship of academic orthodoxy to see what history actually holds. The final image takes us back to a 'Berlin Childhood' and the moment of discovery of the suicide of the woman in blue. There in faded and almost dissipating pallor, sits a child on a bed (Figure 7.13).

Notes

1 Walter Benjamin, 'Berlin Chronicle', *One-Way Street*, translated Edmond Jephcott and Kingsley Shorter, London: Verso Books, 1979, 295.

2 Walter Benjamin, 'Berlin Chronicle', *One-Way Street*, translated Edmond Jephcott and Kingsley Shorter, London: Verso Books, 1979, 295. *Erleben* and *Erfahren* are the two German words for experience – one which refers to an accumulation of experience through which the subject has lived; the other has the implications of a kind of accumulation of knowledge resulting from such living through. The forced term lived Berlin, *Berlin vécu*, which comes from the French title of a book *Paris Vécu*, does not have a real translation into English.

3 I have presented Van Gogh as the paradigm case for this biographical collapse in my 'Artists, media and mythologies; genius, madness and art history', *Screen*, vol. 21, no. 3, 57–96, and 'Crows, blossoms and lust for death: cinema and the myth of Van Gogh', in *Mythologies of Van Gogh*, ed. Tsukasa Kodera, Amsterdam: John Benjamins, 217–239.

4 Nanette Salomon, 'The art historical canon: sins of omission', Joan Hartmann and Ellen Messer-Davidow (eds), *(en)Gendering Knowledge: Feminism in Academe*, Knoxville: University of Tennessee Press, 1991, 222–236 and Vanessa Corby, 'Don't look back: reading for the ellipses in the discourse of Eva Hess(e)', *Third Text* (2001–2), no. 57, 31–42. Of course, Roland Barthes, *Sur Racine* (1963) initiated a challenge to what he denounced in literary studies as biographism. Stanley

Fish: 'Biography and intention', in William Epstein (ed.), *Contesting the Subject. Essays in the Postmodern Theory and Practice of Biography and Biographical Criticism*, West Lafayette, Indiana: Purdue University Press, 1991.

5 The first publication was titled *Charlotte: A Diary in Pictures*, New York: Harcourt, Brace and World, 1963. The first major biography of the artist and her work is Mary Lowenthal Felstiner, *To Paint her Life: Charlotte Salomon in the Nazi Era*, New York and London: HarperCollins, 1994.

6 I would love to illustrate this entire argument but limitations reduce the possibility. In lieu I provide the Jewish Historical Museum call number JHM as a means of identification of the images by Charlotte Salomon to which I am referring. These numbers correspond with those on the CD-Rom version that is easily available from the museum.

7 Since I am severely limited in my illustrations while working on a vast painting cycle, I will refer readers to the Jewish Historical Museum (JHM) accession numbers. A CD-Rom is easily available from the museum with all of the paintings identifiable by these numbers which are also used in *Charlotte Salomon Life/or Theatre?* ed. Judith Belifante *et al.*, London: Royal Academy, 1998.

8 See Stephanie Barron, *'Degenerate Art': The Fate of the Avant-Garde in Nazi Germany*, Los Angeles: Los Angeles County Museum, 1991.

9 In the above catalogue Peter Gruenter recalls his impressions of the exhibition which he visited as a seventeen-year-old, passionately interested in modern art.

8

Biography and spatial experience in contemporary diasporic art in Britain

Dorothy Rowe

In her 1976 autobiography Georgia O'Keefe commented that:

> ... *where* I was born and *where and how* I have lived is unimportant. It is what I have *done* with *where I have been* that should be of interest...[1]

I begin with these remarks since I find them a particularly resonant lever for a chapter that attempts to prise open ideas about how biographical facts and spatial experience may be mapped within an arena of contemporary diasporic art in Britain, in a way that dislocates the essentialising conventions of cultural and ethnic identity politics prevalent in much of the critical literature that still accrues to this topic despite vast paradigmatic shifts in other areas of the discipline.[2] Just over ten years ago Sonia Boyce already voiced her frustration with the category of 'black art' for example, when, in an extended interview entitled 'The Art of Identity' (1992), she remarked that:

> ... Whatever we black people do, it is said to be about identity, first and foremost. It becomes a blanket term for everything we do, regardless of what we're doing ... I don't say it should be abandoned, but am I only able to talk about who I am? ... [Am I] not able to say anything else? If I speak, I speak 'as a' black woman artist or 'as a black woman' or 'as a black person'. I always have to name who I am. I'm constantly put in that position, required to talk in that place ... never allowed to speak because I speak...[3]

'Speaking because I speak' from a place that is not pre-determined by fictions of cohesive cultural identity but is predicated upon explorations of the nexus between shifting and historically constituted inter-subjectivities and spatial experiences is also the locus from which Gayatri Spivak has consistently confronted questions of self-representation and multicultural-ism. For Spivak, 'the question of "who should speak?" is less crucial than "who will listen?" and the historically and spatially determined positions from which one is being listened to and by whom.'[4]

It is this exploration of historical and spatial contingency as co-determinants in stories of biographical and autobiographical self-presencing that is central to the signifying practices of a group of works made between 1994 and 1997 by Mohini Chandra, a British-born artist of Indian descent. *Travels in a New World 1 & 2* and *Album Pacifica* all speak of Chandra's engagement with global histories of migration, displacement and diaspora located through a personal anthropology that re-presents her own family as subjects of her investigation and maps their experiences across time and space.

Travels in a New World 1 (Figure 8.1) is a walk-in installation of 1994 which consists of tea-chests that double as light-boxes illuminating trans-parencies of family photographs taken by Chandra as a child, during a trip to Fiji in the 1970s. The boxes are accompanied by a looped soundtrack that repeatedly – and I think also ironically – asks the question, 'Where do you come from?' – an over-determined question, familiar to many ethnic minority subjects within many spatial frames where 'difference' is visibly

Figure 8.1 Mohini Chandra, *Travels in a New World 1*, installation view; photography, photographic emulsion, sound, light-boxes, tea-chests, electric cable, tea, mixed media, 1994.

and/or audibly demarcated, yet still a key question of global subjective enquiry.

Chandra's family history as it is presented here, is one of multiple displacements, in which explorations of their (and her) diasporic dislocation become the structuring principles that frame her work. Chandra's ancestors were taken from India by the British under colonial rule, between 1879 and 1916, to work as indentured labour on the sugar plantations of Fiji in the South Pacific. After the indentured system was abolished, many stayed on as independent farmers and businessmen. After several generations in which a successful community of Indian settlers had become established in Fiji, members of Chandra's family along with many of the other Indian settlers were once again forced to disperse to various countries around the Pacific Rim in order to avoid the conflicts that ensued after a military coup in 1987 in which racial pressures were brought to bear on 'non-indigenous' communities. Whilst today the Indian population in Fiji numbers over 40 per cent, the history of this sizeable community is largely absent from the hegemonic constructions of an exotic pacific idyll designed to attract the Western traveller to this Edenic paradise island. As Elizabeth Edwards has commented:

> ...The Indian presence disrupted notions of the exotic and was marginal in colonial hierarchies in Fiji. They were 'other' but not the untrammelled 'primitive' of the Pacific stereotype. The indentured Indian labourers are absent from its frames, allowed to exist photographically only in terms of the celebration of colonial progress...[5]

It is these silent and marginal histories and the conceptual issues that they raise that are at stake in Chandra's work in her attempts to re-insert their stories into the frame, whilst at the same time reflecting on her own diasporic position in contemporary Britain. However, displacement and dislocation are not merely treated as discursive tropes, but rather biographically connected subjects are positioned as the active producers of that critical discourse, 'of being the diaspora, rather than being passive objects within it'.[6] In discussing this work, Chandra comments that 'as a child, I migrated to several countries, several times, between Australia, Britain and so on and it was always the act of unpacking crates and tea chests that unfolded meaning'.[7] The crates and tea-chests used in *Travels in a New World 1* signify both migration and Indian labour. Materials are used metaphorically to invoke associations of travel and the colonies, yet at the same time they are imprinted with signs of the historically specific biographical narrative of Chandra's own past, via family photographs authored by the artist that serve as indices to personalised and politicised memories. Images and stencilled text on the side of each box reference colonial histories of global trade in goods and people – in African coffee, Indian tea, sugar and enforced labour. The artist's family during the still unreconstructed post-colonial era of the

1970s are shown to be the apex of a constituted history that is predicated upon a global colonial past, yet as *Travels in a New World 2* (1997) (Figure 8.2) and *Album Pacifica* (1999) both go on to demonstrate, that history does not necessarily bind these contemporary actors in an oppressive relationship with their lived and remembered spaces; rather, the overall project seems to be one of re-connection and sometimes even nostalgia, through memory. The nostalgic condition of these memories is yet another layer of the complex relationships enacted between sites and subjects. Chandra uses the methods and tools of anthropological discourse to conduct a personal anthropology that excavates the threads of her family's disparate past to offer a particularised perspective on the South Asian diaspora. Her use of multimedia installation in this context is, as she states, 'highly indicative of the very fluid and amorphous cultural position in which I find myself'.[8] This focus on the self, on her own position in relation to the enormity of the colonial histories that she uncovers, is also not forgotten. The disembodied question 'Where do you come from?' that pervades the space of this installation is a question not only directed by Chandra at her ancestors and immediate family but also by Chandra at herself, in an explication of her own biography *and* by Chandra at the spectators/viewers of the installation. The question also ironically echoes the English language title of Gauguin's 1897 painting *Where do we come from? What are we? Where are we going?* yet significantly displaces the homogenised 'we' of the hegemonic Western masculine subject in a strategy of distancing and displacement that recalls Spivak's reflections on the problems of 'distancing from oneself' that she acknowledges with reservations is sometimes necessary in order to 'speak as' 'Other' for the sake of political expediency.[9] The evocation of Gauguin in the context of Chandra's installation, whilst not overt, is audible enough to further contest the colonial tropes of the exotic fantasies of the South

Figure 8.2 Mohini Chandra, *Travels in a New World 2*. Detail from 6-screen video projection, installation and sound, 1997.

Figure 8.3 Sonia Boyce, *Talking Presence*, 1988, mixed media montage.

Pacific maintained by the transcendental Western myths of art historical modernism and it is also reminiscent of a similar strategy used by Sonia Boyce in a visual rather than an oral, revoking of exoticist tropes in her 1988 mixed media montage *Talking Presence* (Figure 8.3).

Boyce's metropolitan collage on photographic paper fuses the historically and geographically specific with references to an iconography of Western modernity that simultaneously disrupts and satirises the exotic black body of Western colonial visual convention. History and geography, time and place, collide in a meditation on post-colonial London. The viewer bears witness to a British 'order of things' that is dislodged by the dominant 'presence' of black people. Two black nude bodies, male and female, reclining and sitting respectively (in a gender inversion of the visual rhetoric of Western modernity), are placed immediately before the viewer. They are positioned close to the frontal plane and lower edge of the collage, one on each side, framing, presenting and contemplating the scenes in front of them, yet remaining outside them. They look on, situated in what might be termed a 'paravisual' position, both extending Genette's definition of the paratextual as well as alluding to Michel Serres' notion of the parasite as an 'interrupter', a relational catalyst or a secret agent 'who produces disorder and who generates a different order'.[10] For Genette, the paratext is 'neither on the interior nor on the exterior: it is both; it is on the threshold'.[11] Although Genette's definition of paratexts relates to the written word, to the marginalia of the book form, here I think it has resonances for a consideration of the formal visual positions in which the figures are placed, and in turn the cultural positions that are signified by their visual relationship with this London scene. Their poses also recall the languid exoticism of Gauguin's Tahitian nudes, yet Boyce's figures look away from the viewer, highlighting the recurrent trope of bodily objectification central to Western visual modernity by their refusal to present themselves as the sole objects for such commodification. Boyce is 'talking' the 'presence' of black Britishness via her adroit manipulation of visual signs; the figures may be mute but their presence is not. The paravisual boundary from which they enunciate their position resonates with Homi Bhabha's reformulation of Heidegger's concept that 'the boundary is that from which something begins its presencing'.[12] The idea of affirming presence from the boundary also recalls Boyce's interview with Zarina Bhimji, published to accompany Bhimji's 1992 installation *I Will Always Be Here*.[13]

Bhimji's installation consisted of 60 glass shoe boxes, each containing different materials that acted as a trigger to 'a particular set of memories', accompanied by large wall-mounted photographs of 'poignant arrangements – flowers, strands of hair, nipples, tissue paper dresses, white chiffon headscarves'. In responding to a general question put by Boyce about the use of language and accessibility, Bhimji comments:

> I find I'm entering into the area of things that are not structured any more, boundaries are not distinct. I am experimenting with moving the boundaries. I am trying to talk about things which can be difficult to grasp. It is essential to find the universal language, to go beyond personal references, yet it can only come out of personal experience...
> (Bhimji in conversation with Boyce, 1992, *I Will Always Be Here*, p. 1)

Whilst the search for 'the universal language' is a strategy to be regarded with deep suspicion, Bhimji is struggling to articulate a position that is attempting to eschew essentialism, whilst at the same time, to find a symbolic language that addresses macro-histories through a focus on the 'micro'. The transgression, transformation and dissolution of boundaries becomes a tangible position from which Bhimji, Boyce and Chandra can assert existence and presence in their explorations of broader issues of subjectivity, space and diaspora. The montaged scene that viewers are invited to contemplate from the edge of Boyce's image, is a symbolic cultural landscape of the city coupled with an intimation of a distant colonial 'elsewhere'. In the background, icons of the church and the state (signified respectively by St Paul's Cathedral and the Houses of Parliament) and the centrality of river-trade to colonial expansion (Tower Bridge), are juxtaposed with the vernacular architecture of the Victorian tenement and the post-war skyscraper. At the centre, familiarity and estrangement are coupled via the inclusion of a black cab and red bus, indexical signs of the London tourist postcard that implicitly question who the tourists in this city might be.[14] The interrogation of concepts of 'home' and 'elsewhere' are at the heart of this image of modern London and they are further underlined by the inclusion of a fragment of an interior wall, on which is hung a framed picture of an ocean-faring vessel. The ship and the collection of shells and other objects in front of it, hint at distant countries, different homelands and 'the journeys of the colonized and colonizers'.[15] The historical context of colonialism and Empire is also alluded to via the two fragments of birds, cut from a William Morris textile and wallpaper design (the *Strawberry Thief* of 1883). The wallpaper is a reminder of the Victorian drive towards global expansionism and colonisation, whilst the birds are a poignant symbol of migration. The allusion to Morris in this work references Boyce's earlier four-part work on paper, *Lay Back, Keep Quiet and Think About what Made Britain So Great* (1986).[16] This latter work, 'also contextualizes present-day British life within an historical narrative' depicting symbols of the British colonies in three of the panels, with a self-portrait in the final panel.[17] The background pattern within all four images is derived from designs by Morris and co. In both works Boyce excavates Morris's position at the heart of British heritage culture and discloses the colonial narratives that underpin such cultural symbols. In *Talking Presence*, the dislocated interior wall, visually sandwiched between the two black bodies at the front and the metropolitan scene behind, is the fulcrum in this story of 'paravisual' intervention.

Returning to Chandra's work, then, *Travels in a New World* 2 (Figure 8.2) is also a walk-in installation on the theme of diaspora which uses video projections of 'talking heads' to illuminate her theme. On a large interior wall-space, a grid containing one monochrome and five colour images, is projected. Each of the five colour projections is of a different member of Chandra's family who have been filmed against the backdrop of the Pacific Ocean, talking about an image of an Indian family, their family, in Fiji, which had been their home a generation ago. The image about which they are talking is the one shown in the black and white projection. Their head-shots are occasionally replaced by a shot of waves breaking on the beach and their voices have all been merged into a single overlapping soundtrack that accompanies the visual projections. Visually, the scenery against which these narratives occur is unified by legible signs of a stereotypical pacific land-scape: blue ocean, sandy beach and palm trees. However, although Chandra appears to have reunited her scattered family in order to share their memories of Fiji, this is in fact an illusion. The Pacific Ocean seems to unite them against the same backdrop, yet it is also what divides them since, as the audience is gradually made aware, they have all been filmed in the different countries of their current inhabitation: Australia, New Zealand, the UK, the USA and Canada. The Pacific Ocean is both their common link, yet also the source of their physical and geographical distance as well. The Ocean becomes a potent metaphor for the space across which diasporic links are lost or maintained. As Sean Cubitt has remarked, 'either globalisation severs us from one another permanently and to the point of disparate isolation or it must be challenged by other nets of interest such as care and memory' and it is 'these other nets' that Chandra casts across her divided heritage through her work.

Album Pacifica, the third in this series of anthropological investigations into Chandra's family history, was an installation, also mounted in 1997 which consisted of 100 family photographs, framed with their backs to the viewer, the images hidden, facing the wall (Figure 8.4). They are photographs that had been dispersed with different family members across the globe but Chandra reunites them in a single space for the purposes of the installation. Handwritten captions on the back of each photograph are all that is immediately visible. The captions vary – some are descriptive, some factual and others humorous. The captions are the only traces that the viewer has as to what might be represented on their reverse. Displayed together, they constitute both a presence and an absence. They build up an intriguing narrative of relationships, displacements and departures and disavow the cohesive mythologies of family unity signified in the concept of the 'Family Album'. Disrupting the visible as a sign of the real, as staged here in *Album Pacifica*, is a strategy that attempts to address the problematics inherent in what Peggy Phelan has identified as the 'contradiction between "identity politics" with its accent on visibility, and the psychoanalytic/deconstructionist mistrust of visibility'.[18] As Phelan deftly goes on to explore, the investment in the visible as a sign of the real, a sign of presence, that has underpinned the philosophy of much of the identity politics practised by sexual and racial minorities over the past few decades, is tactically problematic since it relies for its effects upon the very system of representation that it seeks to undermine. As she indicates, such tactics assume that 'what one sees is who one is' but as both psychoanalysis and performance theory have demonstrated, what one sees is an unreliable mis-recognition structured through the phallocentrism of the Symbolic. Thus, if the visible is unreliable, recourse to other strategies that disrupt its dominance becomes a mode of de-articulating the fictions of stable visual signifying

Figure 8.4 Mohini Chandra, *Album Pacifica* detail; framed and glazed photograph.

practices and opening up the spaces for more fluid explorations of embodied subjectivities. Chandra's work allows for such possibilities by employing a range of possible media in which dislocating the visible in order to interrogate its function becomes part of an overall strategy in her re-mapping of her biography in the present against the spatial disruptions of her own and her family's past.

Whilst Chandra and Bhimji both interrogate concepts of biography and space through objects of material culture, highlighting their significance in recollections, access to and re-presentations of the effects and legacies of colonial histories on both an intimate personal and a broader socio-cultural level, London-based Israeli born Jewish performance artist Oreet Ashery offers a very different critique of constructs of the self and their location within wider socio-political histories of diasporic communities. A critique of the nexus between biographical construction and spatial location is central to Ashery's performance and photographic practice. Ashery has for a number of years been performing herself Duchampian-style as Marcus Fisher, a trans-gendered Orthodox Jewish man (Figure 8.5).[19] Ashery completed a Masters degree at Central St Martins between 1998 and 2000. It was during this period that she initially created her fictional alter ego as a homage to a former friend in Israel with whom she was losing touch on his conversion to Orthodox Judaism; a faith that limits social contact with those outside its strictly policed parameters. What began as a series of photographic self-portrait stills of Ashery dressed up to approximate a stereotype of an Hasidic Jewish man, gradually evolved into a series of fictional performance pieces in which a whole new identity was researched, constructed and regularly enacted through live interventions and video documentaries. The black and white stills 'were the starting point of visual research into the appropriation of fantasy, desire and play' within the framework of Ashery's own cultural heritage, central to her project as an artist.[20] Research for the creation of 'Mar-cus' (a name which translates in Hebrew as 'Mr cunt') began as a series of voyeuristic encounters observing the ritualistic practices and symbolic dress-codes of Orthodox Jewish men in the public spaces of Jerusalem and discussing their meanings with her father, a secularised Jewish man.[21] The construction of Marcus beyond the stage performances and Cindy Sherman-inspired photographic 'self-portraits' was conceived via a video work executed in documentary style and ironically alluding to the death rather than the birth of its subject, a 16-minute film entitled *Marcus Fisher's Wake* (2000), celebrating a life in the alluded-to context of its death.[22] The film is a fictional pastiche of various aspects of Ashery's own family circumstances combined with Fisher's performative existence and overlaid with a fictional narrative structure devised by Ashery and narrated in a fake American accent by trans-gendered performer, Del la Grace Volcano. Visual production strategies of disruption, subversion, fragmentation, fiction, pastiche and critique are all knowingly employed by Ashery at every level of the work's content, format and medium imbuing

Figure 8.5 Oreet Ashery, *Self Portrait as Marcus Fisher*, III, 2000, photographic print; collaboration with photographer Manuel Vason.

the work with qualities of an amateur home-video – a production device employed in order to question the authenticity of the medium and thereby also cast doubt on the authenticity of its 'biographical' content.

The video opens with a view across Jerusalem from Marcus's/Ashery's parents' flat followed by the introduction to his/her father who is cooking fish, and overlaid with reference to the gendered division of labour in the house in which Marcus's father is cast in a feminised role of cook and cleaner, whilst his mother, who we are told ran away from Jewish orthodoxy as a young woman and adopted a secular Westernised lifestyle, is described as 'butch' by the narrator and the one who is in control of the household accounts. The viewer is shown incidental footage of children playing and some photographs of an emergent orthodox boy, all of which are employed in the film as evidence of the life-story of the young Marcus, yet the status of which remain ambivalent. Are these photographs from Ashery's own family archive of a family member whom we can/will never know or are they 'found objects' employed as part of the Duchampian strategy, reference to which is provided in the film's closing frame of *Rose C'est Lavie?* Autobiography and fiction are constantly entwined here within a complex construction of subjectivity and trans-gendered ethnic identity. Marcus's fascination with Orthodoxy is charted in the video alongside a narrative that constructs him as 'Outsider', as never quite 'the same'. A particularly telling moment is the lingering homo-erotic camera focus on a young man wrapping the leather straps of *tefillin* around his arm in the public space of the city street in which the collision of private ritual and public space is made all the more forceful by the fetishistic and erotic charge with which we as viewers are also implicated.[23] The narrative voice-over loses its authorial objectivity and slips into a discourse of subjective desire, evident in phrases such as 'real men wrap it real tight'. Such overt fetishisation of religious practices as presented in Ashery's filmed presentation of the *tefillin* ritual through the mediated voyeuristic gaze of Del la Grace Volcano's disembodied voice-over, is a highly sensitive manoeuvre, one amongst many taboos which Ashery consistently interrogates in her performance, video and photographic practices and which she is not afraid to confront directly. Not least, this particular episode raises the question as to whether such overt fetishisation of Jewish Orthodoxy can avoid accusations of the exoticisation of difference. This, I think, is a crucial question which accrues to many parodic forms of visual performance, yet I would argue that in many cases it is precisely the staged theatricality of such practices that allows their 'author/performers' to interrogate religious, social and political constructs in this way. Certainly for me in *Marcus Fisher's Wake*, Ashery avoids exoticising Orthodoxy precisely through her parody of the structures of gendered and ethnic difference that the religion literally embodies. If exoticisation implies identificatory desire of the 'Other', Marcus Fisher's constant re-iteration of removal and difference from that with which he is supposed to belong doubly parodies the stability of his constructed ethnicity. Underlining this further, Ashery sets Marcus up as a stereotype of Jewish Orthodoxy, relying on generic visual signifiers of beard, Black hat, sidelocks (*payers*) and fringes (*tzitzit*) that will be read broadly, by gentiles, non-affiliated Jews and the art audience whom she is addressing. As Rachel Garfield has eloquently argued, detailed attention to the actual schisms and factions within Orthodoxy itself and signalled via particular differences of uniform, certain kinds of silk wrap (*kittel*), fur-lined hats (*streimel*), different

coloured stockings and choice of trousers, amongst other issues, are details
that Ashery deliberately avoids in her construction of a stereotyped male
Jew of historicised western European construction.[24] For Ashery, the figure
of the Jew is a complex image circumscribed by taboos which she wishes to
disrupt. As she has explained of Marcus Fisher (quote):

> ...This performative work attempts to de-territorialize and mobilize
> geographical, sexual and religious zones. I'm interested in working with
> the *image* of the orthodox Jew. This image is at once a stereotype and
> at the same time, an image which is still relatively untouched within
> visual art. The taboos around 'playing' with Jewish imagery (compared
> for example with the appropriation of Christian imagery) are closely
> connected to the Holocaust and to the history of anti-semitism.
> However, this means that a vast area of this culture remains relatively
> unchallenged by visual art...[25]

The de-territorialisation and mobilisation of sexual, geographic and religious zones are all apparent in the video through the sites of intervention
that the adult Marcus enacts in non-koshar places and public environments
where one would not expect an Orthodox Jewish man to be found. Marcus
performs in gay clubs, visits the streets of London's Soho, a non-Orthodox
beach in Tel Aviv and drinks non-koshar coffee in a Turkish men's café in
Berlin; in each of these districts, Marcus tests the boundaries and limits: of
sexuality, of multiculturalism and street-fashion in Soho, of Jewish ethnicity
in Tel Aviv, and of masculinity and difference in Berlin. The implications of
Marcus's performance in terms of the destabilisation of gender identifica-
tions for both the artist and the viewer can most obviously be mapped
against Judith Butler's groundbreaking critique, *Gender Trouble: Feminism
and the Subversion of Identity*, first published in 1990, in which Butler posed
a series of questions designed to disrupt accepted categories of gender
identity and sexuality and which has had far-reaching implications for subsequent Western epistemes of identity, subjectivity and desire. However,
there are also other significant analyses of gender performance through
which 'Marcus Fisher' can usefully be read and it is these that I should like
to draw on here. Irit Rogoff's essay on diaspora and gender, 'Daughters of
Sunshine' and Francette Pacteau's analysis of androgynous representation,
'The Impossible Referent', both offer suggestive frameworks for interpretation. Pacteau's analysis is useful because of its sustained investigation of the
pre-Oedipal possibilities of androgyny and the pressures on the visible that
androgynous representation provokes, whilst Rogoff's piece grounds my
analysis of Ashery's work within the discursive formations of modern and
historical Jewish feminine identity construction that is also integral to
Ashery's wider cultural project.[26] For Rogoff, 'femininity in Israel is experiencing a crisis not just of identity but also one of context' which she
explores in terms of an analysis of some aspects of Israeli visual culture and

its implications for the feminine.[27] One of the most poignant features of her piece is her quotation from a poem by Esther Fuchs about Fuchs' abortive attempt at suicide; she comments:

> ...Fuchs' poem speaks of the despair of attempting to actually possess an identity of one's own in a society in which collective trauma has served to simultaneously infantilize and bind one to duty ... the concerns of women born long after the war had ended and the state of Israel had been founded, could not be viewed as anything but self-indulgent desires aimed at a form of bourgeois, individual gratification...[28]

Collective struggle, guilt and redemption through the formation of the modern Zionist nation state built on a mythical belief in the ideologies of progressive heroism adapted from the modern West, determined how ideologies of femininity in modern Israel were constructed at the level of dominant visual discourse: as both militant and exotic, pioneers and consumers, different from the West yet in mimicry of the same. Yet as Rogoff also points out, the new culture of belonging central to the successful formation of the modern state of Israel could not be maintained without 'a consciousness of not belonging against which it exists in a permanent state of defiance and self-definition'.[29] In her article, 'Oreet Ashery: Transgressing the Sacred', Rachel Garfield has powerfully drawn out the implications of the conflict of 'not belonging' when she notes that it is precisely by becoming an Orthodox man that Ashery makes visible the conflict inherent in the Zionist project's attempt to 'normalise' the Jew through the construction of a nation state. She comments that:

> ...through becoming an orthodox man, Oreet Ashery takes herself into a simpler past when the Jew was outsider untainted by the burden of choices beholden to the insider. But this turning away is never a simple solution and the conflict continues. For while the Israeli may yearn nostalgically for the Diaspora, s/he, as an Israeli [woman] cannot be at home there ... 'Oreet' is invisible as an 'other' but as an orthodox Jewish man, she is not only visible but also unusual. Oreet Ashery [becomes] a public Jew, defiantly not assimilating and defiantly shocking...[30]

By becoming a public Jew though, she also throws into question the gender identification of what it means to be Jewish.[31] If to be Jewish within a dominant historical formation of cultural memory is to be male, then what place is there for Ashery, in either a modern or historical locus – a question that poignantly underpins her 2002 video-work, *Why do you think I left?* in which she returns to Israel from England to put this question to each member of her family who answer her in turn whilst at the same time revealing a lot about their own positions, biographies and self-constructions as contemporary Jewish subjects living with daily political and personal conflicts in Israel.

Locating a place for the feminine, then, within a Symbolic order of language and representation that is further complicated through signifiers of ethnicity and difference via recourse to a performance of androgyny in *Marcus Fisher's Wake* becomes a significant, though not unproblematic psychical manoeuvre in Ashery's project. In Francette Pacteau's analysis of androgynous representation, 'the androgynous "position" represents a denial, or a transgression, of the rigid gender divide, and as such implies a threat to our given identity and to the system of social roles that define us'.[32] It is the boundaries of this threat that Ashery probes in her performance of Marcus Fisher. However, as Pacteau also comments:

> . . . The androgynous fantasy is a narcissistic 'caress' in which the subject annihilates itself. In this double movement of pleasure and destruction, the fantasy allies itself with the 'death drive', that regressive tendency towards the restoration of a less differentiated, less organised, ultimately inorganic state . . .[33]

In constructing a mobile figure of Marcus Fisher through allusion to his death in *Marcus Fisher's Wake*, it could be argued that Ashery is performing the double act of representation and annihilation central to this psychoanalytic understanding of narcissism in a performance that challenges the taboos of semitic representation in order to materialise her own corporeal subjectivity. The ambivalence of this manoeuvre is apparent in the role that death has to play in the construction of modern Jewish identity. If, after the horrors of the Holocaust diasporic Jewishness became most often 'a cipher for death, loss and victimisation',[34] whose redress was sought in the formation of the modern state of Israel, creating and killing the cipher of the diasporic Jew is a radical, shocking yet enabling move for Ashery – a post-modern Israeli Jewish woman. It is the unspoken annihilation of the narcissistic impulse that haunts the performative explorations of corporeal subjectivity in this work. As Janet Hand has convincingly explained via her reading of Janine Antoni's *Lick and Lather*, the self-shattering implied by narcissism can also be figured as a paradoxical 'structuring' of subjectivity; the desire to disappear implied in the fantasy of disguise for Ashery can perhaps be read through Hand's theorisation as an alternative to 'the omnipotent identity fantasies of self-presence' that have dominated the logic of the Symbolic for too long.[35]

As I hope to have at least touched upon here, if not yet done full justice to, the practices of Chandra, Boyce, Bhimji and Ashery discussed in this essay clearly operate extremely rich and diverse interrogations of the transnational spaces left open to feminine diasporic subjects working in postcolonial Britain today.[36] Although the aesthetic outcomes of their individual practices all differ markedly from one another and although I certainly do not intend to 'lump' all of these artists together under a single and not unproblematic label of 'diasporic art', the concept of 'biography and space' from which this volume originates has afforded me the opportunity to explore and tease out points of intersection as well as divergence between their practices as embodied female subjects inhabiting and negotiating the spaces of their own and their ancestors' lives within the condition of global post-colonial post-modernity in which histories of the present at both macro and micro level can only ever be understood as legacies of the past for the future.

Acknowledgements

I should like to thank the two co-editors of this publication for their patience and the artists Mohini Chandra, Oreet Ashery and Zarina Bhimji for their generosity, warmth and friendship; thank you.

Notes

1 Georgia O'Keefe (1976) cited in Eldrege, Charles (ed.) (1993) *Georgia O'Keefe: American and Modern*, New Haven and London: Yale University Press, p. 17; my emphasis.

2 For further information regarding some of the histories of the essentialising conventions of 'black' art in Britain see Beauchamp-Byrd, 'London Bridge: late twentieth century British art and the routes of "national culture"', in *Transforming the Crown: African, Asian and Caribbean Artists in Britain 1966–1996* (1997 exhibition catalogue), New York: Franklin H. Williams Caribbean Cultural Centre/African Diaspora Institute, p. 25.

3 Boyce in Manthia Diawara (1992) 'The art of identity', *Transition*, no. 55, Oxford: Oxford University Press, pp. 194–195.

4 Gayatri Chakravorty Spivak (1986) 'Questions of multiculturalism', in Harasym, Sarah (ed.) (1990) *The Postcolonial Critic: Interviews, Strategies, Dialogues*, London and New York: Routledge, p. 59.

5 Elizabeth Edwards, 'Mohini Chandra: travels in a new world', in Ghosh and Lamba (eds) (2002) *Beyond Frontiers: Contemporary British Art by Artists of South Asian Descent*, London: Saffron Press, p. 71.

6 Edwards in Ghosh and Lamba (eds) 2002, op. cit. p. 73.

7 Chandra, 'Cannibals and coolies: notions of fixity, colonial vision and identity in contemporary art practice', in Merali, Shaheen and Mulvey, J. (1995) *Radical Postures; Art, New Media and Race*, London: University of Westminster/Panchyat, p. 32.

8 Ibid., p. 27.

9 Gayatri Chakravorty Spivak (1986) 'Questions of multiculturalism', in Harasym, Sarah (ed.) (1990), op. cit. p. 60.

10 I would also suggest that the formal properties of montage are an ideal medium for highlighting the juxtapositions implied by the notion of the 'paravisual' as I conceptualise it here: the idea of adding something on top of or next to something else in order to transform the meanings of both. See Serres (1982), cited in Kear, Adrian (2001) 'Parasites', *Parallax*, vol. 7, no. 2, p. 38.

11 Genette (1997), p. xvii cited in Stewart, Janet (2000) *Fashioning Vienna: Adolf Loos Cultural Criticism,* London and New York: Routledge, p. 26.

12 Heidegger cited in Bhabha (1994) *The Location of Culture,* London and New York: Routledge, pp. 1–5.

13 Zarina Bhimji (1992) exhibition 'I Will Always Be Here', Birmingham, Ikon Gallery, 4 April–9 May 1992. A full transcript of the interview can be found on the artist's file at the African and Asian Visual Artists Archive (AAVAA), University of East London.

14 For a more sustained analysis and deconstruction of the visual role of the postcard in the construction of consumable urban identities, see Miles (2000) *The Uses of Decoration,* Chichester: Wiley and Sons, chapter 1, pp. 9–35.

15 King (ed.) (1999) *Views of Difference, Different View of Art,* New Haven and London: Yale University Press with the Open University, p. 260.

16 Arts Council Collection; charcoal, pastel and watercolour on paper; four parts, each 152.5×65 cm, in Araeen, R. (ed.) (1989) *The Other Story,* London: Hayward Gallery. The country in the title of the work is listed as Britain but in Beachamp-Byrd, M.J. (1997) essay 'London Bridge: Late Twentieth Century British Art and the Routes of "National Culture"' from *Transforming the Crown,* op. cit. p. 23, the country in the title is listed as 'England'. Here I have chosen to use Araeen's earlier listing.

17 Beachamp-Byrd (1997), op. cit. p. 23.

18 Peggy Phelan (1993) *Unmarked: The Politics of Performance,* London and New York: Routledge, p. 6.

19 In her doctoral thesis Rachel Garfield indicates that although 'there is no evidence that Ashery's character is Hasidic, it would be recognised as Haredi rather than Modern orthodox'.

She also notes that 'Orthodoxy is full of schisms, the most well known of which is Hasidic and Mitnaged. Hasidism began in seventeenth century Poland by the Baal Shem Tov and is an ecstatic form of Judaism. The Mitagned form of Orthodoxy originates in Lithuania and is a scholastic orthodoxy. Both of these forms are collectively known as Haredi, which also includes Sephardi and middle-Eastern orthodoxy' (Rachel Garfield (2004) 'Oreet Ashery' from unpublished doctoral thesis, *Performativity and Identity Politics: Encounters in Recent Jewish Art* (Royal College of Art, London)).

20 Oreet Ashery, 'Marcus Fisher – Background', e-mail correspondence from Ashery in 2003.

21 This interaction with her father also touches on other key aspects of Ashery's work in which the artist's ongoing explorations of identity and subjectivity are imbricated within a wider discourse of the tensions between home and belonging, and between Judaism and Zionism, explored in her 2002 video work *Why do you think I left?* available to view in the library of the Live Art Development Agency (LADA), London.

22 For a more detailed reading of Ashery's debt to Cindy Sherman see Garfield, Rachel (2004) 'Oreet Ashery', op. cit.

23 *Tefillin* are small black boxes containing passages of scripture with black straps attached to them, worn by men over the age of 13 at weekday morning prayer. One box is placed on the head to remind Jews to subject their thoughts to God's service and the other is placed on the left arm, near the heart to remind Jews to subject their hearts' desires to God's service so it is particularly telling that it is the *tefillin* associated with desire that is foregrounded in this particular scene.

For more information about the practice of wearing *tefillin* see Jacobs, Louis (1995) *The Jewish Religion: A Companion*, Oxford: Oxford University Press, p. 537.

24 Rachel Garfield (2004), op. cit.

25 Oreet Ashery, 'Marcus Fisher – Background', e-mail correspondence from Ashery in 2003.

26 See for example Ashery's 2001 twenty-minute video work, 'Why do you think I left?' in which Ashery returns to her parental home in Israel and poses the question to each member of her family individually whilst filming their replies. Ashery moved to England from Israel when she was 19 and has lived in England ever since.

27 Rogoff, 'Daughters of Sunshine', in Bloom, Lisa (ed.) (1997) *With Other Eyes: Looking at Race and Gender in Visual Culture*, Minneapolis: University of Minnesota Press, p. 173.

28 Ibid., p. 165.

29 Ibid., p. 159.

30 Garfield (2002) 'Oreet Ashery: Transgressing the Sacred', *Jewish Quarterly*, Summer 2002, pp. 4–5.

31 Ashery comes from a family in which on her mother's side she is a third generation Israeli woman but on her father's side she identifies herself as being from an indigenous community who have never left Palestine, her father being a fluent Arabic speaker. This latter identification is very important to her sense of identity and is also particularly significant in relation to one of her current research interests in which she sets out to interrogate 'the ways in which visual and performative fictional characters can be used to articulate multiple Oriental Jewish identities and their relations to the Arab world through historical narratives and visual representations'; (email correspondence with the author over the period of a few months from August to December 2006).

32 Francette Pacteau, 'The impossible referent: representations of the androgyne', in Burgin, Donald and Kaplan (eds) (1986) *Formations of Fantasy*, London and New York: Routledge, p. 63.

33 Francette, Pacteau, 'The impossible referent: representations of the androgyne', in Burgin *et al.* (eds) (1986), ibid., p. 82.

34 Meskimmon (2003) *Women Making Art*, London and New York: Routledge, p. 22.

35 Janet Hand, 'Disappearing acts: an impossibility of identity', in Steyn, Juliet (ed.) (1997) *Other than Identity: The Subject, Politics and Art*, Manchester: Manchester University Press, p. 224.

36 As always in my thinking and writing I am using the term 'post-colonial' cautiously since as Sara Suleri has observed it too often becomes a convenient abstraction 'into which all historical specificity may be subsumed', p. 757. Suleri's critique is particularly resonant in its attempts to articulate the epistemological problems attendant on the articulation of a 'black' feminist discourse within Anglo-American academia. See Suleri, Sara, 'Women skin deep: feminism and the postcolonial condition', *Critical Inquiry*, vol. 18, no. 4, pp. 756–769.

9

The art of reconciliation

Autobiography and objectivity in the work of Aldo Rossi

Belgin Turan Özkaya

Architecture is the most abstract of all the visual arts. Despite its fairly obscure mimetic origins and perennial flirtation with classicism and figuration it remains an art that resists easy symbolization and straightforward representation. On the other hand, one of the oldest genres of architectural writing is biography: architecture has long been explained and classified on the basis of individual artists and architects. We are used to perceiving architecture as a product of the lives and works of individuals. But what about autobiography? How can the abstraction of architecture and the self-representation of autobiography come together and what does it mean for architecture to be autobiographical? In this paper I am tackling these questions in relation to the work of the Italian architect Aldo Rossi. Rossi not only built and designed but also painted, drew, wrote and even shot a film, but his persona remains elusive.[1] When he died in 1997 he left behind an abundance of archival material, not only many versions of his published and unpublished theoretical writings, journal articles, editorials, lecture and conference notes, but various personal notes and diaries. The excess in the archive together with Rossi's solipsistic and aphorismic mode of writing that draws inspiration from myriad sources and brings together short pieces of writing without leading to a logical, coherent whole complicates any attempt to come up with a definitive portrayal of him. So, should we take the often stated claims about his 'autobiographical architecture' at face value, which is also associated with an attempt to develop objective architectural principles beyond individual architects' 'whim'? My aim is to inquire into such tensions between the subjective and the objective, between autobiography and architecture, and finally between the creation and the reception of architecture in order to demonstrate how these tensions might have been reconciled in Rossi's work.

Architect's study

The 1992 Aldo Rossi monograph by Electa opens and closes with photographs of Rossi's two Milanese offices. With the aid of Luigi Ghirri's 1988 photographs, first we peek into the former studio on via Maddalena, and at the end we 'leave' the volume after glancing at his later office on via Santa Maria alla Porta in 1992 (Figure 9.1).

The images with the exception of the last one disclose bright interiors painted at different hues of blue; azure, celeste, light blue, the color to which Rossi attributed an almost sensate doleful quality. Inspired by the title of Georges Bataille's book *Le bleu du ciel*, he adapted the phrase *L'azzurro del cielo* (The blue of the sky) as his motto for one of his most significant projects, the cemetery of San Cataldo in Modena, where the roofs would be covered with blue sheet metal. Throughout his life from the legendary diaries, *i quaderni azzurri* (the blue notebooks) that he kept for more than 20 years in the same simple blue notebooks, to the bedroom walls of his lakefront residence outside Milan, the color blue, with all its melancholic associations, remained his favorite color.[2] Nevertheless, in the offices, the atmosphere is cheerful and the blue paint seems to be colluding with the joyful environment, animated by sundry models, drawings,

Figure 9.1 The former studio of the architect in 1988 (photograph by Luigi Ghirri, Collection Centre Canadien d'Architecture/Canadian Centre for Architecture, Montréal).

paintings and all those objects, odds and ends that Rossi collected and cherished. By bearing in mind that they are not casual snapshots but photographs taken by an acclaimed artist, by Luigi Ghirri, a reminder to their 'constructed-ness,' it is still possible to see these images as presenting us bits and pieces of the architect's life: we get an idea about the favorite models preferred over others, the Segrate monument, the San Rocco housing in Monza or the Scandicci municipality; paintings and drawings put on display in the office, those of the cemetery of San Cataldo or Monte Amiata Housing in Gallaratese with other favorite images, that of the Kaaba alongside his collage 'Interno Veneziano' and a model of the Milanese Duomo; the favorite knick-knacks, the busts of Shakespeare and Buddha, some books, a radio, an ashtray, working drawings hung here and there.[3]

The last image of the book shows a window that looks on to the seventeenth-century church of Santa Maria alla Porta across the street from Rossi's last office. In a composition that emulates one point perspective, our gaze by gliding over the grand table positioned in the middle of the darkened reception room passes through the gigantic vertical window and stops at the baroque façade of Santa Maria alla Porta, which Rossi himself often photographed.[4] The image appears to be the enactment of a trope that Rossi wrote about: 'the window.' He writes:

> In architecture every window is the window both of the artist and of anybody at all, the window children write about in their letters: 'Tell me what you see from your window.'... Moreover, the window, like the coffin, presents an incredible history. Of course, from the point of view of construction, the window and the coffin resemble one another; and the window and coffin, like palace, like everything else, anticipate events which have already happened, somewhere, here or some other place.[5]

The difference is blurred, Rossi's window becomes our window; we 'inhabit' a place that he often occupied to look out, take pictures and ponder before 'leaving' the book by looking out from his window. The images of the office cause a shift in our status as 'readers,' who are supposed to be outside the 'picture' – we are invited to take place in the 'picture,' to 'occupy' Rossi's study – but also they signal a shift from the work to the architect. All the projects, buildings, paintings, drawings, furniture and designs that constitute the real bulk of the book, i.e., objects architectural or otherwise, get encircled by scenes alluding to the life of the architect. The office images operate as the signature of the architect. They sign and seal the work as his.

Biography, autobiography, and other difficulties

Similarly as one of the oldest genres of architectural writing, biography, demonstrates, architectural production has long been 'signed and sealed' as the work of individual architects.[6] We are used to perceiving architecture as the individual creation of architects. But, what is the exact relation between the architect and the architectural production? Architecture encompasses diverse conceptual, representational, textual and spatial practices. At the level of the conceptual project attribution to individuals, to the architect and draftsman, might be easier but when it is the built form that is at issue we are facing a collective production by different individuals, from groups of architects and draftsmen to structural, mechanical and electrical engineers, from site engineers to simple onsite workers, even to clients, patrons and financiers. In that case can the final product be easily seen as the exclusive production of the architect?

Even in the cases where the architectural product can be attributed to an individual architect the forcefulness and consistency of biography as an explanatory model for architecture remains debatable. As cultural critics Mieke Bal and Norman Bryson have argued:

> [t]he concept of 'author' brings together a series of related unities that, though assumed as given, are precisely the products and goals of its discursive operations. First is the unity of Work. Second is the unity of Life. Third, out of the myriad of accidents and contingent circumstances, and the plurality of roles and subject positions that an individual occupies, the discourse of authorship constructs a coherent and unitary Subject. Fourth is the doubly reinforced unity that comes from the superimposition of Work upon Life upon Subject in the narrative genre of the life-and-work; for in that genre, everything the Subject experiences or makes will be found to signify his or her subject-hood.[7]

Along those lines architectural authorship too assumes that the work and life of the architect are coherent meaningful totalities and constructs an Architect Subject, which it places in, another 'unity,' the biographical narrative.

What happens when we take this one step further and envisage architecture as directly signifying the subject-hood of the Architect Subject? As autobiographical? When the issue of autobiography is raised in relation to twentieth-century architecture the first name that comes to mind is arguably that of Aldo Rossi. In contradistinction to the majority of twentieth-century architects who did not write much neither on her/his own architecture nor on architecture in general, Rossi produced a considerable amount of writing – in his youth he wrote in different journals from communist publications to architectural journals, prepared essays and dossiers for the journal *Casabella Continuità* from 1955 to 1964 as one of the editors when his mentor Ernesto Rogers was the chief editor, he penned one of the most influential architectural theory books of the late twentieth century, *L'Architettura della Città*, but also and more importantly kept diaries and wrote what he called 'autobiographies,' part of which was published under the title *A Scientific Autobiography* in 1981. Another short manuscript titled *Note Autobiografiche sulla Formazione ecc.* is now at the Getty Research Institute in Los Angeles alongside the first 32 of his diaries, *i quaderni azzurri*.[8] What Rossi does in these autobiographies and diaries, which are actually notes rather than full-fledged texts with a beginning and end, is to record his ruminations on architecture in a non-linear fashion. Rather than explaining his work through more conventional technical and architectural criteria, as for instance Le Corbusier does in his *Oeuvre Complete*, Rossi mostly talks about things, not only buildings, projects, cities but also paintings, books, films, events, anecdotes, objects, utensils, odds and ends that had caught his attention and made him ponder since his childhood, some of which apparently became important during the design process of some of his work. His 'autobiographies' are repetitious fragmentary texts between memoir and meditation which resist closure and made up of notes that are put side by side through free association. I would argue that there is a common structural logic between his architectural work and the way his 'autobiographical' texts are conceived – both are based on the principle of montage, i.e., on putting, related unrelated, fragments side by side.[9] How should we come to terms with these two parallel productions, written and architectural? Should we take the former as an explanatory account of the latter? Or, are they singular but analogous productions not explaining but momentarily 'lighting up' each other? My contention is that while the architect's own writings might fleetingly illuminate his architecture they cannot exhaust the meaning of the architectural object.

It is obvious that as in the case of the opening and closing photographs of the 1992 monograph Rossi's persistent production of 'autobiographical' writings helped in 'signing and sealing' his architecture as 'autobiographical.'[10] Along those lines it was argued by many but also by none other than the influential architectural historian and close friend of Rossi, Manfredo Tafuri, that his architecture is characterized by 'subjective nostalgia.'[11] Tafuri wrote, 'Rossi's *mémoire* was heir to the overwhelming autobiographical trend of the fifties, but it preferred archaic silence to the opulence of [Carlo Emilio] Gadda's rhetorical flourishes.'[12] Yet, particularly his early work is also seen as an attempt to develop objective architectural principles beyond individual architects' 'whim.' Indeed, in the sixties and seventies Rossi was involved in typological and morphological studies of architecture and the city, and throughout his oeuvre types, those relatively objective anonymous architectural forms beyond individual architects' creation, remained an important starting point for his architecture.

These apparently contradictory characterizations of Rossi's architecture both subjective and 'objective' point to the difficulties of conceiving architecture, the most abstract of the visual arts that resist straightforward representation, as the medium of subjective creation or 'autobiographical' expression of the architect. To the tensions between architecture and autobiography between the subjective and the objective the tension between 'creation' and reception should be added. Even if we accept architecture as a medium for subjective expression or 'autobiography,' the meaning of which is shaped by the intentions of the architect, we still have the problem of whether that 'meaning' can be conveyed to the third party, to the inhabitant or the beholder.[13] I would argue that in the case of Rossi what we have is something different: the intentions and 'memories' of the architect and those of the beholder meet midway. Rossi might be subjective in his preferences of some types, the universal 'objective' forms and figures, over others but what his architecture conveys to the beholder is not Rossi's own subject-hood or his memories. Rather, as I will try to show below, those universal, primeval architectural types that he utilizes trigger individual memories for each beholder. In that sense Rossi's architecture reconciles the subjective and the objective, autobiography and architecture.

The familiar and the unfamiliar

It is difficult to overlook the intense visual pleasure that accompanies the uneasiness the Rossian architecture propels. His drawings, often depicting shadowy, frozen views and his architecture which operates as settings for similar scenes resonate with solitude and silence. His 'empty landscapes,' and 'still lives,' often work as *mementi mori* reminding us of the transience of life. On the other hand, despite this melancholy side to his work, Rossi comes at the forefront of twentieth-century architects whose work has been associated with a distinctive pictorial and figurative 'style' and whose work was disseminated via that idiosyncratic image.

What is the appeal of the Rossian imagery? What I am trying to define is of course easier to 'feel' than explain. And, when I ask the above question I am aware that visual appeal, hence visual perception, is as much about the beholder as the perceptual object. Yet, as it had been argued by German literary critic Walter Benjamin in the context of literature and recently brilliantly endorsed by psychoanalytical theorist Kaja Silverman for visual texts, some objects are more encouraging than the others in triggering certain responses and 'it is moreover, not the perceiving subject, but rather the perceptual object which plays the initiating role in this scopic transaction.'[14] The strikingly simple forms and figures of Rossi, the basic beach cabin, the quintessential Italian tower, the rotunda, the cube, the conical smokestack, the lighthouse with all the shades of their potential meanings appear to be visually very evocative (Figures 9.2, 9.3). They seem to strike a chord with each and every addressee provoking personal responses.

The lure of the Rossian imagery can be explained on the basis of two seemingly inimical dynamics that operate in his work. The reception of his images seems to hinge on the evocation of the senses of both familiarity and unfamiliarity.[15] In other words, the images operate via the perpetual oscillation between the familiar and the unfamiliar. The familiarity is due to the

Figure 9.2 Aldo Rossi, Cemetery of San Cataldo, Modena, Italy, 1971–78. (Photograph by author.)

Figure 9.3 Aldo Rossi, Cemetery of San Cataldo, Modena, Italy, 1971–78. (Photograph by author.)

fact that Rossi's primeval, archetypal figures and forms are situated at the point where the realm of collective images, hence collective past, meets personal memory. Rossi's engagement in archetypal forms 'the imitation of [which],' in Quatremère de Quincy's words, which Rossi quotes 'involves nothing that feelings or spirit cannot recognize' is very well known.[16] The term Benjamin coined in relation to rituals is apposite for Rossian images as well: in their latent capacity to trigger real or fictive/implanted recollections in the beholder, they work as 'handles of memory.'[17] As in the case of the taste of *madeleine* that unleashes a host of childhood memories for the narrator of Marcel Proust's *Remembrance of Things Past* Rossian images seem to suggest things which appear to be personal. In *On Some Motifs in Baudelaire*, Walter Benjamin suggests that aura, that quality which differentiates a work of art from other objects – hence the 'aestheticity' of an aesthetic text – is the result of the associations that tend to cluster around the work of art.[18] Likewise, the Rossian imagery can unleash an associative network which may be 'filled in' individually by each person. Among his universal, perennial forms the chance of encountering that object in which 'the past is unmistakably present' for us is quite high.[19] In his very suggestive but otherwise complicated text Benjamin probes two aesthetic categories; *mémoire involontaire* (involuntary memory) suggested by Marcel Proust and *correspondance* (correspondence) by Charles Baudelaire and intimates that *Remembrance of Things Past* and Baudelaire's *Les Fleurs du mal* are actually the sites where these are at work. Benjamin further argues that Proust and

Baudelaire through *mémoire involontaire* and *correspondance* which work like unconscious memory were capable of evoking certain 'memories' not consciously lived by the reader. Kaja Silverman, on the other hand, in her reading of Benjamin, while rejecting Benjamin's equating of *mémoire involontaire* and *correspondance* with unconscious memory, nevertheless agrees with him on the possibility of a work of art's providing an associative network which would set the unconscious and the preconscious of the addressee – the reader or the viewer – to work, first through implanted recollections which would later be replaced by more authentic, indigenous ones.[20] This is, as in Proust's *mémoire involontaire* and Baudelaire's *correspondance*, what the Rossian images, due to the associative network they launch, are capable of doing as well. They are capable of setting in motion a chain of 'remembering' via interactions between fictive and authentic recollections and between the preconscious and the unconscious.[21] Yet, what 'lights up' the Rossian image is not always a past, personal or otherwise, long gone and perhaps nostalgically, and unconsciously, searched. What about the immanent poignancy of these images?

Rossi's interest in the mundane and the ordinary is well known. In his 'art' he employs the typical – the ubiquitous high-rise of modern architecture that alludes to the Lombard tenement house, those indispensable elements of the Italian landscape: the tower and the arcade, the rotunda and the lighthouse. The use of such forms regardless of their functions is his trademark. Thus a hollowed-out urban block can become a depository of bones, and can make part of a cemetery as is the case in the cemetery of San Cataldo (Figure 9.3). In relation to a less known cemetery project he has done in 1989, for the cemetery of Ponte Sesto in Rozzano, Rossi writes:

> A main avenue unites the entrance to the church and along which the crematorium and the columbariums are found. And among them are trees, benches, lamps as *it has to be in the avenues of the city for the living. This is the authentic civil character of the cemetery*, that part of the city where hope has not escaped – in our poet's words – but where it is sublimated into that incomprehensible sentiment that we have towards the dead.[22]
>
> (my emphasis)

The analogy he facilely establishes between the city of the living and the city of the dead, hence an easy shift from one realm to the other, is symptomatic of Rossi's work. Likewise, in *i quaderni azzurri* he talks about a high school he happened to visit during summer intermission.[23] He finds the school, the abandoned classrooms and objects fascinating. He then remembers all those former 'inhabitants' of the building, students who 'somehow at one point have to pass to another state.'[24] The word he uses, 'trapassare,' in Italian has the double meaning of 'to pass beyond' and 'to pass away,' which makes Rossi's musing redolent of things beyond its immediate meaning. The liveliest of all the places for the living, a school, is imagined as a realm belonging to the dead and departed. Such double coding is at work in many other projects as well, one example being the Segrate monument, parts of which can be alternately read as alluding to, among other things, a pitched roof, a hut or a sarcophagus.[25]

How to understand this alternating exposure, concealment of the typical, mundane, and banal with the strange, eerie, and otherworldly? As in his symbolic and literal conversion of the dwelling for the living to the 'shelter' for the dead in the cemetery of San Cataldo, hence his rendering of the house 'un-homely,' the shift from the familiar to the strange and eerie corresponds strikingly with how Sigmund Freud explained the workings of the uncanny feelings in the psyche. In his canonical 1919 text Freud argues that the feeling of 'uncanniness,' *das unheimlichkeit* (which, in German, literally means 'un-homeliness') is related to the repressed fantasies of the childhood.[26] Freud in his argument, in addition to psychological observations, ethnological claims and literary and aesthetic analyses, heavily relies on linguistic scrutiny so as to conflate 'the un-homely' with 'the homely.' He ascribes the invoking of the sense of horror and dread to encountering with something familiar which needs to remain concealed. For us what is important in Freud's scheme is the susceptibility to inversion, to become de-familiarized, he assigns to the familiar. Rossi's work in its 'relays' of evoking the familiar and the un-familiar, simultaneously causing pleasure and distress provides a visual analogue to Freud's scheme.

Now the puzzle is how to account for the visual hence aesthetic pleasure catered by Rossian images despite their 'uncanny' side. Whether one is in the courtyard of the cemetery of San Cataldo or that of the school of Fagnano Olona, or just in front of a drawing such as *Catedrali Americane II* there is a captivating quality which engulfs the beholder and lures him or her into melancholic contemplation. The answer may emerge again from Freud's text and its not readily manifest implications that link 'the uncanny' to the 'the aesthetic.' As argued by French philosopher Sarah Kofman in her critical reading of Freud, between the lines Freud hints at the inseparability of uncanny feelings and 'positive' aesthetic feelings on the basis of aesthetic pleasure's connection to the return of repressed infantile fantasies. Kofman suggests that according to Freud 'All works of art would provoke feelings of uncanniness if artists did not use the seductive artifice of beauty which diverts the ego's attention and prevent it from guarding against the return of repressed fantasies.'[27] In other words the effects of 'uncanniness' and mere 'aestheticity' (hence the emergence of negative or positive feelings) depend on the level of disguise the work of art has in relation to its repressed (hence uncanny) content. Moreover, Kofman argues that, for Freud, '[the] "negative feeling," itself, is also, conversely, a source of pleasure: it is a pleasure from beyond the pleasure principle.'[28] She writes, 'The uncanny can also give rise to a masochistic type of pleasure, a satisfaction (jouissance) arising from the very source of anxiety itself; a pleasure which also leads back to the death instinct since it is linked to return and repetition.'[29] Thus, by extension, Kofman points out, for Freud, '[there] is no aesthetic feeling in which the death instinct is not implicated ... death is always already at work in the "positive," that Eros and the death instinct are indissociable.'[30]

Rossi's work by providing 'handles of memory' for our own 'memories,' becomes a source of pleasure and distress for us. As in his window which momentarily becomes our window at the end of the 1992 monograph, with the aid of Rossi's architecture we are invited to 'occupy' a place that initially belonged to him. We go and 'look out from his window.' Yet, what we see is all about us rather than Rossi.

Notes

1 A different and longer version of this paper titled 'Memory and Loss in the Architecture of Aldo Rossi' was delivered as part of the Visiting Scholars Seminar series at the Canadian Centre for Architecture in Montreal in December 2000. Translations from the Italian unless otherwise noted are mine.

2 Karen Stein, 'Portrait: Aldo Rossi, Italy's leading architect at his lakefront retreat,' in *Architectural Digest*, 51:1, January 1994, 50. We learn from Stein that the master bedroom is painted *il celeste della Madonna* blue, 'a signature color for Rossi, who also used it for his Milan office.'

3 Even in the case of casual snapshots photograph is always a mediated depiction of its object.

4 Francesco Dal Co, ed., *Aldo Rossi: I Quaderni Azzurri 1968–1992*, no. 45, facsimile, Electa/The Getty Research Institute, Milan, 1999.

5 Aldo Rossi, *A Scientific Autobiography*, Cambridge and London, 1981, 45.

6 For a critical and innovative engagement with biography as a resilient genre of architectural historiography see Dana Arnold, *Reading Architectural History*, London and New York, 2002, 35–81.

7 Mieke Bal and Norman Bryson, 'Semi-otics and art history: a discussion of context and senders', in *The Art Bulletin*, 73: 2, June 1991.

8 *Note Autobiografiche sulla formazione ecc.* December 1971, Aldo Rossi Papers, The Getty Research Institute, Los Angeles.

9 For an explication of montage as a structuring device in Rossi's work see my 'Visuality and Architectural History', in Dana Arnold, Elvan Altan Ergut and Belgin Turan Özkaya, eds, *Rethinking Architectural Historiography*, London, 2006, 183–199.

10 In the Italian context the word 'autobiographical' is used interchangeably with 'subjective.' Rossi also talks about 'autobiography' of his projects in the sense of 'explanation.'

11 Manfredo Tafuri and Francesco Dal Co, *Modern Architecture 2*, New York, 1979.

12 Manfredo Tafuri, *History of Italian Architecture 1944–1985*, Cambridge and London, 1990, 137.

13 Furthermore, as in the case of any creative work the intentions of the 'creator' cannot be constrained to the conscious ones by overlooking unconscious impulses.

14 Kaja Silverman, 'The Language of Things,' essay presented in the Evening Lecture Series, Summer Insti-

tute in Art History and Visual Studies, University of Rochester, July 1999, 2–3. It was later published in *World Spectators*, Stanford, 200, 129. In this section I am relying on Kaja Silverman's argument in *The Threshold of the Visible World*, New York and London, 1996 (particularly on pages 93–105) and Walter Benjamin, 'On some motifs in Baudelaire,' in Hannah Arendt, ed., *Illuminations: Essays and Reflections*, New York, 1968, 155–201.

15 For a different treatment of the familiar and the unfamiliar in Rossi's work see Jean La Marche, *The Familiar and the Unfamiliar in Twentieth-Century Architecture*, Urbana and Chicago, 57–78.

16 Quatremère de Quincy cited by Aldo Rossi, *The Architecture of the City*, 40.

17 Benjamin, 'On some motifs in Baudelaire,' 159.

18 Benjamin, 'On some motifs in Baudelaire,' 186.

19 Benjamin, 'On some motifs in Baudelaire,' 186.

20 Silverman, *The Threshold of the Visible World*, 100–101.

21 For a slightly different argument on the reception of Rossi's work see my 'Visuality and Architectural History,' particularly the section, 'The affective space of Aldo Rossi.'

22 Alberto Ferlenga, *Aldo Rossi: Architetture 1988–1992*, Milan, 1992, 190.

23 *Aldo Rossi: I Quaderni Azzurri 1968–1992*, no. 23.

24 *Aldo Rossi: I Quaderni Azzurri 1968–1992*, no. 23.

25 For an article that assesses the myriad sources of Rossi's work particularly in relation to the cemetery of San Cataldo see Eugene J. Johnson, 'What remains of man – Aldo Rossi's Modena Cemetery', in *Journal of the Society of Architectural Historians*, 41:1, March 1982.

26 Sigmund Freud, '*The "Uncanny"*,' in James Strachey, ed., *The Standard Edition of the Complete Psychological Works of Sigmund Freud*, vol. XVII, London, 1986, 219–256. For a text that critically engages with that of Freud see Sarah Kofman, *Freud and Fiction*, Cambridge, 1991, 121–162. For a work that mobilizes the concept in relation to architecture and the city see Anthony Vidler, *The Architectural Uncanny: Essays in the Modern Unhomely*, Cambridge, 1992.

27 Kofman, *Freud and Fiction*, 123.

28 Kofman, *Freud and Fiction*, 123.

29 Kofman, *Freud and Fiction*, 123. The text '*The "Uncanny"*,' published in 1919, a year before 'Beyond the Pleasure Principle,' a text even more controversial than the former, was produced in the context of World War I, when Freud was trying to come to grips with war, death and the death instinct. Accordingly, the implications of both texts (particularly the place of the death instinct in the overall psychoanalysis) are still far from being definitively settled. Accordingly Kofman in her deconstructive reading of '*The "Uncanny"*' eventually hails the text as not being convincing enough due to its internal inconsistencies, which, I would argue, should not be a pretext to overlook its interesting insights.

30 Kofman, *Freud and Fiction*, 123.

10

Disinter/est

Digging up our childhood. Authenticity, ambiguity and failure in the auto/biography of the infant self

Joanna Sofaer and Joshua Sofaer

This essay arises from the Disinter/est project, a collaboration between sister and brother, archaeologist Joanna Sofaer and artist Joshua Sofaer. The project had its genesis in a common interest in cultural models for the communication of specific subjectivities but we came to it with two different, albeit intersecting imperatives, each related to our own location within discipline-specific areas of enquiry. For Joanna this meant the exploration of the role of material culture in the construction of identity and an opportunity to explore the boundaries of archaeological method. For Joshua, the stake was in thinking through the possibilities of a developed methodological approach – in this case archaeology – as a way of expanding the possibilities of art and writing and as an alternative method for understanding the construction and deconstruction of subjectivity.

Collective auto/biography was the point of departure for our joint practice: specifically, the period of our infancy. Infancy is a mysterious era that is both of ourselves and of other. A focus on infancy challenges traditional models of autobiography based on an experiential narrative; the recounting of incidents, the recalling of memories. Like most people, neither of us have any memories of our earliest childhood from which to attempt such introspection. Even if we claimed to have remembered our own births, as some people do, the quality of those memories and recalled fragments are open to question.[1] Infancy therefore lends itself to a rethinking of the relationship between self and autobiography. In tracing infancy we necessarily have to negotiate an understanding that runs counter to an established tradition. As a time about which we remember nothing, it permits an exploration of the self as other; a biography of the self.

Before memory: auto/biography and infancy

Traditionally, infancy has received little attention in auto/biographical narratives. This contrasts with the perceived importance of infancy in much of the educational, psychological and sociological literature where the infant years are seen as a critical period in human development.[2]

In her sociological study of the genres of auto/biography, Mary Evans remarks on the refusal of many auto/biographers to deal with the importance of childhood:

> ...childhood is given almost no discussion and, more significantly, allowed no influence on adult personality or behaviour. The refusal of childhood (and with it, of course, the implicit refusal of the most radical development in understanding in the twentieth century which is psychoanalysis) is so striking a feature of auto/biography that it should – but seldom does – invite comment. Indeed, comment is scarcely sufficient to denote the misrepresentation that this facet of conventional auto/biography amounts to; it might be more appropriate to suggest that in this general refusal lies not just a problematic literary convention but a dominant cultural fault.[3]

For Evans, the way to insert infancy into auto/biography lies in the possibilities provided by psychoanalysis which, she suggests, offers a means of accessing the missing years. The problem with such a solution is, however, that psychoanalysis positions the adult's infant life through a set of standardized negotiations often predicated on loss (in particular loss of infant memories) and recovery on behalf of the now adult child.[4] This has resulted in a generic conception of the 'autobiography' of early childhood that closes down, rather than expands, potential meaning. Early childhood only has meaning in particular adult terms rather than having meaning in itself. Furthermore, it places self-knowledge at the heart of authenticity. In other words, unless I tell you about myself then there is no other way of accessing my past. Thus from a psychoanalytic perspective, an infant autobiography is possible, if retrospective, but a biography is not. The issue at stake: who has access to the world of the infant?

A contrasting approach is embedded within Marcel Proust's discussion of infancy in *In Search of Lost Time* where he discusses this question of access. Proust refers to infancy as follows:

> Those years of my earliest childhood are no longer a part of myself; they are external to me; I can learn nothing of them save – as we learn things that happened before we were born – from the accounts given by other people.[5]

For Proust, the documentation of infancy becomes a process of historical reconstruction that follows a traditional historical methodology which relies on the written and oral accounts given by other people. In this case one is bound to hand the self over to the interpretation of others completely. An exploration of infancy seems to place the subject outside the 'auto' of autobiography. In other words, I cannot have direct access to myself. Instead my history can only be constructed by others. Biography is possible; autobiography is not.

Georges Perec takes a slightly different stance on the autobiographical dilemma, although it is one that still lies within the historical genre. In *Je suis né*, he comments on the difficulty of autobiographically describing infancy. 'To begin one's story with a date of birth is a beginning that invites a whole history but continuing the story after making this opening statement is a near impossibility'.[6]

Perec is interested in how childhood is 'given back' to the author[7]; the missing memory invites fictionalization. The primacy attached to memory in the biographical genre is predicated on the notion of proximity and access to the subject. For Perec, memories can be relayed through the detailed investigation of one's own past (in his case through descriptions of photographs).[8] Perec thus takes on a process of historical research but autobiography still eludes the author; false neutrality or 'fictive memory' emerge.[9] For Perec, what matters is not so much what actually happened but what we believe to have happened.

A possible alternative to both psychoanalytical and historical methods comes from the work of Rom Harré.[10] In a discussion of the temporality of the body, Harré suggests that there are three interconnected strands to the life course: the biological life-span, the social life-span and the personal life-span. Each has its own beginning and end that need not overlap with those of other strands. The biological life-span begins at conception and ends at death. Harré argues that although these two points are absolutes in the human time frame, they are external to a sense of self and therefore stand outside the social and personal.[11] Social identity may begin before bodily identity takes shape (as in the parental definition of a child to come), and may persist after death. The social life-span is thus longer than the biological. The personal life-span, on the other hand, fits within the time span of the physical body. Reflective of consciousness, it begins in late infancy and often ends in old age in senility, before the death of the body. Conception and death lie outside the period of self-knowledge.

Harré's approach fragments the traditional view of biography as being a single linear trajectory with a single origin point and a single end point, and replaces it with three parallel strands, each of which, while interconnected, may be described independently and to which different forms and degrees of access may be obtained. For a given person there are, therefore, not just multiple interpretations of a single set of unique narrative events but rather three distinct narrative strands, each of which is subject to interpretation and reinterpretation. For Harré, conciousness or self-knowledge constitute the personal. Without these there is no auto/biography. The implication of

Harré's approach is that traditional autobiographical accounts predicated on personal recollections need not even attempt to engage with infancy. Such an understanding of the period of infancy necessarily means that any attempt to access it through the autobiographical genre is inevitably doomed to failure. Instead, infancy belongs to the biological and social realms.

For Harré, human life is a discontinuity, rather than a continuity, that recognizes the disjunction between our current selves and our infant selves. Yet rather than this being a point of closure, this approach opens up a series of new areas for investigation. It places infancy within the realm of the social and thus pushes us to consider infancy not as something personal but as something intersubjective. Infancy is thus a social identity rather than the articulation of subjectivity. Harré's insights invite us to consider a method for accessing the past that relies on the communication of shared meanings and the relational construction of identities rather than on the expression of the subjectivities 'I' or 'you' as single discrete individuals.

The contrasting ways of thinking about auto/biography described by Evans, Proust, Perec and Harré create a series of tensions between knowing and not-knowing, fact and fantasy, the subjective and the intersubjective. Above all, they raise questions about how we should access infancy or, indeed, whether it can be accessed at all. The failure of traditional auto/biographical models to account for early childhood arises from a gap between the theoretical identification of the infant years as a formative period that is deemed so fundamental to human development that it sets the tone for what comes after, and the impossibility of articulating that experience in adult memory or hindsight. How can we ever hope to bridge that gap?

The Disinter/est project set out to explore alternative ways of accessing infancy. In the spirit of experimentation, we wondered what would happen if we took a developed methodological approach to auto/biography that did not rely upon recollections. What would happen if we took an archaeological approach to the investigation of our own infant pasts? What possibilities and tensions would it provoke? How would these relate to the approaches of Evans, Proust, Perec and Harré? In this sense the Disinter/est project was not about establishing the 'truth' of our infant existence, but rather about exploring the potentials and problems of focusing on the materiality of our infancy and the conditions of knowledge production.[12]

Archaeology and auto/biography

An archaeological approach differs from that of history in that its focus on material culture allows it to access deep time or prehistory from which there are no written records or oral testimonies.[13] In effect, archaeology studies what is no longer remembered. As a method by which to explore infancy –

a time about which we remember nothing – it therefore appears particularly apt. Archaeology offers the possibility for a literal prehistory of the self. Since we are no longer infants, it is an investigation of the self as other where autobiography turns into biography; a metaphor for archaeology as a whole, since the exploration of the relationship between 'us' and 'them' sits at the heart of the discipline.[14]

Emphasis on the material allows a methodological reclamation of the 'auto' or self since the study of the subject is not predicated on the accounts of third parties or on the indexical qualities of the photographic image; the photograph promises much yet it acts as proof rather than as experience.[15] The study of material culture provides the possibility to directly examine our infant selves without the filter of other people's comments, positioning the infant self as other.

Material culture provides the means by which social relations are visualized, for it is through materiality that we articulate meaning and, as such, it is the frame through which people communicate identities. Without material expression social relations have little substantive reality, as there is nothing through which these relations can be mediated.[16] Material culture thus mediates between people and it is the culturally specific established meanings of material culture that archaeologists aim to explore and recognize.

Since material culture acts as a way of expressing shared meanings, what became critical to our choice of archaeology as a method for studying infancy is that an archaeological approach focuses not on the personal but on the social; despite recent interest in individuals in archaeology the discipline finds great difficulty in accessing the individual in the past. This immediately produces a significant reconfiguration of auto/biography since the use of archaeology as a model meant that we were not searching for self but rather using elements of the life course that might as well have been anyone, not necessarily us, to think about wider issues. The choice of archaeology thus necessarily rejects the psychoanalytical approach of Evans as the personal become less critical to auto/biographical description and places our model closer to that of Harré.

The choice of archaeology as a method for auto/biography also has metaphorical significance, accentuating the underlying drive of discovery, rescue, restoration and interpretation.[17] Archaeology has also often been used as an effective metaphor for deconstruction and revelation. Thus in Michel Foucault's *Archaeology of Knowledge* we dig only to find that in doing so we disrupt pre-given categories like 'development' and 'tradition' with no single origin point.[18]

Disinter/est: digging up our childhood

The specific spaces of our joint childhoods were the loci for the intersection of our joint practice and investigation: the common spaces that linked our auto/biographies as infant sister and brother. In summer 2000 we met in Cambridge, England to explore the city, the places of our early childhood; the places we were before we can remember.

Space 1: the city of Cambridge

The first spatial location that we investigated was the city of Cambridge itself. The initial stage in investigating any archaeological site is to carry out prospection and recording to see where to start digging. We followed standard archaeological practice and went to the aerial archive (Figure 10.1).

Whereas the archaeologist looks at the aerial image to prospect and record sites, what became interesting to Joshua about this aerial photograph (originally taken to record the Roman road and the expansion of Addenbrooke's Hospital) were the implications of the particular time that it was taken. This aerial photograph was taken on 20 October 1971 at about midday. As the photographer pressed the cable release, Joanna Sofaer, a 14-month-old infant, was probably playing with her toys having just watched

Figure 10.1 Aerial evidence. The arrow indicates the house owned by the Sofaer family on the outskirts of Cambridge.

the 11 am screening of Playschool's *Pets' Day* on BBC2. Forty weeks on, her younger brother Joshua was born.

This photograph acts as a quasi-record of Joshua's conception, which must have taken place, probably in this house, within a week of this photograph being taken. This image is the first in Joshua's bio-chronology. It marks the start of the biological life course. The biological life course is, however, as Harré puts it, 'relative to the main acts of the drama of life as it is lived, merely "noises off"'.[19] While the photograph marks a biological origin point, it says very little about the social or the subjective.

Yet on seeing this photograph, Joshua admitted the need to satisfy a desire to find an origin point, albeit an imagined belonging, since he has no affinity or experiential connection that he can recall with the location marked on the image.

As Perec puts it:

> I would like there to exist places that are stable, unmoving, intangible, untouched and almost untouchable, unchanging, deep-rooted; places that might be points of reference, of departure, of origin ... such places don't exist, and it's because they don't exist that space becomes a question, ceases to be self-evident, ceases to be incorporated, ceases to be appropriated. Space is a doubt: I have constantly to mark it, to designate it.[20]

The aerial photograph thus points to a psychological need but does not offer a satisfying answer to the question 'where do I come from?' Instead of offering meaning to the notion of origin, the aerial photograph highlights the tension between a need to find a single origin point (the place to which we belong), the contemporary reality of dislocation, and the fragmentation of the life course as highlighted by Harré; if the life course has three separate strands then there can be no single origin point so it is fruitless to search for it. Here, as throughout our 'excavations', archaeology had not offered an answer but had rather provoked a tension between material evidence and the auto/biographical. We had, in Perec's words, 'marked' and 'designated' the space but it had failed to speak to us of our infancy. We had uncovered a psychological need but failed to provide a psychological answer.

Space 2: the Sofaer family house

The second space that we investigated was the Sofaer family house. We went to the house that we had lived in and were guests of the current owners. Again, we followed traditional archaeological methods, recording and documenting objects and space (Figure 10.2).

But when we looked through the material remains of our time in Cambridge, without informants, we found it difficult to reconstruct who used particular objects or spaces. At this point in the research process we were

Figure 10.2 Surveying the Sofaer family house.

tempted to engage with historical method using other forms of evidence, in particular oral histories and photographic documentation, in order to try to make sense of the material archaeological findings that otherwise seemed to say very little about the personal or specific subjectivities. In going down this road, however, as with Proust's discussion of infancy, we would only find the perceptions, experiences and memories of others rather than of self; the photograph does not bring us back the sensation of being in Cambridge; we have no memory of those experiences (Figure 10.3).

> The photograph does not call up the past (nothing Proustian in a photograph). The effect it produces upon me is not to restore what has been abolished (by time, by distance) but to attest that what I see has indeed existed.[21]

The photograph, then, highlights a point of fact. The Proustian effect, of which Barthes considers there to be 'nothing' in the photograph, is that of involuntary memory. Unlike voluntary memory where the past exists within the present, involuntary memory does not recall the past in the present. Rather, as with the tea-soaked madeleine which Proust's narrator brings to his lips where the taste of the madeleine *is* Combray, the past is inseparable from the present. The photographs of our infant selves deny both voluntary and involuntary access to past memories. It is outside conscious memory, it eludes it.[22]

How then should we proceed in understanding the archaeology of the photograph? We faced a dilemma. Should we now, on the basis of our

Figure 10.3 Joanna and Joshua in the Sofaer family house.

research, imagine ourselves in Cambridge and, like Perec, fictionalize our lives? Should we try to take the photograph at face value? The premise of both of these questions seemed fraught. In the former, our becoming fiction relies on a literary imperative; in the latter we must acknowledge that the specific subjects of our study (ourselves) have changed out of all recognition, to all intents and purposes they no longer exist. The children in the photographs have become adults. Rather than edging closer to the material under study, we were dealing with subjects who lacked any material form in a traditional archaeological sense. The photograph becomes something else – a record of an event that happened, almost as if to someone else.

Christian Metz says of the photographic subject: 'The person who has been photographed, not the total person, is dead, dead for having been seen.'[23] Roland Barthes augments this argument when he describes the being in the photograph as having 'become Total Image, which is to say, Death in person'.[24] The body in photographic representation that Metz and Barthes configure as dead, is analogous to the archaeological body that is literally dead. Looking at photographs of ourselves during this time in Cambridge is like looking at a dead self and there is a strange vertiginous instability in hailing the subject in the domestic family snapshot as being oneself.[25]

Perhaps the problem here is the elision of body, self and social identity. Harré points out that the separation of the body from the person is 'routinely accomplished' by a series of 'separation practices'.[26] Such processes include anaesthetization for surgery and states of drug-induced disembodiment. While acknowledging that lived social identity and experiences of the body are closely related,[27] by concentrating on the living body and focusing on embodiment, to the exclusion of its counterpoint disembodiment, the fallacy that the biological death of the body means that the individual has ceased to be is reinforced.[28] Such an emphasis, with its conflation of body and self, fails to deal adequately with situations where people have a social presence, yet lack a living body, as for example in the case of ancestors,[29] a corpse in preparation for disposal,[30] or even when a body becomes a focus for archaeological study.

Harré suggests that a person's social identity may begin before their bodily identity has taken shape in the parental definition of the child to come and that it may persist long after the decay of the body.[31] The importance of the social presence of the deceased for the living is familiar to archaeology in, for example, work on the funeral and the display of the corpse as an arena for the mourners.[32] Though such archaeological studies are often presented in terms of the manipulation of the dead in the political strategies of the living, they also offer a clear challenge to the notion that people become social beings only through their living embodiment. Here 'the biologically deceased can retain an influential social presence in the lives of others'.[33] Attitudes to death and commemoration also illustrate how meanings and identity can detach themselves from the living body,[34] while Alfred Gell has argued that the biographical careers of people may be prolonged long after death through memories, traces, leavings and material objects.[35] Such arguments extend the materiality and boundaries of the archaeological body and bring into question the boundaries between life and death.

At this point it may be useful to return to Harré's model of the life course as fragmented. If social identity pre- and post-dates the physical existence of the person, then while we are not materiality the people in the photograph, our social identities as children can remain as parallel threads to our adult identities. We never lose our identities as children. Rather, we simply accumulate strands of parallel identities. The photograph then represents our continuing social presence as infants.[36] In so doing, it reveals tension in conventional notions of biography and autobiography, suggesting that biographies and life courses are multiple, fragmented and overlapping, but it seems to say little regarding our experiences of infancy.

Space 3: the Sofaer family bathroom

The third and smallest of the spaces that we studied was the bathroom in the Sofaer family house which, remarkably, remained the same as when we had lived there (Figures 10.4 and 10.5).

In this family photograph, mother and daughter wash the infant son. Peering into this scene from the perspective of the hidden photographer (presumably the father) three and a half decades after it was taken, our adult gaze again effaces our childhood experience.

Figure 10.4 Joanna and Joshua Sofaer record the family bathroom in 2000. The bathroom fittings are the same as when they lived in the house in 1971/2.

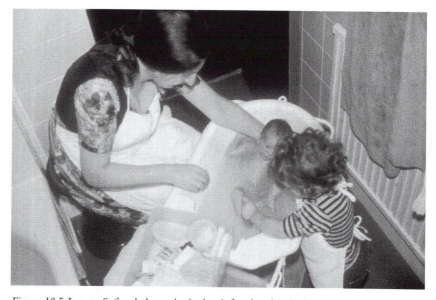

Figure 10.5 Joanna Sofaer helps to bathe her infant brother Joshua.

In an earlier article in *Performance Research* we have discussed how, instead of pursuing the hopeless attempt to understand the image in terms of one's own past experience, the common archaeological device of 'reconstruction' might aid in seeing oneself through the eyes of another. In other words, to achieve self-knowledge through the identification with others by momentarily inhabiting their eyes.[37] To pick up again from Metz and Barthes, if the body in the photograph is dead, then necessarily the eyes which gaze into those of the image must belong to someone else. If this 'someone else' is the transformed but same self then the process becomes one of self-reflection, in which assessments are made as to the value of the self-image in relation to self-identity; the 'look at me then, look at me now'.

We hired an archaeological illustrator to recreate the bathroom scene from the viewpoints of each of the participants within it – seeing oneself through the eyes of another by literally offering up their vision (Figures 10.6, 10.7, 10.8).

Seeing through the eyes of the mother and daughter forces contemplation of the typically gendered domestic filial and sibling relations of 1970's Britain – the social and spatial dynamics of bathing and learning to bath the baby. But this only goes to confirm what we think we know from the photograph itself. The infant's view is blurred as young infants have blurred vision. They experience the world differently – not just in terms of their particular subjectivity but physiologically, from the adult and the older child. The blurred baby perspective highlights the non-individuated worldview of the neonate. It illustrates how, in choosing to deal with the infant child, we immediately call into question the notion of the individual.

Figure 10.6 Mother's view.

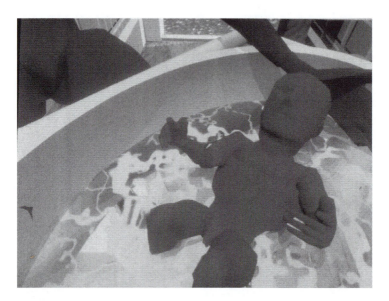

Figure 10.7 Joanna's view.

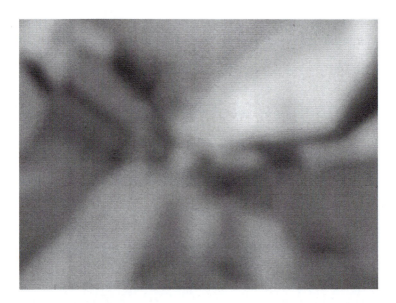

Figure 10.8 Joshua's view.

Infants are individuals in the sense that they are separate unique bodies, but they are dependent on others for their very survival.

Such a non-individuated world-view brings into question conventional notions of the constitution of the person as a single, bounded entity. According to Harré, the personal life course (the autobiographical strand of the life course) begins with self-knowledge or consciousness.[38] Personal being has itself three complementary strands. The first of these is a sense of personal identity through which a person conceives of himself as a singular being with a continuous and unique history. The second is self-consciousness, which involves both knowing what one is experiencing as well as noting that one is experiencing it. This requires the capacity to make some form of self-reference and the ability to identify something, rather than to simply react to it as a stimulus. The third component of personal being is agency. For Harré, to be an agent is to conceive of oneself as being in possession of the power to make decisions and take actions and to be capable of deciding between alternatives.[39] The personal life course only emerges in late infancy when each of these three strands are in place, and it is for this reason that, according to Harré, infancy cannot be considered part of the personal life course.

Yet Harré does concede that early infancy has an interesting position as it offers the possibility of being a period of 'preprepositional knowing'[40] in which one knows what one is experiencing without at that moment being ready to declare it. It is the period in which our knowledge of categories is formed and our ability to act as agents becomes clear. Thus small children will scream and kick, refuse or demand to eat or sleep, and make a mess.[41] The bathing scene questions the non-agency of the infant. Who is central in this scene, who has agency? The infant may not have asked to be bathed but the carers are adjusting themselves to the infant's responses and demands. The bathing image asks us to question the primacy attached to the verbal and to focus on somatic communication.[42] As John O'Neill puts it:

> Our bodies commit us from the first moment of life to the company of those who have grown up and who, in turn, oblige themselves to care for our physical well-being. Of course, the care we receive as children is to bring us to care for ourselves, to free us from the dependency of an immature body and an uneducated mind. Thus the satisfaction of our bodily needs is never intended by those who care for us to yield in us a merely selfish pleasure. Human care initiates us into a *tradition of caring* whereby we learn to give back what we ourselves have received. This is an essential condition of society.[43]

In short, infancy is a period of inter-subjectivity rather than subjectivity. It is the time when the foundations of the personal are laid and personal identity is built upon social relations with others. The notion of the infant as inter-subjective (or perhaps rather an 'inter-subject') raises an interesting question for the auto/biographer. If we want to write about infancy then who should we be writing about? An account of infancy cannot be limited to the infant (to the 'I' or 'auto' of autobiography) but must encompass several different people (the sister, the mother, the father, as well as the son). Such a perspective is echoed in the anthropological work of Tim Ingold[44] and Christina Toren[45] who explore the ways that humans grow in an environment provided by the presence and activities of others. There is a growing corpus of literature showing that social relations affect how a child develops in later life, suggesting that those early experiences become 'biologically embedded'.[46] Our experiences are thus related to those of our parents and carers. We literally embody our history and because our history is created through our relations with others, we also embody the history of our relations with them, thereby tapping into their histories too.[47] As Paul Connerton puts it, the pasts of people are 'sedimented' in their bodies.[48]

Toren makes this point in relation to the spatial disposition of children's bodies in her ethnographic work on child cognition and the learning of hierarchy in Fiji.[49] Here, hierarchical relations are described by people's relative position on an above/below spatial axis within buildings. Children learn routine behaviours that are performed by adults concerned with maintaining the rules of hierarchy and who enjoin youngsters to follow the rules. Children have to accommodate adult concerns by sitting, crawling, walking, clapping or taking food in the prescribed manner. The embodiment of behaviour is key to the process by which these behaviours are understood over time, and to the reproduction of ritual and ritualized behaviour. Toren's concern is with building a theory of mind where cognition is not abstract but part of an autopoietic (self-creating) organism whose development is a material phenomenon. This is a function of a certain kind of biological organization, but one that is mediated by intersubjectivity and an artefact of the way that humans embody the history of relations with others.[50] Traditions and conventions do not exist in any external sense but are bodily phenomena whose practice (or rejection) actively leads to particular kinds of bodies. Process and structure are inseparable.[51] Because materiality is brought about through intersubjectivity, body and mind are linked in a material way.[52] The body is not a pre-existing passive biological container to be filled with culture.[53] Infancy is not then, as Proust suggests, external to us, rather it is embodied within us. It becomes a material part of us – it is just that we cannot remember the process of that embodiment. As O'Neill puts it: '... our own bodies are the permeable ground of all social behaviour; our bodies are the very flesh of society'.[54]

O'Neill goes on to describe how Charles Horton Cooley spoke of this permeable ground when he drew attention to the notion of 'the looking glass self'. What we see in the mirror is what others see. This constitutes 'the incarnate bond between self and society'.[55] What sociologists call the socialization process (the bringing up of an infant or child by those who care for it in accordance with the prevailing standards of behaviour), rests upon the infant's visceral knowledge of what is required of it, conveyed as early as its feeding, cuddling, handling, toileting experiences with its mother. 'From its earliest moments, and long before it can apprentice to the rules of perception, language, and conduct, the child's body resonates with its social experience… What Cooley called the "looking glass sel" is actually part of the complex acquisition of what is now called the *body image*, which involves passing through a crucial *mirror stage* that enables the infant to become aware of its own body and the other person's experience of it as *a body*. Thus from infancy we acquire the ability to mirror our intentions in the facial and linguistic expressions of the mother as the *prima facie* basis for their elaboration according to the mother's sense of their meaning.'[56]

Such an analysis suggests that biographies are as much about the relationship between the subject and others as they are about the subject themselves and reveals an underlying tension in conventional notions of biography. In other words, there is a general perception that biography is about specific subjectivities, yet it is this very notion that causes difficulties with regard to infancy as subjectivities do not exist in isolation but are brought into being through social relations with others. A central problem in conventional notions of auto/biography in relation to the period of infancy is thus that they focus on subjectivities alone, rather than intersubjectivities. While corporeal personhood is bounded in space,[57] social personhood need not be[58] and the elision between body and self need not be complete. Embodying our histories means embodying the histories of others as well, so there can be no singular biography. What becomes important about the bathing scene is not the experience or memory of the bathing but the understanding that the intersubjectivity that it represents is a moment in the development of self. The development of the self through interactions between people and material culture. By literally reflecting the past, the bathing scene reminds us of the 'looking glass self'.

If the inability of the infant to articulate notions of 'I' as an individual and the intersubjectivity of the infant in the bathroom scene contest conventional Enlightenment notions of the individual, then the choreography of this intersubjectivity also provokes consideration of a further tension arising from the relationship between materiality and conventional notions of auto/biography – a tension between the non-discursive and the discursive. The bathroom is the domestic space most involved in body care and the maintenance of body cleanliness is a key aspect of infant care. Here intersubjectivity is mediated through the use of a particular kind of space (in this case the bathroom) and material culture choreographs the use of the space (the centrally positioned baby-bath with the infant and the mother and daughter bending over it). Materiality, rather than words, 'speaks' to the way in which this body care is organized. Furthermore, since the infant cannot speak, the learning about his body and sense of self that the image reminds us of must necessarily be non-discursive. Yet biography and autobiography are essentially discursive genres, raising the question of whether, and how, one can 'translate' between the materiality and auto/biography.

Once again, our 'excavation' of infancy had failed to reveal specific insights into our infant experiences. Rather than solving the problem of how to admit infancy into auto/biography, it raised more questions than it had answered. It had suggested the impossibility of accessing infancy rather providing a route into it. If the study of the infant self is in any case doomed to failure because there is no 'self' at that point and if biographies are not so much about us as about those around us, then the investigation of our infancy was bound to fail. To see a blur, as the infant does, is to acknowledge that this blurring, this not quite in focus, is not only a physiological model for the recreation of infant experience, but is also all one can hope for in the adult attempt to disinter the infant self. Configured as such, the bathroom image of the infant is not physiognomic but rather a site for the contestation of experience. The blurred recreation of infant vision becomes a metaphor for the attempted reclaiming of the experience of that moment by self and other. It is a metaphor for the inevitable failure of the Disinter/est project.

Up against a brick wall: productive failure and the Great Wall of China

The methodological approach employed in the Disinter/est project was embarked upon in the knowledge that it would most probably collapse. Not only were the boundaries of archaeological method challenged, but the methodological application of archaeology failed to yield the kind of experiential accounts sought after in auto/biography. There was also a necessary negotiation of the pleasures and problems of working with family as both co-researcher and research subject.

It was, however, in the moments where archaeology failed – at the point of collapse – that the productive engagement of destabilization allowed for an expansion of potential meanings for the area under study through the exposure of a series of tensions between the material and the auto/biographical. The Disinter/est project was a productive failure. To explore this concept further, we turned to an iconic archaeological monument – the Great Wall of China. Notions of productive failure surrounding the wall set a precedent for understanding what 'productive failure' might be.

Wall 1: the material wall

The Great Wall is a symbol of modern Chinese national unity, integrity and historical continuity. Its scale and physical presence demand explication, yet the notion of a single continuous Great Wall built as a defensive barrier against external aggressors and surviving intact to the present day is a carefully cultivated political storyline.[59] Rather, the Great Wall is a series of walls that were built in different geographical areas in different eras, at different points in time, with differing strategic imperatives. Furthermore, the wall did not achieve those strategic goals. It failed to keep out Genghis Khan and his Mongol Hordes in the thirteenth century, and the Manchu warriors who entered China in 1644 and ended the Ming dynasty, the greatest wall-builders of all.[60] Indeed, the wall has carried predominantly negative connotations on both popular and elite levels for most of Chinese history. The wall has stood for the corruption of the entire traditional moral and political edifice of feudal China and this has lent it persistent emotional power in Chinese folklore and intellectual life.[61] In one of the most famous legends surrounding the wall, Meng Jiang Nü sets out to bring winter clothes to her husband who was seized and forced to build the wall. She discovers that he has died of exhaustion and has been buried beneath it. She weeps profusely until part of the wall collapses to reveal his bones, which she carries home for proper burial. In this story of devotion and anguish, Meng Jiang Nü epitomizes the cruel and unjust sufferings of Chinese women throughout the ages, yet her emotional power is such that she can bring down the wall (representing crumbling political power) with her tears.[62]

It was only in the twentieth century, via a 'detour' of mythologization by the West that the wall took on national-historical significance.[63] As Arthur Waldon puts it:

> The Great Wall of China, it turns out, is a fascinating vision, and one not surprisingly deeply imbedded in learned and popular imaginations, in both China and the west. Yet at the root of the commonly accepted idea of the Wall lie some fundamental misunderstandings. The reality is quite different from the vision, and the whole topic is in need of comprehensive revision.[64]

The shock about the Great Wall of China is, therefore, that there is no Great Wall at all, at least not in the way that it has been conceived and promulgated by both China and the West, 'as having a unified history and a single purpose'.[65] Like other celebrated archaeological monuments such as Stonehenge or the Parthenon, the Great Wall is highly contested.[66] It eludes definitive interpretation and belongs as much to the realms of myth and imagination as it does to historical or political discourses. A series of different discourses oscillate around the wall including history, archaeology, legend, literature and tourism. It is an extraordinary intercultural matrix attracting a plethora of methodologies which it nevertheless escapes. The convergence of these diverse cultural discourses has conspired to create a vision of The Great Wall of China for propagandist purposes. What Waldron identifies are the ways in which legend, literature, folklore, tourism, orientalism and Chinese national identity have, in effect, failed the 'truth' of the wall, just as the wall itself failed its various builders, or as despotic rulers failed the Chinese people.

Even Waldron, as he himself acknowledges, forms part of this cycle of failure. As a historian, he has relied primarily on extensive written documentation for his study but he acknowledges that this methodological approach will also ultimately collapse.

> But the written record has definite limits, and in the Chinese case the kinds of cartographic and archaeological work that have made it possible for students of comparable topics in the west to fill in its omissions and resolve its inconsistencies have not yet been carried out.[67]

The methodological approaches of cartography and archaeology that could provide a closer understanding of the wall have not yet been applied. So for both the wall itself, 'useless militarily even when it was first built' which 'symbolized the failure of Ch'in rule, the way the emperor had failed'[68] and the methodology employed to understand it, failure is encountered time and time again. These failures are not, however, absolute but lead to new directions or understandings. In many cases, the diverse significations and meanings of the Great Wall in historiographic and contemporary discourses seem to evince meaning through an embodiment of productive failure.

Wall 2: the literary wall

The short story *The Great Wall of China* by Franz Kafka was never meant to be published. It was the failure of his executor Max Brod to carry out the instructions of the testament that has resulted in its publication. This failure, Walter Benjamin argues, was always one that was anticipated. 'Kafka presumably had to entrust his posthumous papers to someone who would not want to do his will.'[69] It was a forgone productive failure, contributing to the corpus of Kafka's work.

This 'productive failure' which is external to the diegesis mirrors that within it. *The Great Wall of China* is a series of parables, and parables within parables which deal with the failure of different methodologies – of military strategy, of geography, of national communication – but nevertheless paradoxically produce a desired effect. The narrator identifies himself as a builder of the wall. His account commences with a description of its 'piecemeal construction', a method which went against its aim.

> After all the wall was intended, as was universally proclaimed and known, to be a protection against the peoples of the north. But how can a wall protect if it is not a continuous structure?[70]

This theme of inexpedient method to aim continues on various levels of the narrative. In the case of the wall construction itself, the narrator is forced to come to the 'strange conclusion' that 'the command willed something inexpedient'; which is to say that they embarked purposefully on a project that they knew was bound for failure, that failure was courted and somehow seen as productive. It is not until the end of the story that this failure is understood as 'one of the greatest unifying influences among our people', that the perpetual threat from outside which the piecemeal construction of the wall engenders, with its gaps and geographical inconsistencies, neutralizes alterity within the community. And yet even this productive failure is destabilized by the parable within the parable. There is the account of the Emperor's death-bed message that can never be delivered because the messenger will be met by an endless journey 'through the chambers of the innermost palace; never will he get to the end of them' let alone the city, let alone the country. There will always be another court, another stair, another palace. This fable within the fable ruptures the possibility of a unified community protected by the wall, by articulating alterity from within. In this way, Kafka's metaphor for productive failure itself fails, and it is through this kind of double failure that a literary resolution is attained. Benjamin observes this failure as the binding thread of Kafka's work.

> One is tempted to say: once he was certain of eventual failure, everything worked out for him *en route* as in a dream.[71]

This ultimate failure within the diegesis now refers back to an external productive failure in its political and social intent. As Ewa Ponowska Ziarek has written:

> This failure not only destroys the possibility of grounding the exemplary meaning of the text in the common ways of speaking but also exposes the violence inherent in that kind of grounding. Thus, for Kafka as for Benjamin, it is the ghostly beauty of failure that disrupts the aestheticization of politics and enables a turn towards the politicization of aesthetics.[72]

Wall 3: the performative wall

Another incarnation of failure at the Great Wall of China can be found in the work by artists Marina Abramovic and Ulay who walked from either end to meet each other in the middle. The walk, which commenced in March 1988, had been fraught with problems from the moment of its conception. It took them over eight years and a massive amount of bureaucratic negotiation and compromise before they could embark on the piece, as well as a considerable amount during the walk itself. Restricted by the Chinese authorities from walking through certain areas of national security and others of dangerous terrain, Ulay identified the practical exemplification of the walk as failing its initial aim: 'It had been impossible to carry out the pure concept'.[73] Not only was there no consistent wall to walk, but they had hoped to walk alone, yet they were forced to be accompanied; they had hoped to camp on or beside the wall, yet they were forced to use hotels and guesthouses.

Greater still was the failure of the relationship between the two that had given rise to the piece in the first place. Initially called *The Lovers* the piece had been conceived of as 'the apotheosis of romantic love' with the possibility that they might even get married at the end of the walk. But after years of a working collaboration and love relationship, Marina and Ulay split, less than a year before the walk was due to take place. This threw the conceptual basis of the project into disarray; the failure of the relationship seemed to signal the failure of the project.

> Before [there] was this strong emotional link, so walking towards each other has this impact ... almost epic story of two lovers getting together after suffering. Then that fact went away. I was confronted with just bare Wall and me. I had to rearrange my motivation. Then I always remember this sentence of John Cage saying, when I throw the I Ching, the answers I like less are the answers [from which] I learn the most.
>
> I am glad we didn't cancel the piece because we needed a certain form of ending. Really this huge distance we walk towards each other where actually we do not meet happily, but we will just end – it's very human in a way. It's more dramatic than having this romantic story of lovers. Because in the end you are really alone, whatever you do.

Abramovic's retroactive reconfiguring of the conceptual foundations of the piece is a model of productive failure. Embarking on the walk in the knowledge that the original aim has collapsed both in terms of its conceptual foundation (love) and its practical exemplification (the walk – the wall) nevertheless produces the condition to 'learn the most'; even if her understanding of the project resolves itself (if only for that moment) in a nihilistic aphorism 'in the end you are really alone'.

Abramovic and Ulay's work has often been about the anticipation of collapse – of failure – where the body is pushed to a boundary from which it can continue no further. It is in that space of collapse that a productive sense of corporal engagement is established. Whether or not she had read Kafka's story is unclear, but at one of the most stressful moments of the walk, when she has run out of water and is physically exhausted, Abramovic is reported to have said to a visiting journalist 'Kafka is good literature here'. In this statement is the acknowledgement of the beauty of failure and how that might become a productive force. The collapse of methodology, the failure of intent, exponentially opens up the possibility of meaning.

Of course, success and failure are always, and only ever, context specific. One person's success is still another's failure. Maybe it is the fear of failure which produces the impetus to embark upon a project which is bound for failure – a construction which makes failure success – which cannot fail, because from the outset failure is courted: a strange paradox. Perhaps that is what productive failure is: the exemplar of paradox.

Encountering the Great Wall of China on the terms of these material, literary and performative productions leaves open the question of the wall itself. What is the Great Wall of China? Just as the productive failure of the Disinter/est project leaves us with the question: who were our infant selves?

Conclusion: autoambioguity

Traditional models of auto/biography are predicated on 'knowing'. They are historical or psychoanalytical narratives where what is important is the uncovering or revealing of facts relating to a specific subject. An archaeological approach highlights the difficulties of accessing specific subjectivities or ambiguities and brings the impossibility of knowing the personal to the fore. On one hand this can be viewed as a failure of archaeology: by choosing archaeology as the method by which we chose to approach the project we simply picked an inappropriate model. On the other hand, however, highlighting sociality and the ambiguity of the personal may be a more authentic model for human lives. In recognizing and actively seeking out intersubjectivity and fragmentation the auto/biographical project might become richer, more complex, and more, rather than less, real.

The Disinter/est project failed to uncover any turning points or seminal auto/biographical moments materialized in the archaeological record. Nor, indeed, did our 'surveys', or 'excavations' generate traditional forms of archaeological data. We did not end up with a set of interpretations or any kind of narrative along a time line or chronology that could be considered auto/biographical in the way that auto/biography is traditionally conceived. We found that we were working not with tropes or specific subjectivities but with structural categories of people – infant, daughter, mother, father – that might as well be anyone, not necessarily us. Yet this very collectivity,[74] and indeed ambiguity, offered our project levels of understanding: an 'autoambioguity'. Where archaeology failed in the exploration of subjectivity, arts practice picked up and there was a constant dialectic between the two fields. The constant zigzagging back and forth between archaeology and arts practice produced a series of conceptual and methodological tensions – some predictable, some unexpected – that led to a reconfiguration of notions of auto/biography, and of how we write the prehistories both of ourselves, and of others.

As the notion of auto/biography in relation to infancy is made meaningful through the *inability* to produce a singular coherent narrative, so too the archaeological methodology used to disinter the Cambridge years becomes itself a model under study – that of productive failure. Like Abramovic and Ulay's performance where the tension of the piece lies in the interplay between intersubjectivity and being alone, the same tension plays beneath notions of auto/biography and the practice of archaeology, as indeed, it does within the very notion of infancy itself.

Notes

1 See, for example, Yukio Mishima, *Confessions of a Mask*, trans. by Meredith Weatherby (London: Panther, 1972), p. 7 in which Mishima begins his autobiography with an account of his belief that he could remember his own birth.

2 Psychologists and sociologists consider infancy to be one of the most important formative periods in human development. See, for example, Richard Tremblay, 'Developmental health as the wealth of nations', in Daniel Keating and Clyde Hertzman (eds), *Developmental Health and the Wealth of Nations* (New York: Guildford, 1999), pp. 337–347.

3 Mary Evans, *Missing Persons: The Impossibility of Auto/biography* (London: Routledge, 1999), p. 135.

4 As Adam Phillips observes '...the child [has become] someone for whom something essential is missing, or lost, or destroyed'. Adam Phillips, *The Beast in the Nursery* (London: Faber & Faber, 1998), p. 20.

5 Marcel Proust, *In Search of Lost Time*, vols 1–6, trans. by C.K. Scott Moncrieff and Terence Kilmartin, revised by D.J. Enright (London: Vintage, 1996), vol. 3, p. 5.

6 Georges Perec, *Je suis né* (1990), in Georges Perec, *Species of Spaces and Other Places* (London: Penguin, 1999), pp. 99–102.

7 Georges Perec, 'The Work of Memory', an interview with Frank Venaille (1979), in Georges Perec, *Species of Spaces and Other Places* (London: Penguin, 1999), pp. 99–133.

8 Georges Perec, *W or the Memory of Childhood*, trans. by David Bellos (London: Collins Harvill, 1989).

9 Georges Perec, 'The Work of Memory', an interview with Frank Venaille (1979), in Georges Perec, *Species of Spaces and Other Places* (London: Penguin, 1999), pp. 99–133.

10 Rom Harré, *Physical Being: A Theory for a Corporeal Psychology* (Oxford: Blackwell, 1991).

11 Ibid., p. 35.

12 The project was therefore a form of historical epistemology in the sense that it was about probing the conditions of knowledge production. For a discussion of historical epistemology see Arnold Davidson, *The Emergence of Sexuality: Historical Epistemology and the Formation of Concepts* (Cambridge, Mass.: Harvard University Press, 2001), Mary Poovey, *A History of the Modern Fact: Problems of Knowledge in the Sciences of Wealth and Society* (Chicago: University of Chicago Press, 1998) and Ian Hacking, *Historical Ontology* (Cambridge, Mass.: Harvard University Press, 2002).

13 The term 'material culture' includes the built environment as well as objects.

14 See Colin Renfrew, *Figuring it Out: What are We? Where do We Come From? The Parallel Vision of Artists and Archaeologists* (London: Thames and Hudson, 2003).

15 Joshua Sofaer and Joanna Sofaer Derevenski, 'Disinter/est: digging up our childhood', *Performance Research* 7(1) (2002), pp. 45–56.

16 For discussions of this point see Marie Louise Stig Sørensen, *Gender Archaeology* (Cambridge: Polity Press, 2000); Colin Renfrew, 'Symbol before concept: material engagement and the

early development of society', in Ian Hodder (ed.), *Archaeological Theory Today* (Cambridge: Polity Press, 2001), pp. 122–140; Joanna Sofaer Derevenski and Marie Louise Stig Sørensen, 'Becoming cultural: society and the incorporation of bronze', in Barbara Ottaway and Emma Wager (eds), *Metals and Society. British Archaeological Report International Series 1061* (Archaeopress: Oxford, 2002), pp. 117–121; Joanna Sofaer, 'Introduction: materiality and identity', in Joanna Sofaer (ed.), *Material Identities* (Oxford: Blackwell, 2007), pp. 1–9.

17 Haiyan Lee, 'Tears that crumbled the Great Wall. The archaeology of feeling the May 4th folklore movement', *Journal of Asian Studies* 64:1 (2005), pp. 35–65.

18 Michel Foucault, *The Archaeology of Knowledge*, trans. A.M. Sheridan Smith (London: Routledge, 2000).

19 Harré, *Physical Being*, p. 35.

20 Georges Perec, 'Species of Spaces' (1974), in Georges Perec, *Species of Spaces and Other Places* (London: Penguin, 1999), p. 91.

21 Roland Barthes, *Camera Lucida* (London: Vintage, 1993/1980), p. 82.

22 See Joshua Sofaer and Joanna Sofaer Derevenski, 'Disinter/est: digging up our childhood', *Performance Research* 7.1, 'On Editing' (2002), pp. 45–56.

23 Christian Metz, 'Photography and fetish', in *October*, no. 34 (Fall 1985), pp. 81–90.

24 Barthes, *Camera Lucida*, p. 14.

25 For a more detailed discussion of the role of the photograph in accessing the infant self, see Sofaer and Sofaer Derevenski, 'Disinter/est: digging up our childhood'.

26 Harré, *Physical Being*, p. 15.

27 Mike Featherstone, 'The body in consumer culture', *Theory, Culture & Society* 1:2 (1982), pp. 18–33; Chris

Shilling, *The Body and Social Theory* (London: Sage, 1993); Allison James, 'Embodied being(s): understanding the self and the body in childhood', in Allan Prout (ed.), *The Body, Childhood and Society* (London: Macmillan Press, 2000), pp. 19–37.

28 Elizabeth Hallam, Jenny Hockey and Glennys Howarth, *Beyond the Body: Death and Social Identity* (London: Routledge, 1999), p. 8.

29 Maurice Bloch and Jonathan Parry (eds), *Death and the Regeneration of Life* (Cambridge: Cambridge University Press, 1982); Mike Parker Pearson, 'Fearing and celebrating the dead in southern Madagascar', in Jane Downes and Tony Pollard (eds), *The Loved Body's Corruption: Archaeological Contributions to the Study of Human Mortality* (Glasgow: Cruithne Press, 1999), pp. 9–18.

30 Gail Kligman, *The Wedding of the Dead: Ritual, Poetics, and Popular Culture in Transylvania* (Berkeley: University of California Press, 1988).

31 Harré, *Physical Being*, p. 35.

32 John Barrett, *Fragments from Antiquity: An Archaeology of Social Life in Britain 2900–1200 BC* (Oxford: Blackwell, 1994).

33 Hallam, Hockey and Howarth, *Beyond the Body*, p. ix.

34 Sarah Tarlow, *Bereavement and Commemoration: An Archaeology of Mortality* (Oxford: Blackwell, 1999).

35 Alfred Gell, *Art and Agency: Towards a New Anthropological Theory* (Oxford: Clarendon Press, 1998), p. 22.

36 One might think of this as a kind of auto-transgenerational haunting.

37 Sofaer and Sofaer Derevenski, 'Disinter/est: digging up our childhood'.

38 Significantly, Harré does not refer to memory. Perhaps this is because even in our adult lives there are many things which we do not remember.

39 Rom Harré, *Personal Being: A Theory for a Corporeal Psychology* (Oxford: Blackwell, 1983), pp. 27–30.

40 Ibid., p. 28.

41 John O'Neill, *Five Bodies: The Human Shape of Modern Society* (Ithaca: Cornell University Press, 1985), pp. 21–22.

42 For a discussion of how babies communicate and of the importance of somatic communication see Alma Gottlieb, 'Where have all the babies gone? Toward an anthropology of infants (and their caretakers)', *Anthropological Quarterly* 73:3 (2000), pp. 121–132.

43 O'Neill, *Five Bodies*, pp. 20–21.

44 Tim Ingold, 'From complementarity to obviation: on dissolving the boundaries between social and biological anthropology, archaeology and psychology', *Zeitschrift für Ethnologie* 123 (1998), pp. 21–52.

45 Christina Toren, *Mind, Materiality and History: Explorations in Fijian Ethnography* (London: Routledge, 1999); Christina Toren, 'The child in mind', in Harvey Whitehouse (ed.), *The Debated Mind: Evolutionary Psychology versus Ethnography* (Oxford: Berg, 2001), pp. 155–179.

46 See Peter Dickens, 'Linking the social and natural sciences: is capital modifying human biology in its own image?' *Sociology* 35:1 (2001), pp. 93–110; Daniel Keating and Fiona Miller, 'Individual pathways in competence and coping: from regulatory systems to habits of mind', in Daniel Keating and Clyde Hertzman (eds), *Developmental Health and the Wealth of Nations* (New York: Guildford, 1999), pp. 220–234.

47 Toren, *Mind, Materiality and History*, p. 2.

48 Paul Connerton, *How Societies Remember* (Cambridge: Cambridge University Press, 1989), p. 72.

49 Toren, *Mind, Materiality and History*; Christina Toren, 'On childhood cognition and social institutions', *Man* 29 (1994), pp. 979–981.

50 Toren, *Mind, Materiality and History*, p. 127.

51 Toren, *Mind, Materiality and History*; Christina Toren, 'Anthropology as the whole science of what it means to be human', in Richard Fox and Barbara King (eds), *Anthropology Beyond Culture* (Oxford: Berg, 2002), pp. 105–124.

52 Toren, *Mind, Materiality and History*.

53 Ingold, 'From complementarity to obviation: on dissolving the boundaries between social and biological anthropology, archaeology and psychology', pp. 26–27.

54 O'Neill, *Five Bodies*, pp. 22–23.

55 Ibid., p. 23.

56 Ibid., p. 23. Original emphasis in italics.

57 Harré, *Physical Being*, p. 36.

58 For discussion and examples see Marilyn Strathern, *The Gender of the Gift: Problems with Women and Problems with Society in Melanesia* (Berkeley: University of California Press, 1988); Celia Busby, 'Permeable and partible persons: a comparative analysis of gender and the body in south India and Melanesia', *Journal of the Royal Anthropological Institute* 3:2 (1997), pp. 261–278; Nurit Bird-David, '"Animism" revisited: personhood, environment and relational epistemology', *Current Anthropology* 40 (1999), pp. 67–92.

59 Arthur Waldron, *The Great Wall of China: From History to Myth* (Cambridge: Cambridge University Press, 1990); Julia Lovell, *The Great Wall. China Against the World 1000BC–AD2000* (Atlantic Books: London, 2006).

60 Waldron, *The Great Wall of China*; Lovell, *The Great Wall*.

61 Haiyan Lee, 'Tears that crumbled the Great Wall: the archaeology of feeling in the May Fourth folklore movement', *The Journal of Asian Studies* 64 (2005), pp. 33–65.

62 Ibid., p. 47.

63 Waldron, *The Great Wall of China*.

64 Ibid., p. 4.

65 Ibid., Lovell, *The Great Wall*.

66 Barbara Bender, *Stonehenge: Making Space* (Oxford: Berg, 1998); Keith Brown and Yannis Hamilakis (eds), *The Useable Past: Greek Metahistories* (Lanham and Oxford: Lexington Books, 2002).

67 Waldron, *The Great Wall of China*.

68 Ibid., p. 195.

69 Walter Benjamin, 'Max Brod's book on Kafka', in Walter Benjamin *Illuminations* (London: Pimlico, 1999 [1938]), p. 137.

70 Franz Kafka, 'The Great Wall of China', in *Metamorphosis and Other Stories* (London: Vintage Classics, 1999 [1931]), p. 67.

71 Benjamin, 'Max Brod's book on Kafka', p. 143.

72 Ewa Ponowska Ziarek, *The Rhetoric of Failure: Deconstruction of Skepticism, Reinvention of Modernism* (Albany: State University of New York Press, 1995), p. 150.

73 There are many accounts of this walk. Unless otherwise indicated all direct quotes are from the artists and are taken as reported in Cynthia Carr, 'A Great Wall' (1989), in Cynthia Carr, *On Edge: Performance at the End of the Twentieth Century* (Hanover: University Press of New England, 1993).

74 In *The Work of Memory* Perec states that his writing is 'an approach to my own life-story but only to the extent that that is collective, shareable', p. 133.

Index

Figures are indicated by *italic* page numbers.